LEGENDARY LOCALS

OF

# RALEIGH

## NORTH CAROLINA

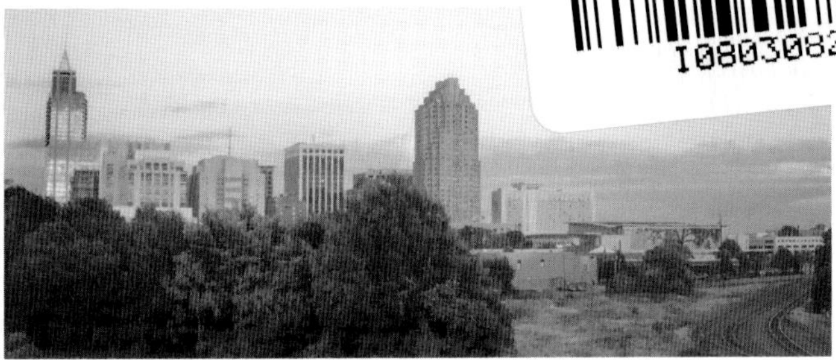

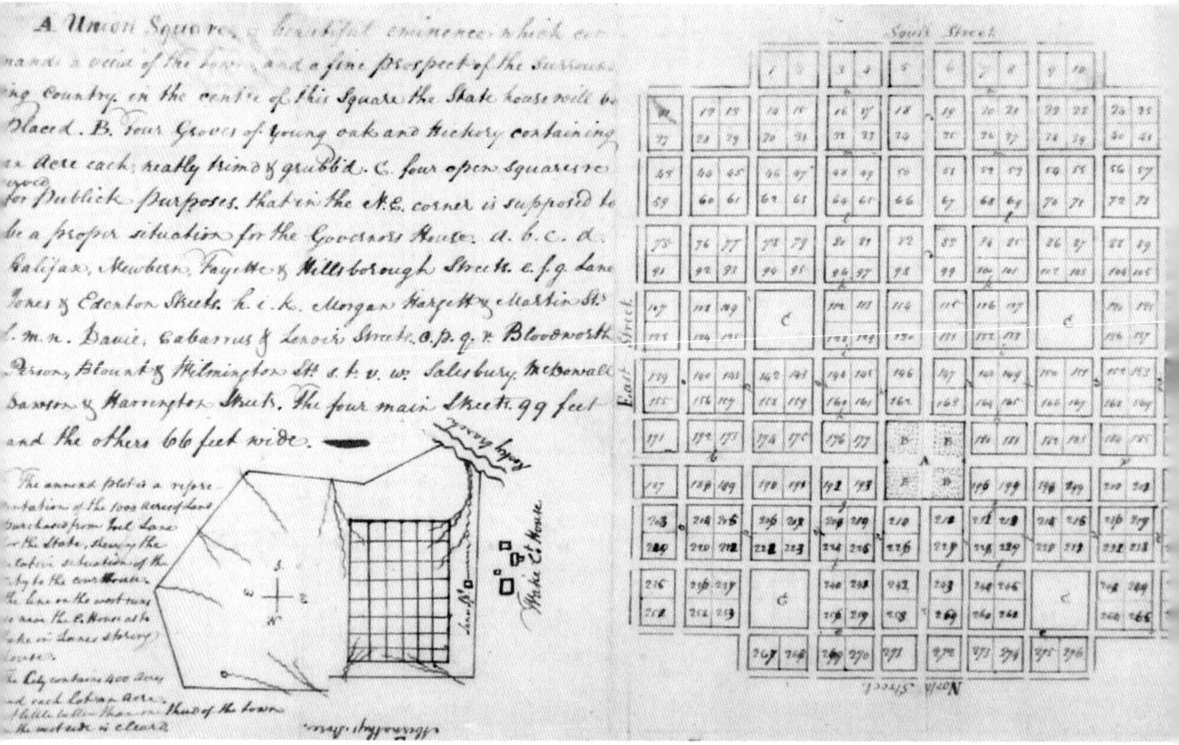


**William Christmas Map of Raleigh, 1792**

In 1792, North Carolina hired William Christmas to lay out and map Raleigh. He based the design on Philadelphia, at that time the nation's capital. Downtown Raleigh includes five squares; Union Square, in the center, houses the capitol building. This original plan is mostly unchanged since the city's first days. (Courtesy of the State Archives of North Carolina.)

**Page 1: The Raleigh Skyline**

Raleigh's current skyline, as seen from the Boylan Street Bridge, includes the city's tallest building, the 33-story PNC Plaza (at left), which was completed in 2008. Raleigh's first "skyscraper" was the Briggs Hardware Building, built in 1874. It stood a towering four stories above Fayetteville Street. (Courtesy of Dmitri Medvedev.)

LEGENDARY LOCALS

OF

# RALEIGH

## NORTH CAROLINA

STORMI SOUTER AND ELIZABETH WEICHEL

LEGENDARY LOCALS

ISBN 978-1-4671-0063-2

Legendary Locals is an imprint of Arcadia Publishing
Charleston, South Carolina

Printed in the United States of America

Library of Congress Control Number: 2012951694

For all general information, please contact Arcadia Publishing:
Telephone 843-853-2070
Fax 843-853-0044
E-mail sales@arcadiapublishing.com
For customer service and orders:
Toll-Free 1-888-313-2665

Visit us on the Internet at www.arcadiapublishing.com

**Dedication**
*This book is dedicated to the memory of Raleigh's inspirational citizens, past, present, and future.*

**On the Cover**: From left to right:
(TOP ROW) Ian Finley, playwright (courtesy of Ian Finley, see page 50); Anna Julia Cooper, educator and feminist (courtesy of RCM, see page 58); Dr. Annie Wilkerson, doctor (courtesy of RCM, see page 40); Berry O'Kelly, community leader (courtesy of RCM, see page 62); AG Bauer, noted architect (courtesy of RCM, see page 85)
(MIDDLE ROW) Thomas Briggs, businessman (courtesy of RCM, see page 124); Lunsford Lane, abolitionist (courtesy of RCM, see page 73); Kate Denson, artist (courtesy of RCM, see page 43); Aldert Smedes, educator (courtesy of St. Mary's School, see page 64); Marshall Wyatt, music historian (courtesy of Marshall Wyatt, see page 45)
(BOTTOM ROW) Dr. Manassa T. Pope, doctor and politician (courtesy of RCM, see page 14); Kay Yow, coach (courtesy of RCM, see page 51); Samuel A. Ashe, journalist (courtesy of Library of Congress, see page 105); Cornelia Petty Jerman, suffragist (courtesy of RCM, see page 16); Josephus Daniels, journalist and politician (courtesy of Library of Congress, see page 102).

# CONTENTS

# ACKNOWLEDGMENTS

Our humble and sincere thanks go to the following people and organizations: Broughton High School; CharGrill; Clyde Cooper's BBQ; East Carolina University; Jugtown Pottery; Library of Congress; Marine Biological Laboratory at Woods Hole; Meredith College Archives; The North Carolina Collection, University of North Carolina Library at Chapel Hill; North Carolina Museum of Art; North Carolina State Library; Oberlin College Archives; the Olivia Raney Local History Library; Quail Ridge Books & Music; Raleigh City Museum; Raleigh Garden Club; Raleigh Hall of Fame; Raleigh Little Theatre; Raleigh Police Department; St. Mary's School Archives; St. Augustine's University; State Archives of North Carolina; Theatre in the Park; William Peace University Archives; Woman's Club of Raleigh; York Wilson Photography; Holly Aiken; Kim Anderson; Mahlon Aycock; Dr. Donald Bitzer; Geraldine Burroughs; Jennifer Carpenter; Mildred Christmas; Earl Clayton; Roger Cook; Ernest Dollar; Tiffany Frary; Ian Finley; Judy Greenberg; Yvonne Holley; Myrick Howard; Gordon Jochem; Karen Lewis; Margaret Maron; Dr. Daniel McFadden; Dmitri Medvedev; Scott Menut; Dr. Rajendra Pachauri; Fabette Smith; Ryon Wilder; Marshall Wyatt; and each of our families and friends.

Images in this volume appear courtesy of the Raleigh City Museum (RCM), the Olivia Raney Local History Library (OR), the State Archives of North Carolina (SANC), and other sources as noted.

# INTRODUCTION

The first state capital of North Carolina was in New Bern, but, following the American Revolution, state leaders sought to establish a new capital city, one that was centrally located and that did not have ties to English rule. A committee of eight men was elected to choose the new capital. Initially, established locations such as Hillsborough and Fayetteville were favored. However, the committee eventually decided on starting a new city dedicated to being the capital. In Wake County, near Wake Crossroads, there was a tavern called Isaac Hunters. The committee found that it enjoyed the libations there so much, it announced that the new capital must be located within 10 miles at the North Carolina Convention of 1788. Another committee was established to decide the exact location. After viewing many parcels of land, the state bought 1,000 acres from local farmer, politician, and businessman Joel Lane.

The new city was named after Sir Walter Raleigh, a famous but long-deceased English explorer who never visited the area that became North Carolina. William Christmas laid out the city, designing it after the then–national capital of Philadelphia. The city had five main squares, with the state capitol building sitting in the middle of the center square, Union Square. Moore Square, Nash Square, Caswell Square, and Burke Square stand around it. The streets were named after cardinal boundaries, the state court districts, the commissioners, other state leaders, and Joel Lane.

The statehouse was soon erected on Union Square. Considered unappealing to the eye, as well as being too small for the city's needs, it was added on to in 1822. In 1831, while workers were on the roof fireproofing the building, it caught fire and burned to the ground. The city erected a new capitol building in 1840, which stands in the center of downtown today.

The new town soon earned the nickname "City of Oaks," due to its impressive and somewhat rare stands of oak groves. The moniker was first used in a toast to the city following the completion of the new capitol building: "Here's to the city of oaks with her Grecian capitol!" Today, residents are proud of the nickname, but in those early days, some people used it as an insult—Raleigh as the city of oaks and deer instead of more refined, urban things.

Until the 1820s, most of Raleigh's business and entertainment centered on the government. While the city was the occasional home to grand celebrations, the population mostly consisted of politicians and their families, and those who ran businesses that catered to them. The city experienced several devastating fires during this period, including one in 1816 and one in 1831, both damaging significant portions of Raleigh. The population dropped following the fires, as people moved to cities they perceived as safer. With the opening of the new capitol building in 1840, however, the population nearly doubled and has been growing ever since.

Raleigh started its first railroad in the 1830s. One of its first uses was hauling in supplies to erect the new capitol building. Raleigh soon became a bustling small city with industry and commerce, entertainment, schools, and crime. In the 1840s, the first state mental hospital, Dix Hill, opened in Raleigh.

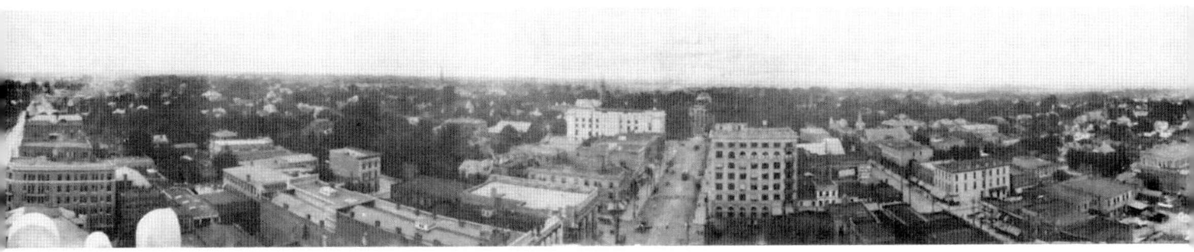

**Raleigh Panorama, 1912** (Courtesy of RCM.)

The city expanded its borders in 1857. Just a few years later, Raleigh would experience the secession of its state from the Union and the effects of the Civil War. It wasn't until the end of the war that Raleigh saw any action within its borders. Gen. William Tecumseh Sherman marched up the East Coast toward Raleigh in April 1865. The war was declared over, and Raleigh officials met Sherman's troops outside the city on April 12 and pleaded for him to spare the city. He did. Sherman stayed in the governor's mansion at the end of Fayetteville Street, which had been built in 1816. Afterward, no North Carolina governor would stay there, and the building was torn down in the 1880s.

Unlike many Southern cities, Raleigh, fortunate to have been spared damage during the Civil War, saw enormous growth and prosperity in the late 19th century. Many businesses that are still prosperous today opened during this boom. During this era, Raleigh installed a streetcar system and continued to expand its borders. Many of the area's colleges and universities opened in the late 19th century, and Raleigh was attracting students from around the country and the world. This academic influx helps to shape Raleigh's diverse culture to this day.

In the early 20th century, Raleigh was a comfortable and charming city that nonetheless experienced the major events that seemed to reach every corner of the world. The Wake County Red Cross was established during World War I, and Raleigh was home to Camp Polk, the only Army tank training base in the United States during the war. A few years later, Raleigh would lose nearly 300 citizens to the Spanish influenza.

In the 1930s, Raleigh opened up two restaurants that are still favorites today, The Mecca and Clyde Cooper's BBQ. On the other hand, it also saw many old businesses succumb to the Great Depression. After World War II, Raleigh developed into a modern city. Its first shopping mall opened in 1949, and Research Triangle Park was established in 1959. In 1965, IBM moved to the area. The population exploded in the middle of the 20th century as a result, and the Raleigh area became known for its technological industries.

During the 1960s, Raleigh, like other cities and towns across the country, was a hot spot for the civil rights movement. Ella Baker and students at Shaw University formed the Student Non-Violent Coordinating Committee (SNCC), which contributed to the movement across the South.

Downtown Raleigh was in decline by the 1970s. Since the opening of Cameron Village in 1949, and subsequent shopping malls and expansion, few people had reasons to come downtown. Raleigh officials closed Fayetteville Street to automobile traffic and established a pedestrian walking mall. The decade saw Raleigh achieving two milestones, with the election of its first female mayor and its first African American mayor.

In 2005, downtown was more depressed than ever, and city officials decided to reopen Fayetteville Street and revitalize downtown. Since then, downtown has come alive, with prosperous new stores, restaurants, and entertainment now residing next to long-established businesses and classics. The Raleigh area is regularly named in lists of the best places to live in America, and is one of the most educated areas of the country.

# CHAPTER ONE

# Getting Political

In 1792, Raleigh was established for the express purpose of being a centrally located state capital for North Carolina, and state politicians began moving within the city's borders. As such, the city has always had an active political scene. Even the land purchased for the creation of Raleigh belonged to an 18th-century North Carolina politician and farmer, Joel Lane. Less then 20 years later, only a block from the statehouse, the United States's 17th president, Andrew Johnson, would be born behind Casso's Inn.

In the 20th century, Raleigh was home to several state figures, such as Gov. J. Melville Broughton, North Carolina's "War Governor," who also improved the standards for public education.

Raleigh's politicians have included a few controversial figures over the centuries as well, such as John Haywood, Raleigh's first mayor, who is now remembered for the money he embezzled, discovered after his death, instead of his time spent in office.

Some of our most accomplished politicians have had to fight just for their right to hold office, such as James H. Young, an African American politician in the Reconstruction Era, or Carrie Broughton, the first female to hold a state position. Others fought for the rights of all, such as Cornelia Petty Jerman, a local suffragist who labored to see the passage of the 19th Amendment. These people and many others cleared the way for later minority politicians, like Clarence Lightner, Raleigh's first African American mayor, and Isabella Cannon, who, at the age of 73, became Raleigh's first female mayor.

Downtown Raleigh is home to the state capitol building, the governor's mansion, and offices and buildings of city, county, and state governments. Every day since 1792, politicians have met in this city to shape and mold the future of the city and state, and many have left behind interesting tales.

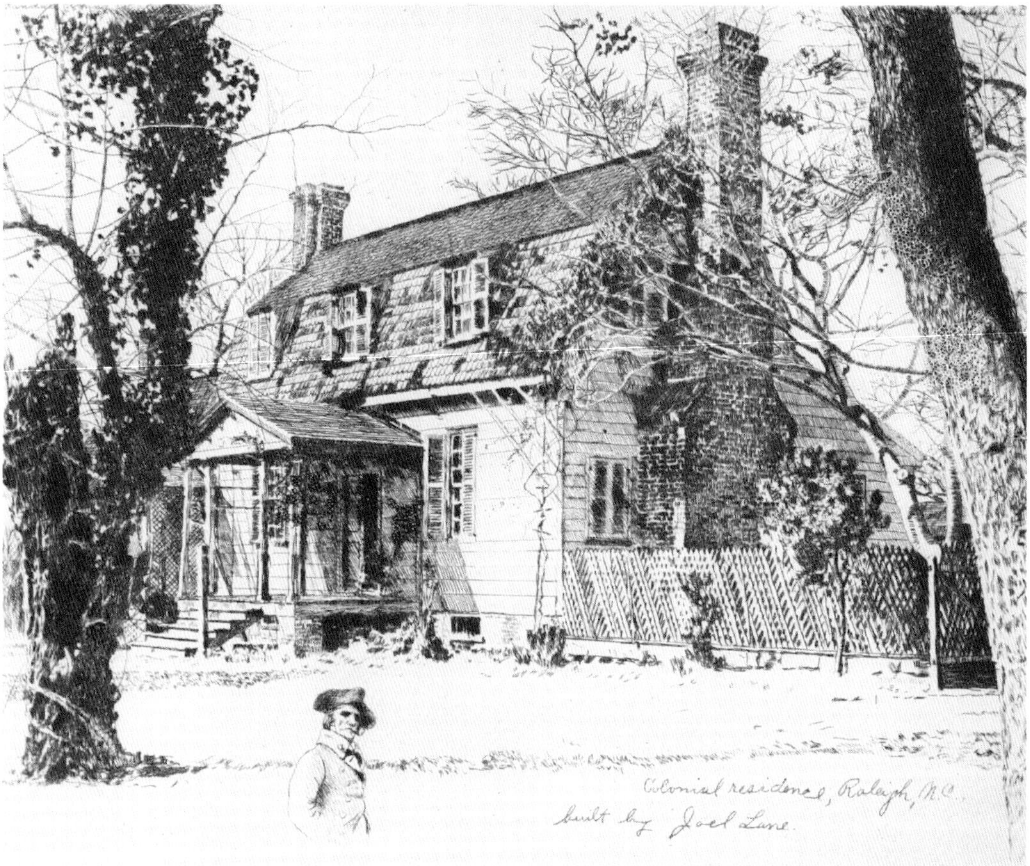


## Joel Lane

Lane (c. 1740–1795), born before Raleigh or even Wake County existed, was important to the establishment of both. After moving from Halifax in 1770, he became a prominent citizen of Wake Crossroads, located in Johnston County. Lane was elected a county representative to the Colonial Assembly in 1770. At the assembly's meeting at Tryon Palace in New Bern, he introduced a bill that would incorporate parts of Johnston, Orange, and Cumberland Counties into a new Wake County. He chose the county's name to honor the wife of Gov. William Tryon, Margaret Wake. His bill was successful. Joel Lane played a vital role in early Wake County, serving as justice of the peace and senator for 11 terms. To this day, Joel Lane is referred to as "the Father of Wake County." The first Wake County courthouse even stood in Joel Lane's yard.

During the Revolutionary War, Lane served as a colonel in the militia. By 1777, North Carolina wanted to change the location of the state capital. It had been in New Bern, but a more centrally located position was desired. Years of debate began. Finally, in 1787, the legislature called a convention to make the decision. The convention decided that the new capital should be located within 10 miles of Isaac Hunter's Tavern and Plantation in Wake County. Local legend says it is because the representatives enjoyed the whiskey-infused Cherry Bounce served at the tavern so much that they wanted to be able to frequent the establishment. It was not until 1792, however, that a location was agreed upon. Several sites in Wake County were being considered, including land belonging to many of the oldest families of the area. Joel Lane proposed that 1,000 acres of his land be chosen as the site of the new capital city and offered it for £1,378 in North Carolina currency. After three votes, his offer was accepted, and the state bought Lane's land. In 1792, Raleigh was established on 400 acres of that purchase, and the capital city has been located there ever since. This drawing depicts Lane's house. (Courtesy of RCM.)

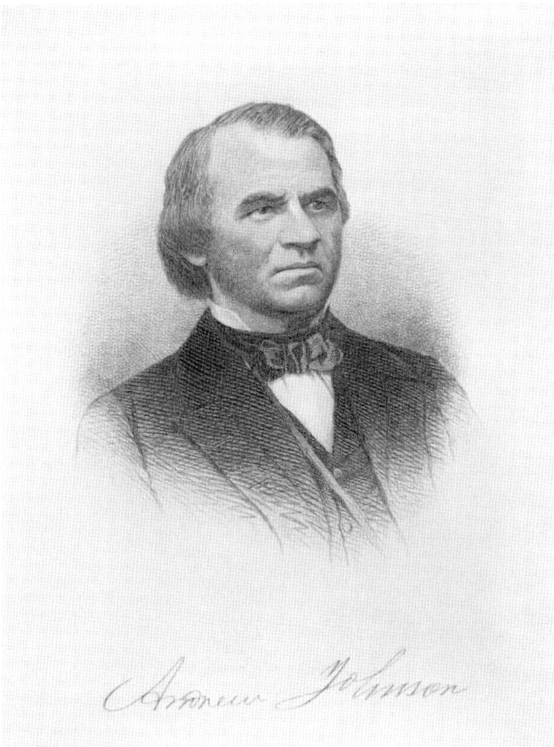

**Andrew Johnson**

Andrew Johnson (1808–1875) was born in a small kitchen house behind Casso's Inn, near the corner of Fayetteville and Morgan Streets. According to legend, his mother, Mary, went into labor while working in the kitchen and gave birth to him on the kitchen floor. In January 1812, his father, Jacob, rescued three drowning men from a lake, but caught pneumonia and died. Andrew and his brother, now fatherless, often got into trouble with local authorities.

When Andrew was 13, he was apprenticed to a tailor in Raleigh, but rebelled against it. He ran away with his older brother to South Carolina. Upon returning three years later, the tailor refused to release him from his obligation. So the brothers, along with their mother and stepfather, headed for Tennessee. There, Andrew started his own tailoring business. He met and married Eliza McCardle, who taught him arithmetic, reading, writing, and other skills he had not learned in his poverty-stricken youth. This additional education enabled the man to start participating in local political debates, which he greatly enjoyed and excelled at.

In 1835, Johnson won his first political position in the Tennessee House of Representatives. In 1843, he won his first campaign for Congress. Though a citizen of Tennessee at the time of Southern secession, Johnson chose to stay with the Union. He ran as vice president for Abraham Lincoln's second term, during the height of the Civil War. Following Lincoln's assassination in April 1865, Andrew Johnson became the 17th president. However, the Republican Party, on whose ticket Lincoln and Johnson ran, did not agree with many of Andrew Johnson's policies. He had been a supporter of slavery and now took a very lax standing with the Southern states reentering the Union. He faced a challenging group of radical Republicans, who eventually called for his impeachment. He was acquitted by one vote.

Raleigh decided to welcome Andrew Johnson back into town during his presidency and hoped to capitalize on having a native son in the White House. The city decided to reinter Johnson's father in the City Cemetery and hold a proper funeral for him. At this time, the president's father did not even have a gravestone. Andrew Johnson came for the event, but stayed less than a full day before departing again by train, much to the disappointment of Raleigh citizens. (Courtesy of RCM.)

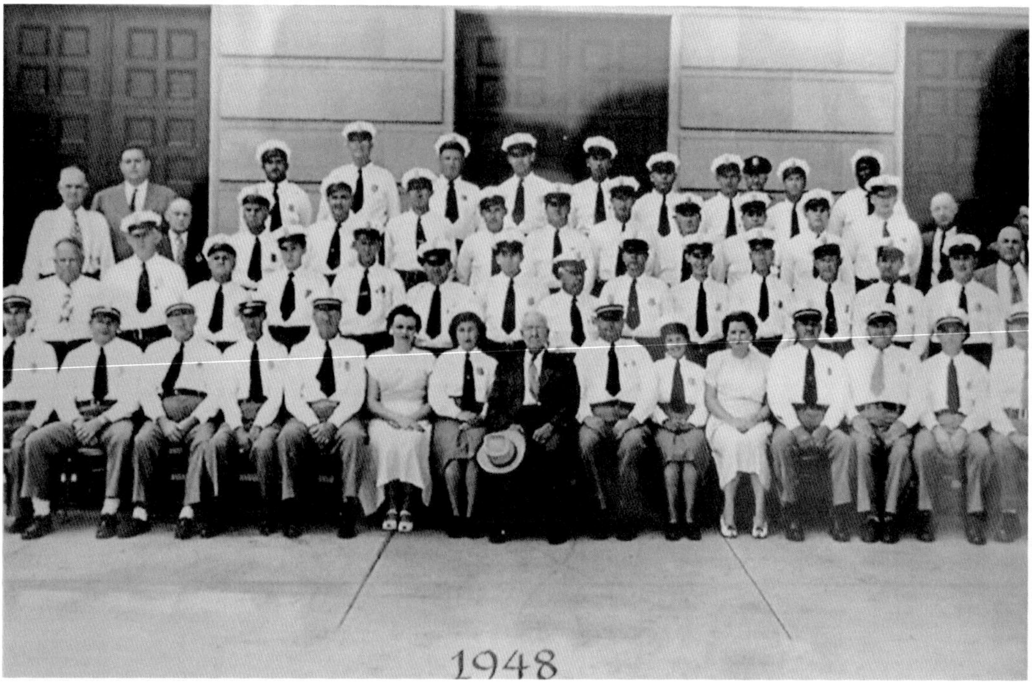


### John H. Baker Sr.

Baker (1914?–1985), a Raleigh native, served the public as his hometown's first African American police officer of the modern era. Hired during the 1940s, he helped the city transition through the racially charged decades of the 1950s and 1960s with relative quiet. For his contributions, the city of Raleigh and the Raleigh Police Department dedicated the John H. Baker Police Training Center in his honor in 1987. (Courtesy of Raleigh Police Department.)

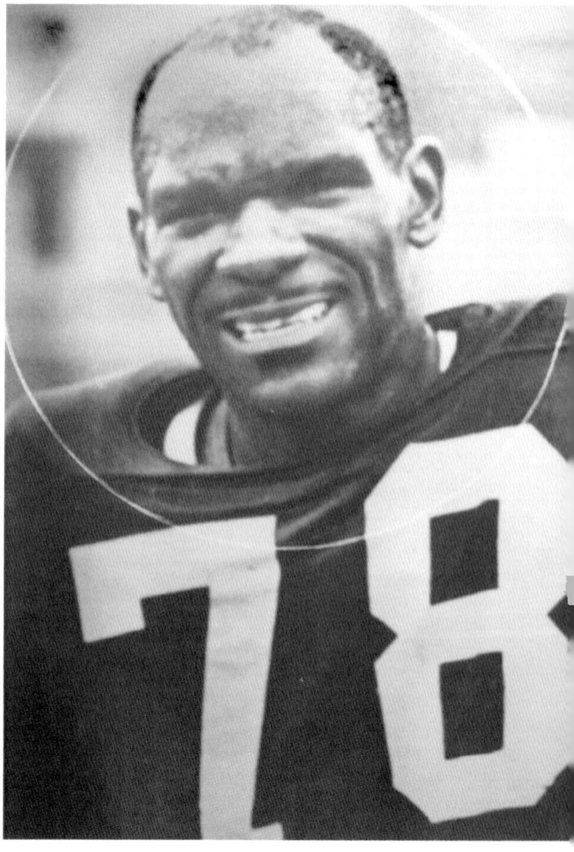


### John H. Baker Jr.

John H. Baker Sr.'s son followed him as a trailblazer on Raleigh's police force. After an 11-year All-Pro career in the NFL, Baker (1935–2007) counseled inmates in the North Carolina Department of Correction. His appointment to the State Parole Board in 1970 was a first for an African American, and in 1978, Wake County elected him as its first black sheriff since Reconstruction, a position he held until 2002. (Courtesy of RCM.)

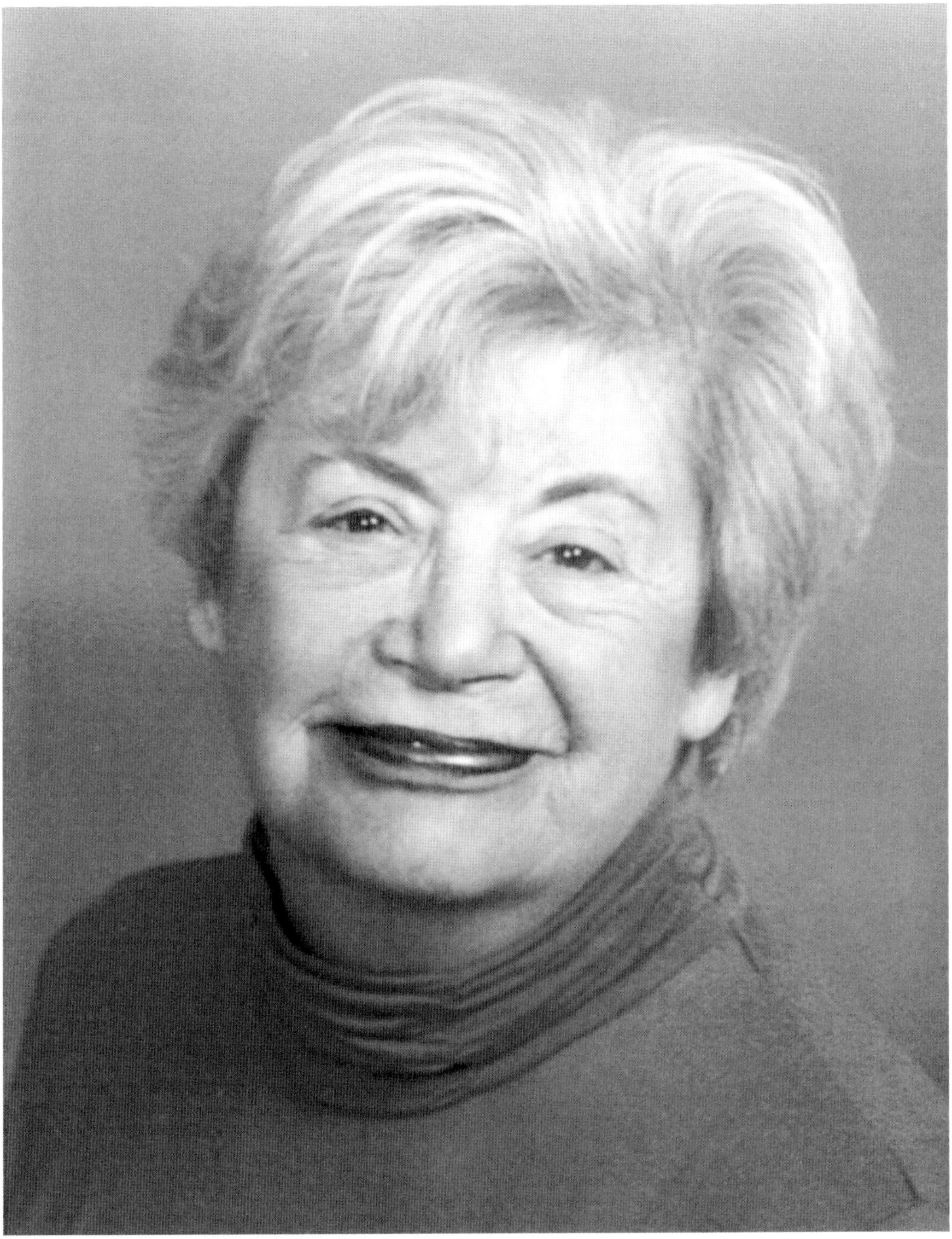

**Ruth E. Cook**

The first woman to represent Wake County in the General Assembly fought for the rights of children, the poor, and the mentally ill for five terms, but she almost never made it to Raleigh. Born Jewish in Berlin, Cook (1929–2011) and her family had to flee the Nazis in 1939 just to survive. In the words of her son, "My mom was not afraid to speak truth to power. She was an incredibly intrepid person." (Courtesy of Roger Cook and Judy Greenberg.)

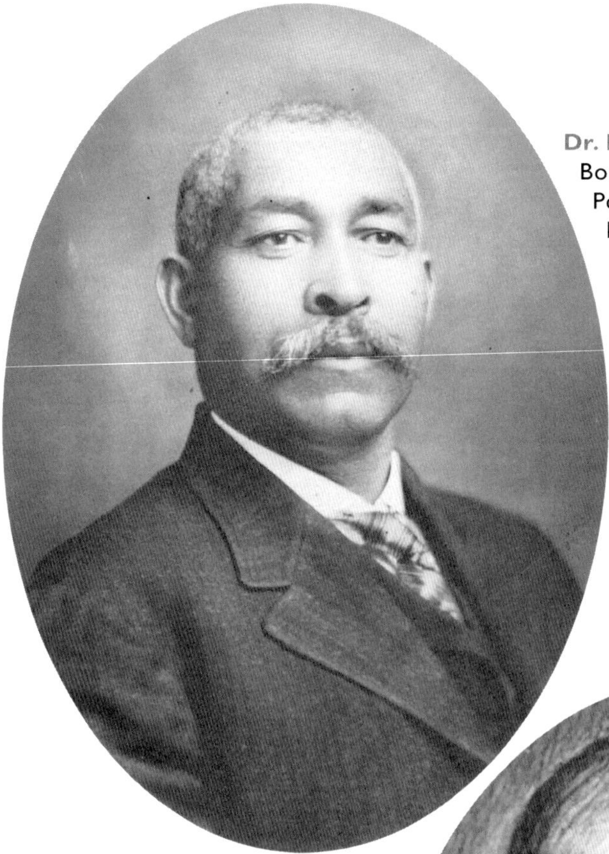

**Dr. Manassa T. Pope**
Born to freemen in 1858, Dr. Manassa T. Pope (1858–1934) moved to Raleigh in 1899. He was the only African American resident in the city who could vote under a grandfather clause. Pope graduated from Shaw University and served as an officer in the Spanish-American War. In 1919, he ran for mayor. He was defeated at the polls, but was instrumental in bringing much of the African American community out to vote. (Courtesy of RCM.)

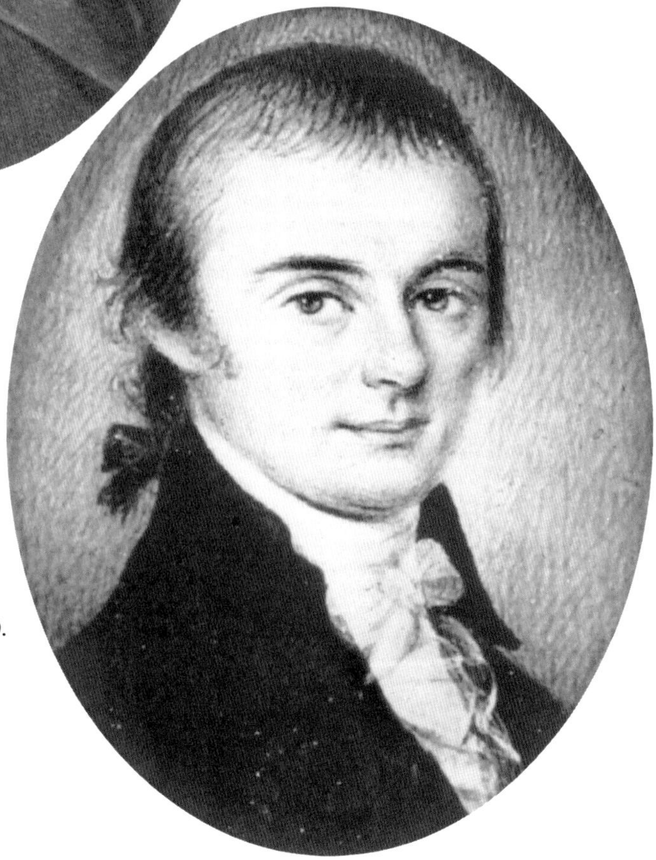

**John Haywood**
Haywood (1754–1827) purchased one of the original plots of land in Raleigh. He built Haywood Hall in 1800, which still stands only yards away from the capitol building. In 1795, he was named the intendant of police, or mayor, of Raleigh. He remained in that position until January 1803, the date of the city's first popular election. After 40 years as state treasurer, Haywood died in 1827, having embezzled $70,000. (Courtesy of OR.)

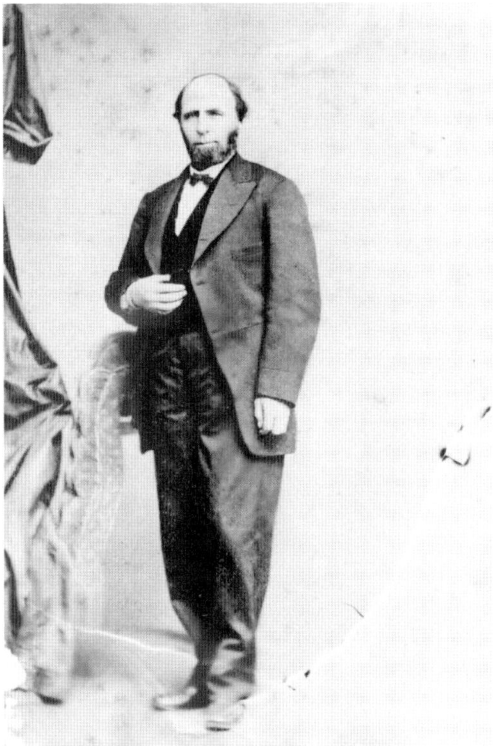

**William W. Holden**

Holden (1818–1892) began his up-and-down political career as a newspaper man in Raleigh, editing the *Standard* in 1843. Holden used his influential position to urge his readers to support the railroads and the state fair and to "Watch and Wait" before calling for secession prior to the Civil War. As it turned out, the war would be the cause of Holden's highest and lowest moments.

North Carolina voted to join the Confederacy when seceding from the Union, doing so by unanimous vote on May 20, 1861, after shots were fired at Fort Sumter. As the fighting progressed, Holden continued to support less extreme positions, pleading for deserters to be reinstated in the army rather than hanged, and opposing the Confederate policies of waging the war, calling it a "rich man's war and a poor man's fight."

Holden's positions led him to run for governor in 1864 for the Peace Party, but his subsequent loss led to violence and vandalism against himself and his office. He continued to print editorials in support of reunification, and after war's end, Pres. Andrew Johnson, a Raleigh native, appointed him provisional governor in May 1865 to oversee the transition to elected leadership. Holden lost the election that fall, but he was triumphant in 1868, becoming the state's first Republican governor.

Coinciding with the rise of Republicans and African Americans in public office, however, was the rise of terrorist acts by groups like the Ku Klux Klan. In order to stop these groups, the legislature took the extreme measure of passing the Shoffner Act in 1869–1870. This act granted unprecedented powers to the governor, which Holden used to send the state militia, under Col. George W. Kirk, to fight in the hotbed of activity (which came to be known as the Kirk-Holden War). The Shoffner Act permitted this military intervention, but it did not allow Holden to jail his dissenters in the press and suspend the writ of habeas corpus to keep them there.

As a result of his actions, the General Assembly impeached Holden in 1871. He became the first governor in the country to be convicted. The legislature repealed the Shoffner Act and declared secret societies like the KKK illegal. Holden spent several years in Washington, DC, after his removal from office before returning to Raleigh, where he served as postmaster from 1873 to 1881. (Courtesy of SANC.)

### Cornelia Petty Jerman

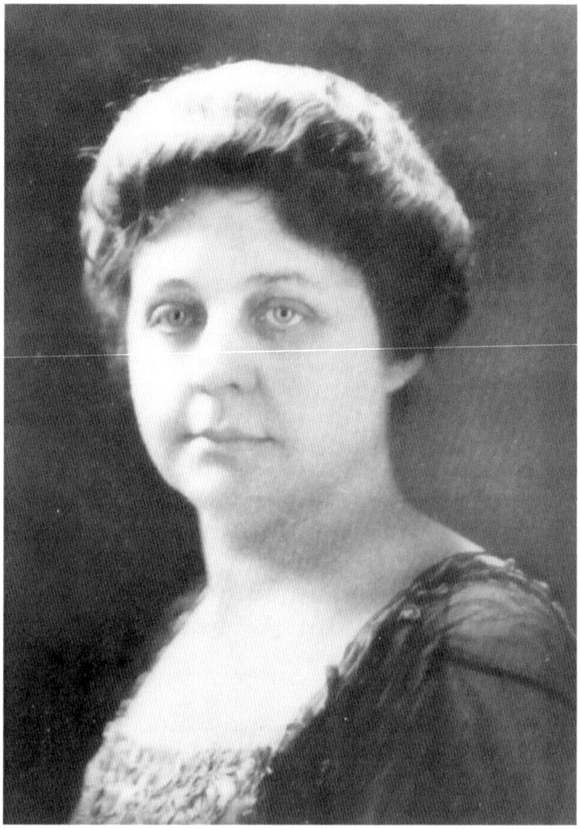

Cornelia Petty Jerman (1874–1946) was a local suffrage movement leader. In 1913, she joined the Raleigh Equal Suffrage League, whose stated belief was that "women need the vote to protect their homes and families." The league's membership grew to 50 women and at least three men, including North Carolina Supreme Court chief justice Walter Clark. Jerman served as the corresponding secretary with the North Carolina Equal Suffrage League, shown below, working in its office in the Yarborough House on Fayetteville Street. There was some tension with anti-suffragists, who deliberately set up their office right next to the league's, but relations were generally polite. In 1918, Jerman was voted vice president and chairman of the legislative committee of the North Carolina Equal Suffrage League and served as a local delegate at state conventions. The suffragists' hard work paid off in August 1920, when the 19th Amendment was passed. (Courtesy of RCM.)

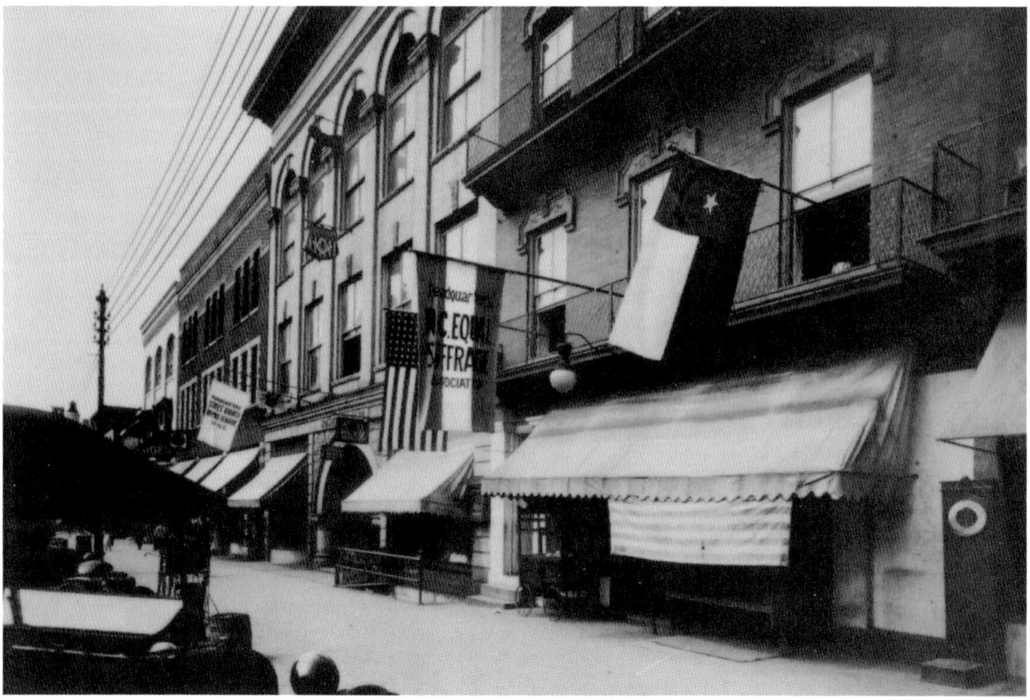

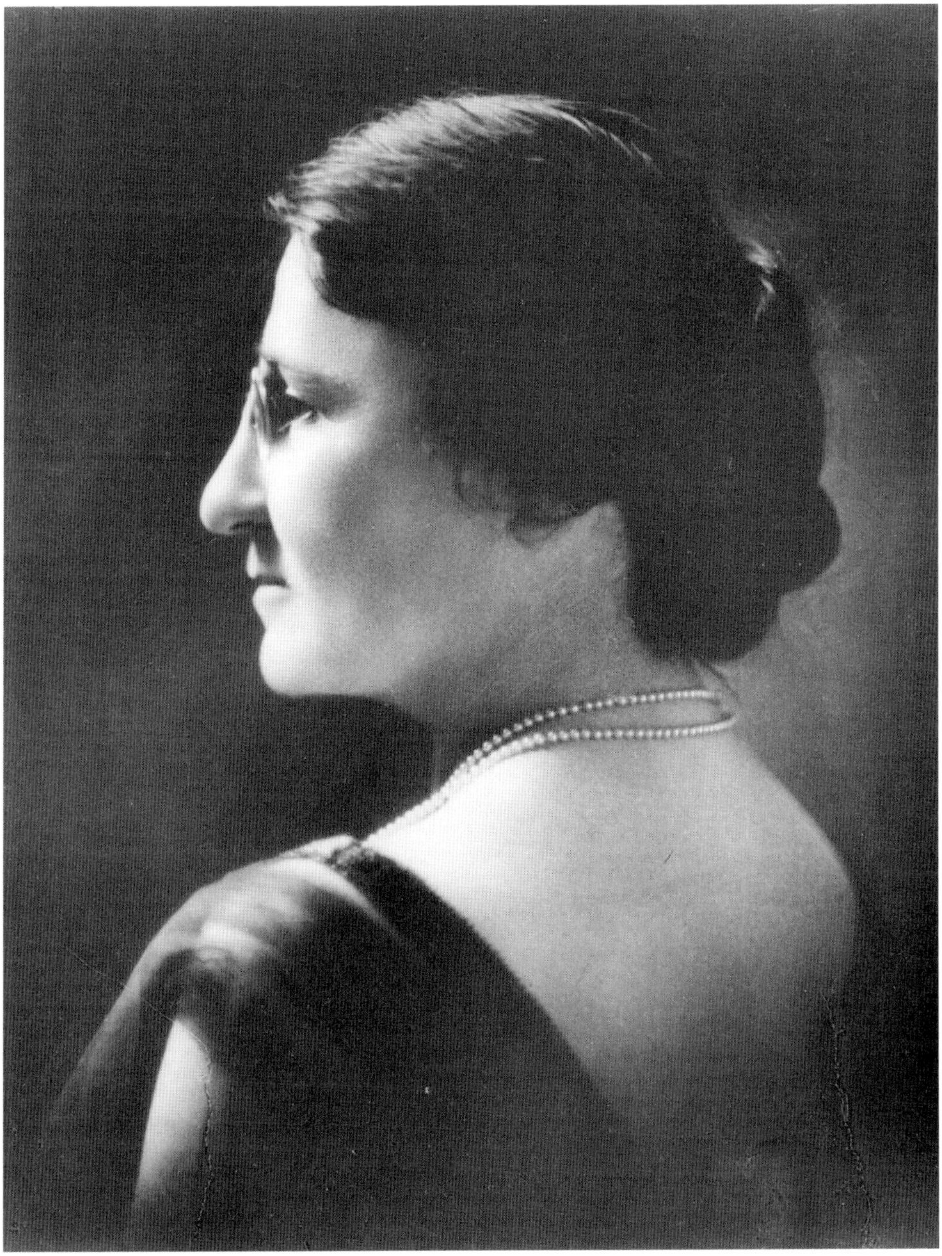

**Elsie G. Riddick**

While working for the government as secretary for the North Carolina Utilities Commission, Riddick (1876–1959) led women from the Raleigh Equal Suffrage League to ambush Raleigh's Democratic precinct meetings in March 1920, arguing that because the 19th Amendment would soon be passed, "and it is a certainty that we will vote in the next election . . . we have [the] right, therefore, to vote in this precinct meeting—just as any man would who will become twenty-one years old prior to the next election." Their argument succeeded, and Riddick and four other women were delegates to the state Democratic convention in 1920. She became the first woman to chair a precinct in Raleigh. (Courtesy of University of North Carolina Library at Chapel Hill.)

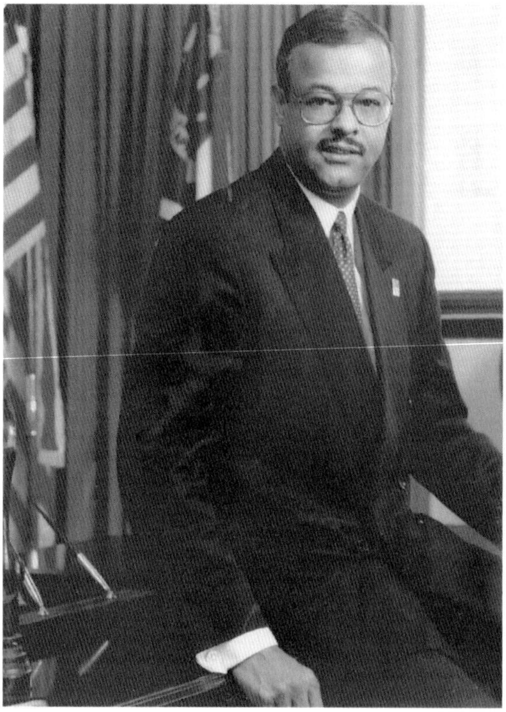

**Ralph Campbell Jr.**
Following his parents' example as civil rights organizers in Raleigh during the 1960s, in 1985, Campbell (1946–2011) ran for and was elected to the first of four terms on the city council. In 1992, Campbell became the first African American to hold a statewide elected office in North Carolina by winning the race for the office of state auditor, which he held for three terms. (Courtesy of Mildred Christmas.)

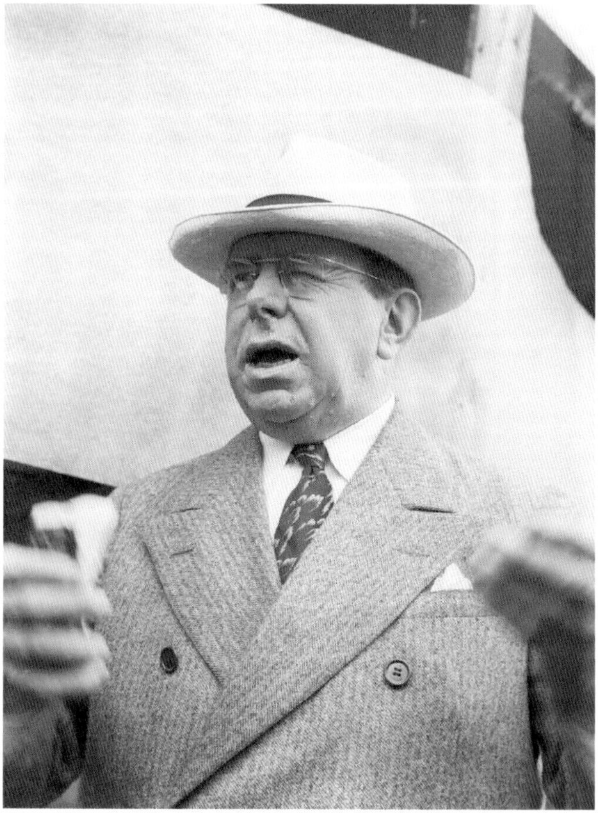

**J. Melville Broughton**
Broughton (1888–1949) is the only native of Wake County to have served as North Carolina governor. He was elected to office in 1941 and served until 1945, successfully bringing the state through the war years and earning the title of the "War Governor." He is remembered for extending the school year from six to eight months. (Photograph by Hugh Morton, North Carolina Collection, University of North Carolina Library at Chapel Hill.)

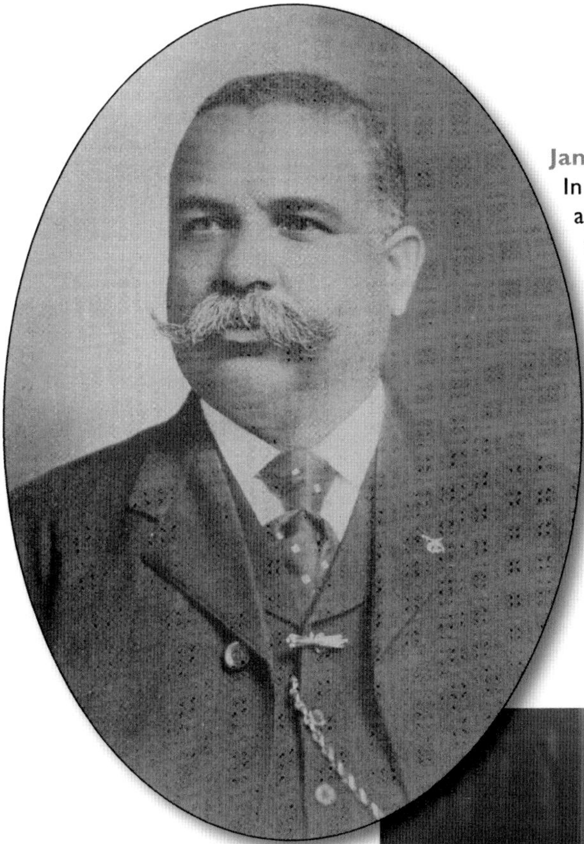

**James H. Young**
In the 1880s, Young served several federal appointments, was active in local politics, and was appointed colonel of North Carolina's African American regiment during the Spanish-American War.

After white supremacist Democrats took over the general assembly, they resented his successes so much that they removed his name from the cornerstone of the North Carolina Institution of the Deaf and Dumb and the Blind's building on Caswell Square, despite his advocacy for the students. (Courtesy of SANC.)

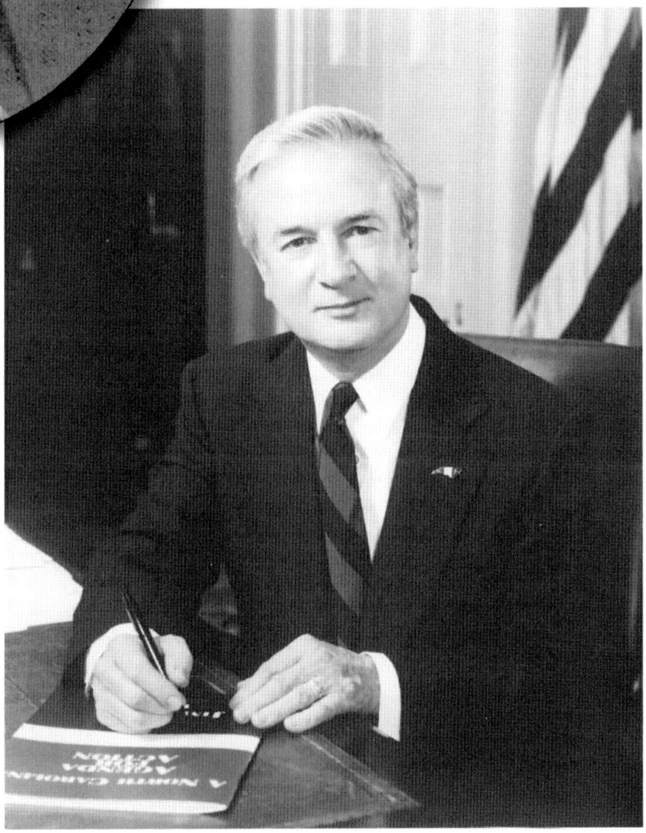

**Jim Hunt**
Hunt (1937–present) is North Carolina's longest-serving governor, winning two terms (1977–1985 and 1993–2001). After losing what was described as "the meanest Senate campaign in [North Carolina's] history" to Jesse Helms in 1984, Hunt left politics until 1993. In office, Hunt started the nationally recognized Smart Start program for pre-kindergarteners and the School of Science and Math to encourage technology-based business growth. (Courtesy of SANC.)

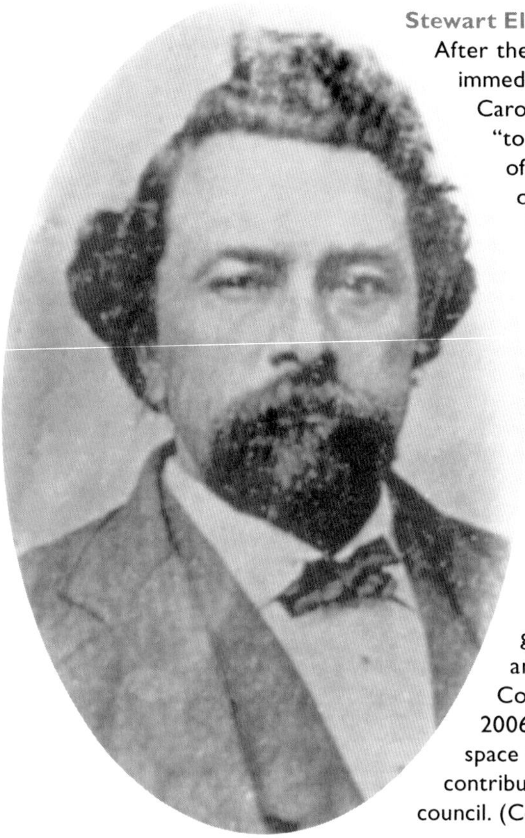

### Stewart Ellison

After the Civil War, Ellison (1834–1899) entered politics immediately. In 1866, he was vice president of the North Carolina State Equal Rights League, whose purpose was "to secure, by political and moral means . . . the repeal of all laws . . . State and National, that make distinction on account of color." Ellison remained politically involved, serving in the state legislature from 1870 to 1880 and becoming one of Raleigh's first black city commissioners. (Courtesy of OR.)

### Miriam Preston Block

Block (1920–2005) won a seat as the first woman on the Raleigh City Council in 1973, and served 10 consecutive terms. She fought for parks and greenway creation and the installation of sidewalks, and she advocated for the Citizen's Advisory Councils and mentored other women in politics. In 2006, the Raleigh Arts Commission named its display space the Miriam Preston Block Gallery in honor of her contributions. She is seen here being sworn in to the city council. (Courtesy of OR.)

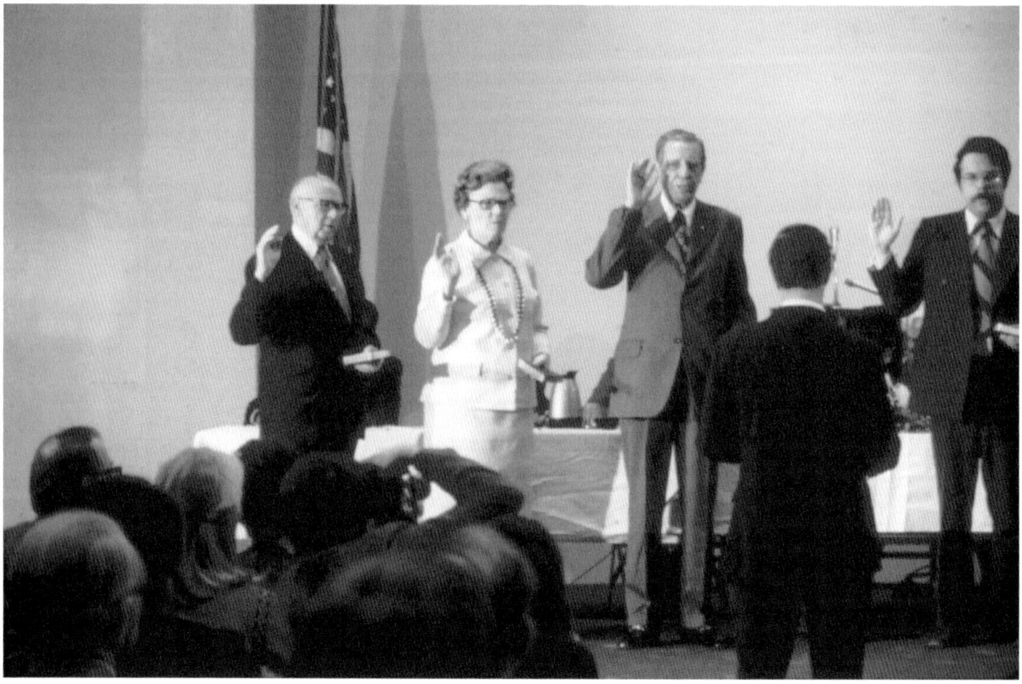

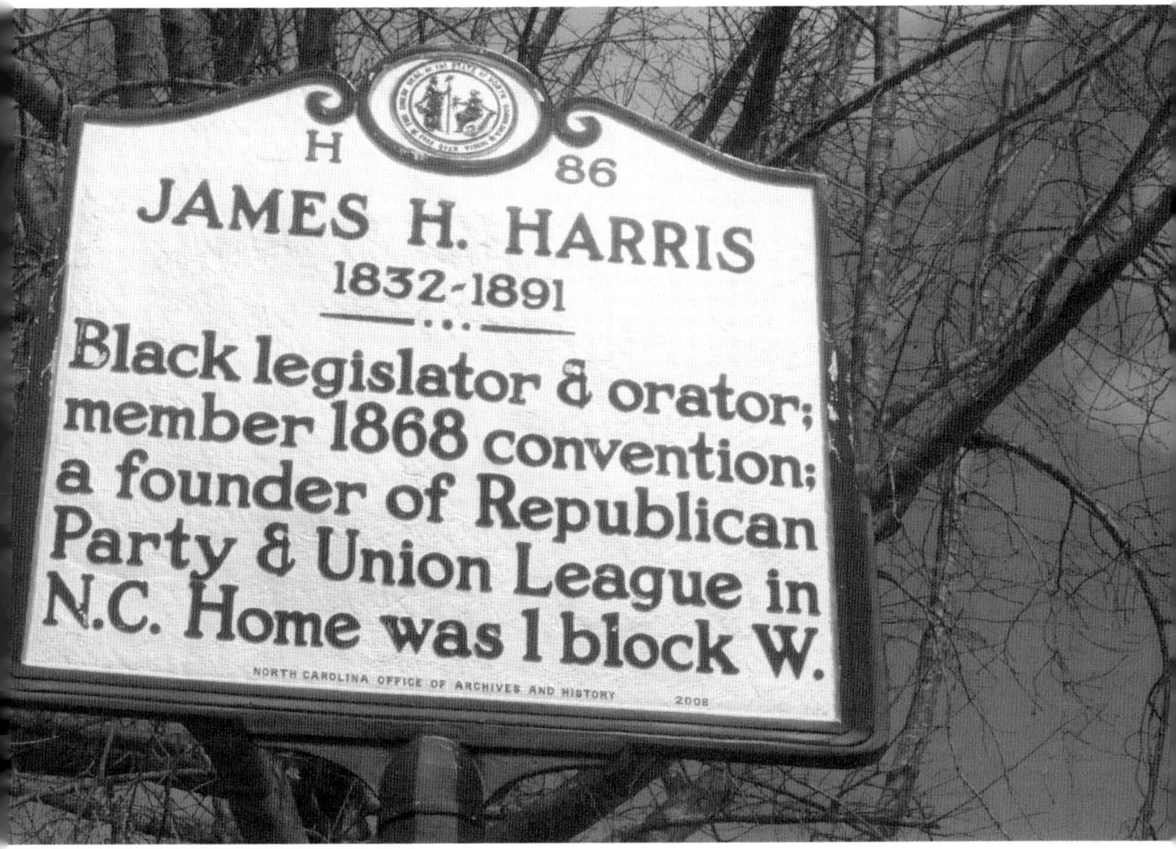


**James H. Harris**
Harris (1832–1891) grew up enslaved in Granville County, commanded an Indiana unit of the US Colored Troops during the Civil War, and then returned to Raleigh in 1865 as a leader of the new Republican Party. He was the first African American state representative elected from Wake County, in 1868 (among 14 African Americans that election), and he went on to serve in the state senate and as a Raleigh alderman over the next two decades.

Harris encouraged the development of the Oberlin community, where former slaves owned their first homes, and the creation of the African American branch of the state Institution of the Deaf and Dumb and the Blind. During the 1880s, however, James H. Young began taking over Harris's political audience, as Harris moved on to national party politics. Harris died in Washington, DC, and is buried in Raleigh's Mount Hope Cemetery. (Authors' collection.)

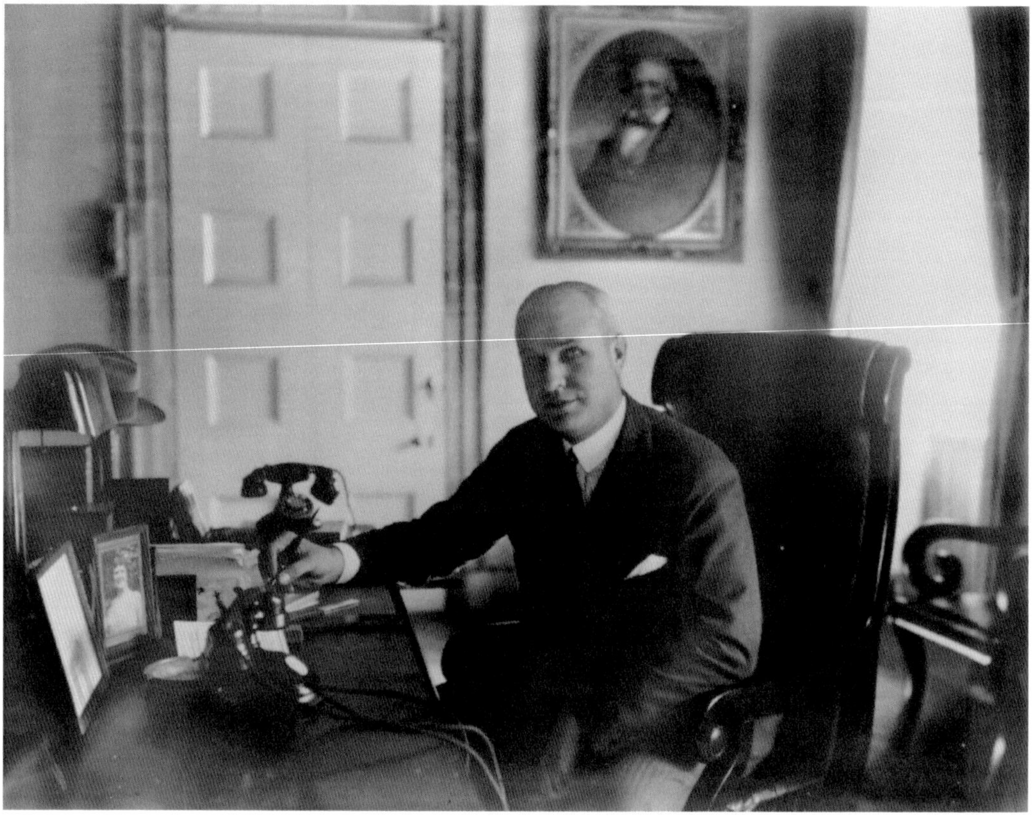

### O. Max Gardner

Gardner (1882–1947) bridged the progressive and conservative politics of North Carolina during his term as governor (1929–1933). He supported women's suffrage, but he also supported (and owned) textile mills and opposed both unions and child labor laws. He balanced North Carolina's budget during the Great Depression while also supporting Pres. Franklin Roosevelt's deficit-based New Deal programs, although he privately opposed their relationship with labor unions. (Courtesy of SANC.)

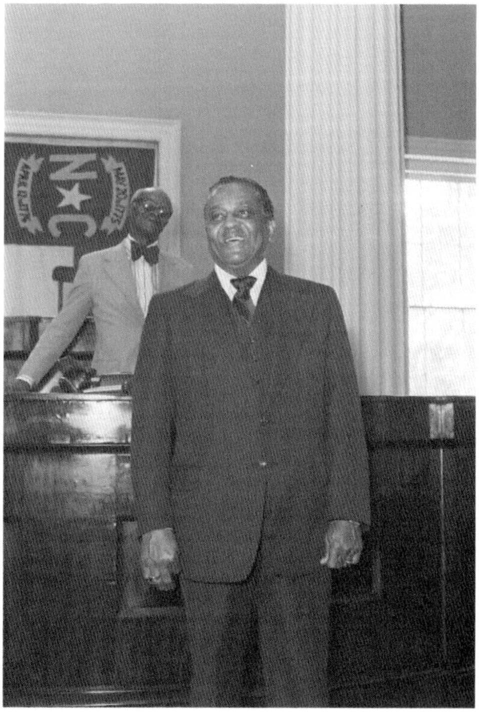

### Clarence Lightner

Lightner (1921–2002) was elected Raleigh's first African American mayor in 1973, having served on the city council since 1967. This election made him the first African American mayor of a Southern city with a population greater than 50,000. He worked for civic affairs on both the local and national levels. Lightner was the son of Calvin Lightner and the father of MLK Garden's designer, Bruce Lightner. (Courtesy of RCM.)

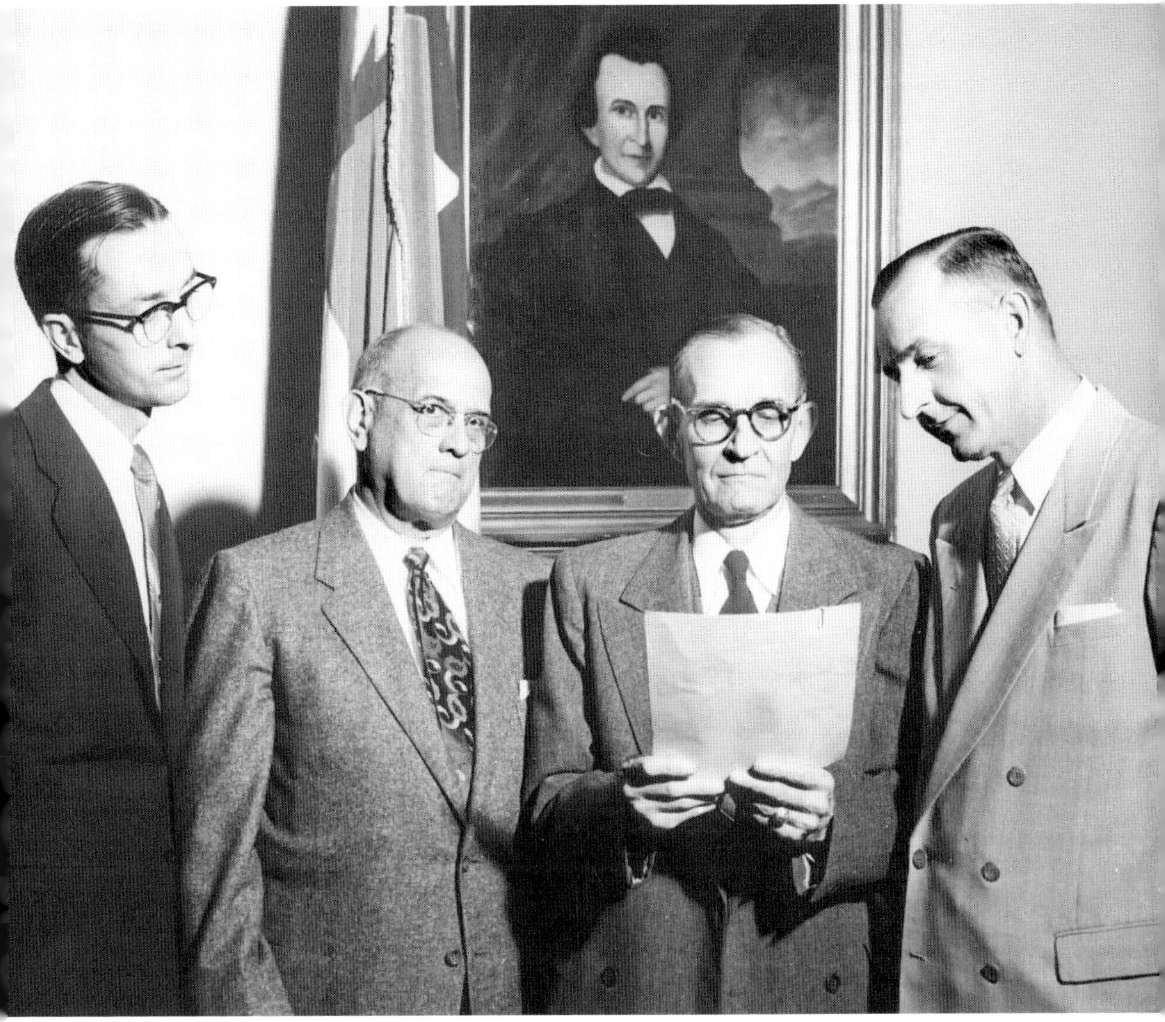

**Jesse Helms**

Helms (1921–2008) made his mark as an outspoken conservative who fought against communism and civil rights. His political career began in 1957, winning a seat on Raleigh's city council, where he immediately gained a reputation for opposing almost everything. In 1960, Helms started giving nightly editorials at the end of the WRAL-TV newscast about various conservative and racially charged topics. This wide audience base elected him to his first Senate term in 1972 and made him the first Republican senator from North Carolina since 1903.

Helms chaired the Senate Foreign Relations Committee during his 30-year career, but he also held a 16-day filibuster against establishing Martin Luther King Jr. Day as a federal holiday. He relished the nickname "Senator No," and when he retired in 2001, he was called the "last prominent unabashed white racist politician in this country." In this photograph are, from left to right, Helms, John Stedman, Gov. William B. Umstead, and G. Harold Myrick. (Courtesy of SANC.)

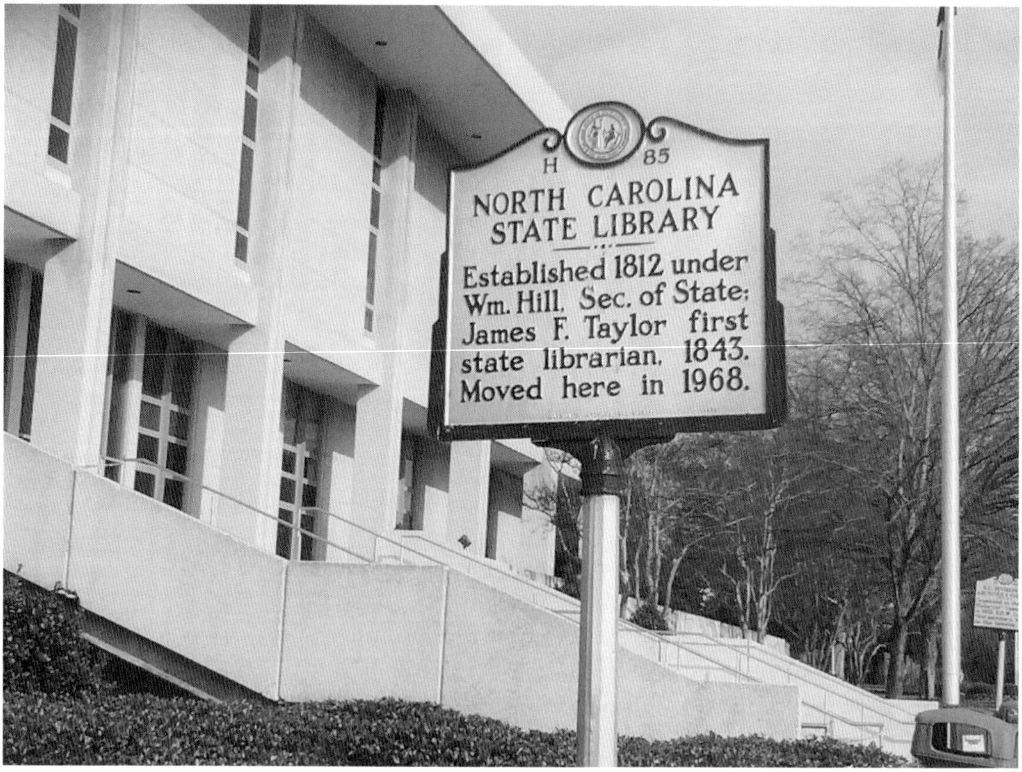


**Carrie Broughton**
Raleigh native Carrie Broughton (1879–1957), the daughter of Needham Broughton, was the first woman to hold a statewide office in North Carolina. In 1917, she started working for the state library, without full pay. The state was under pressure from the North Carolina Library Association, the State Library Commission, and others to make Broughton official. In 1919, she was appointed the state librarian. (Authors' collection.)

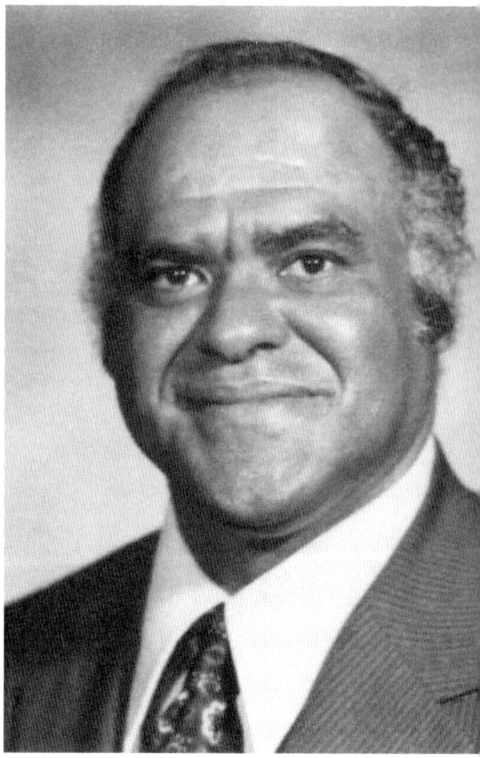

**John Winters**
Winters (1920–2004) served in many local political offices, but he is best remembered as the first African American member of the Raleigh City Council, first elected in 1961. He was also on the North Carolina Good Neighbor Council, and in 1964, was elected a North Carolina senator, serving two terms before being appointed to the North Carolina Utilities Commission. He also served on the boards of Shaw University and the University of North Carolina. (Courtesy of OR.)

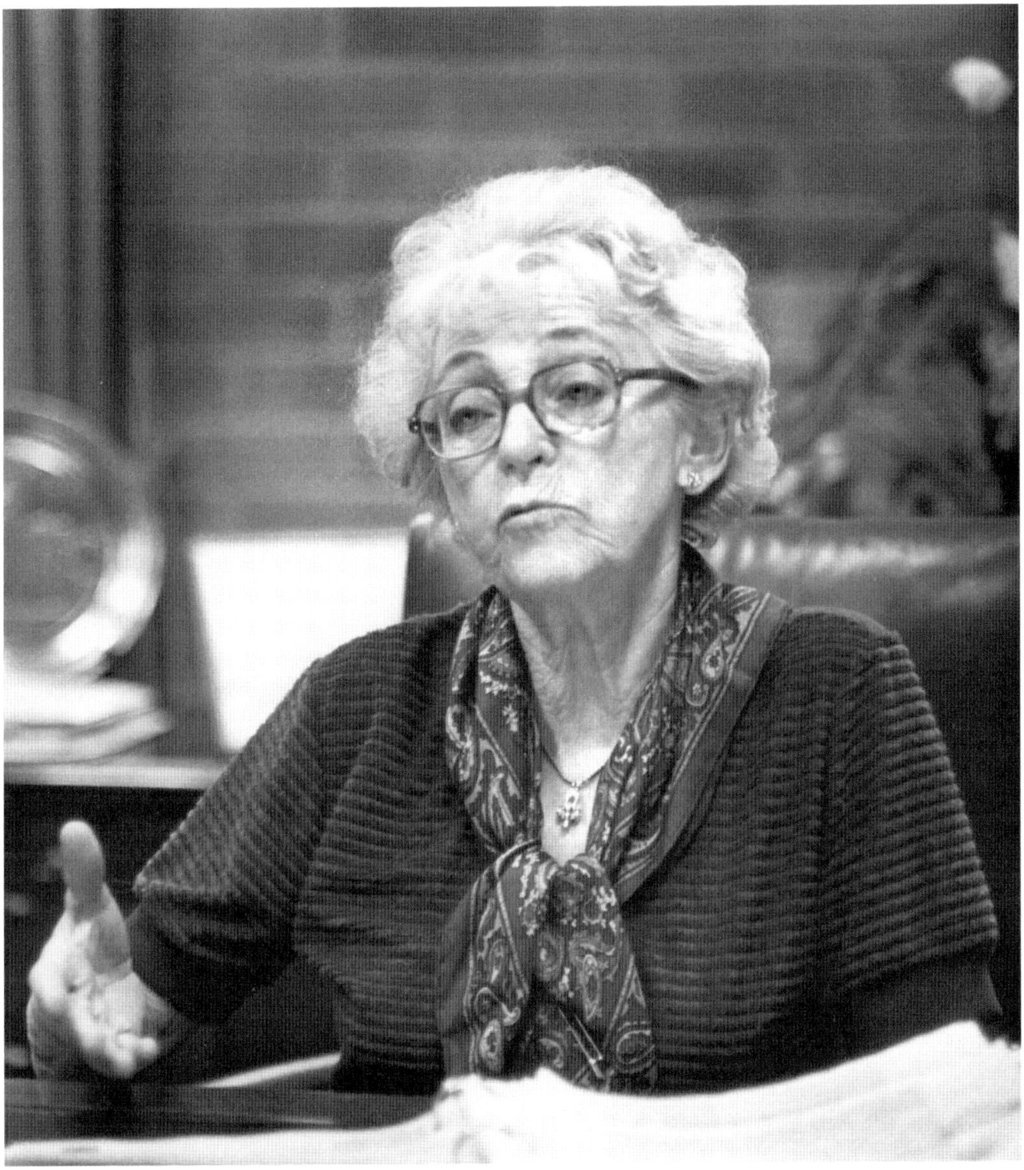

**Isabella Cannon**

Raleigh's first female mayor, Cannon (1904–2002) won her election in 1977 at age 73 with a truly grassroots movement. Her supporters came from outside the business community, and almost all of their donations were $100 or less. She actively participated in civil rights and peace movements before deciding to run for mayor herself. She went door-to-door as "the little old lady in tennis shoes," to prove that her appearance did not negatively affect her ideas or effectiveness.

Cannon only served one term as Raleigh's mayor, but her legacy includes establishing the first-ever comprehensive plan for development and growth in Raleigh, plus dealing with affirmative action issues, strengthening the bonds between the city and the state, and establishing parks. Gardner Street Neighborhood Park was renamed Isabella Cannon Park in 2011, mere months before the election of Nancy McFarlane, Raleigh's second female mayor. (Courtesy of People: administrators, faculty, and staff, c(UA023.024.013), 0001313, Special Collections Research Center, North Carolina State University Libraries.)

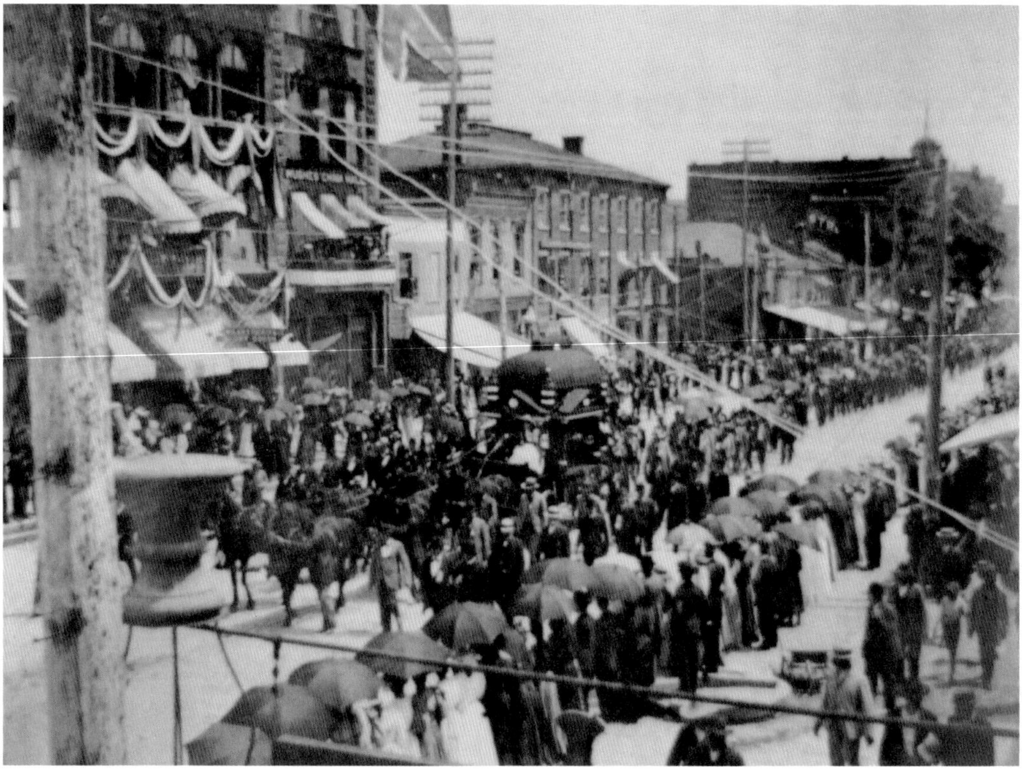

### James Jones

The unique life of James H. Jones (1831–1921) proves that there was no single narrative to African American life in the 19th and early 20th centuries. Born a free man in Wake County in the heart of the slave-owning South, Jones earned an impressive reputation as a brick mason and contractor during the building season. During the winter months, he hired himself out as a gentleman's servant to Raleigh's elite. He continued working through the Civil War, and when Confederate president Jefferson Davis's wife and children moved to St. Mary's in 1862 after the capital of Richmond came under attack, she hired Jones to help them, on the recommendation of his previous employers. He moved back to Richmond with the family and became Jefferson Davis's personal body man for the remainder of the war, driving his carriage, sending his private letters, and otherwise taking care of him. It was Jones who was driving the family south when Davis was arrested at the end of the war.

Jones moved back to Raleigh in 1865 and participated in the Freedmen's and Constitutional Conventions to shape North Carolina's new government. He served as deputy sheriff of Wake County for over 10 years and was elected a Raleigh city alderman during the 1870s and 1880s. He helped form the Victor Fire Company in 1869, which serviced Raleigh's African American community, and was its first foreman until 1882.

With his public works contracting business, Jones worked in cities all across the South, creating their infrastructure as they tried to rebuild after the war. While traveling, he remained involved in Republican politics, and his support of Gen. William Ruffin Cox, who became secretary of the US Senate, led to Jones's appointment to a post in the Senate Stationery Room, where he stayed until his death. He also remained connected to the Davis family. Jones drove Davis's funeral car during a memorial service at the US Capitol in 1893. Davis's funeral procession through Raleigh is pictured here. Before his death, Davis's widow gave Jones her husband's favorite buck horn–handled walking cane, which he donated along with other Davis artifacts to the North Carolina Museum of History.

Jones died in Washington, DC, and is buried in Mount Hope Cemetery in Raleigh. (Courtesy of OR.)

# CHAPTER TWO

# At the Frontier

Keeping Raleigh relevant during its 200 years has at times required people with foresight, creativity, compassion, or courage—and sometimes all of these traits. Whether bravely defending the city from his own men, as Gen. John A. Logan did during the Civil War, or displaying tireless dedication to patients' health, in the case of Dr. Lawson Andrew Scruggs, who taught and practiced medicine at the turn of the 20th century, Raleigh's people have always been willing to make sacrifices for social improvement and the greater good.

Military heroes have defended their country and represented their hometown, like John Lumsden and William Oliver Smith, heroes of World War I who selflessly protected their men against attacks by the enemy. The crusade for health and safety, defending against disease and disrepair, has likewise been led in Raleigh, with Dorothea Dix campaigning for the state's first hospital for the mentally ill in the 1840s, and Dr. Catherine P. Hayden braving the wreckage of a fire to perform necessary surgery.

Breakthroughs in technological research, like North Carolina State professor Dr. Donald Bitzer's work in television engineering, contribute to the advancement of entire industries. The advocacy of fellow NC State professor Dr. Rajendra K. Pachauri regarding the effects of climate change across the globe, especially in third-world countries, resulted in his winning the 2007 Nobel Peace Prize.

Separately, these are all notable accomplishments by admirable individuals. Taken together, however, they exemplify the heart of this city. Raleigh is a close community because so many of its citizens are willing to give selflessly. Whether or not their contributions come on a national stage, Raleigh's citizens believe they are a part of something larger than themselves.

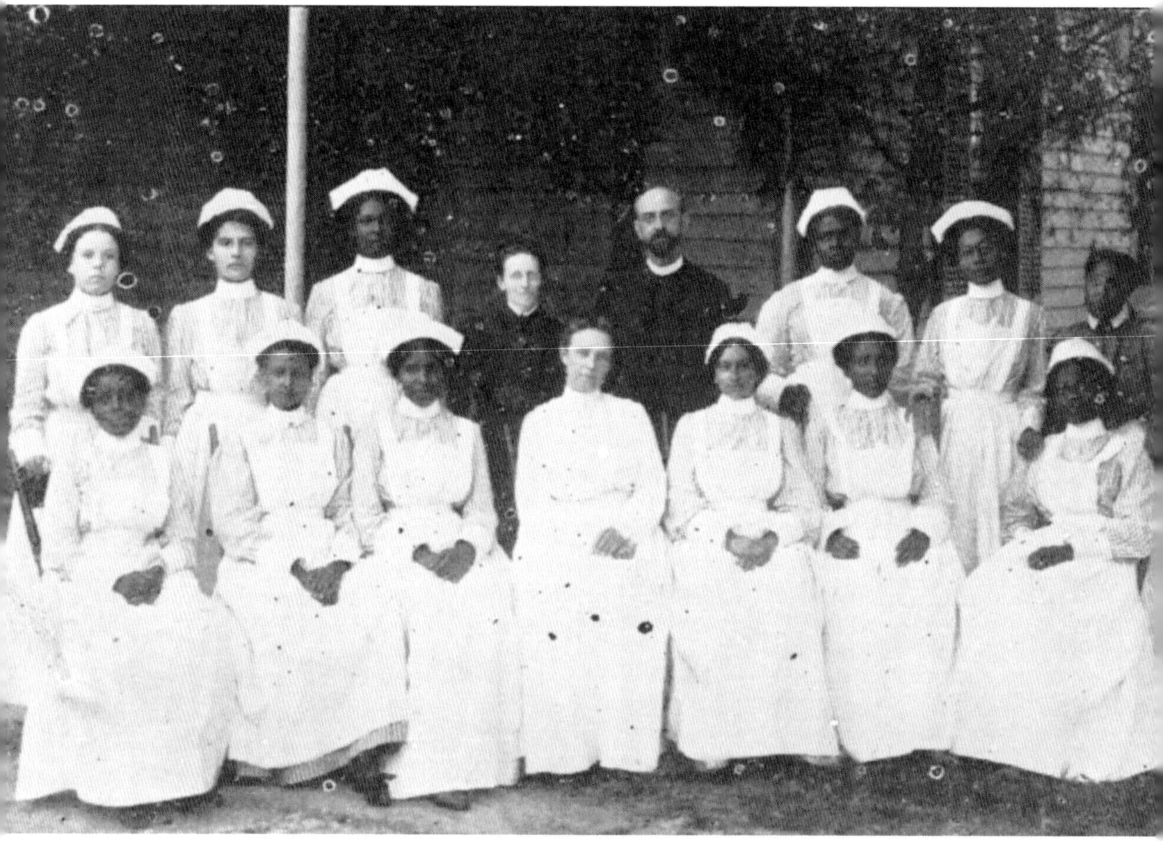

### Dr. Catherine P. Hayden

Dr. Hayden was the first resident physician at St. Agnes Hospital and Nursing School. The hospital began operation in 1896 in the former home of the president of St. Augustine's College. Its purpose was to serve black patients outside Raleigh's city limits. The 1906 nursing class of St. Agnes is pictured here. Through the 1940s, it was the only hospital that would open its doors to black patients in eastern North Carolina, and the only one owned by African Americans in the entire state. Hayden started her work there in 1900, six years after graduating from the University of Colorado. In 1904, a main part of the building burned down. Shortly thereafter, when an emergency patient arrived, Hayden patched up a sterilizing machine from the wreckage and performed surgery in the burned-out building. (Courtesy of SANC.)

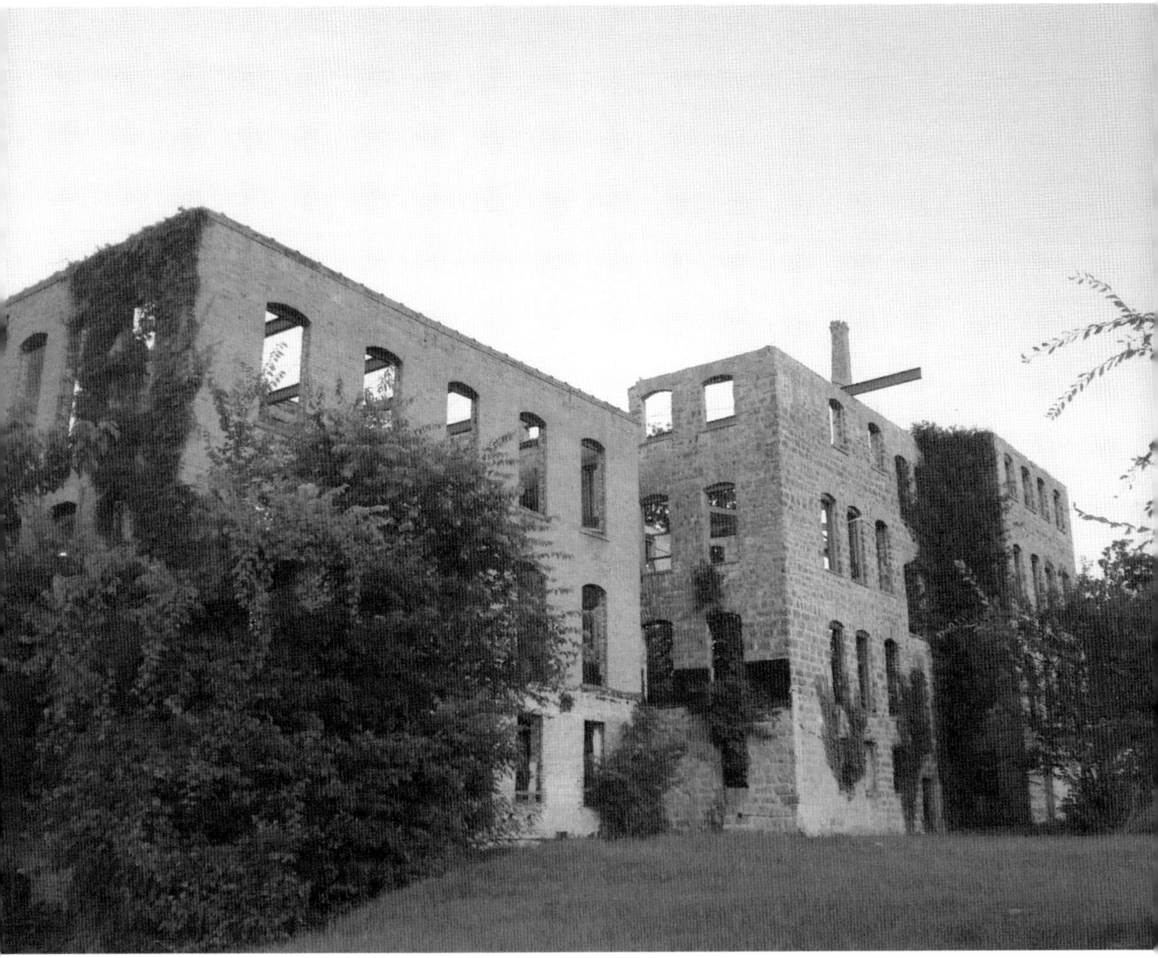

**Dr. Lawson Andrew Scruggs**

Despite being born into a life of slavery and receiving only rudimentary schooling upon gaining his freedom, Scruggs (1857–1914) graduated from Shaw University as a two-time valedictorian—first with a literary degree, and then as a member of the first class of doctors in the Leonard Medical School in 1886. Scruggs went on to become a pharmacist as well, and served as the first black physician and lecturer at both Shaw and St. Agnes, the ruins of which are pictured here. In between, he operated a private practice and actively participated in Raleigh's literary society and in Republican politics. (Courtesy of Scott Menut.)

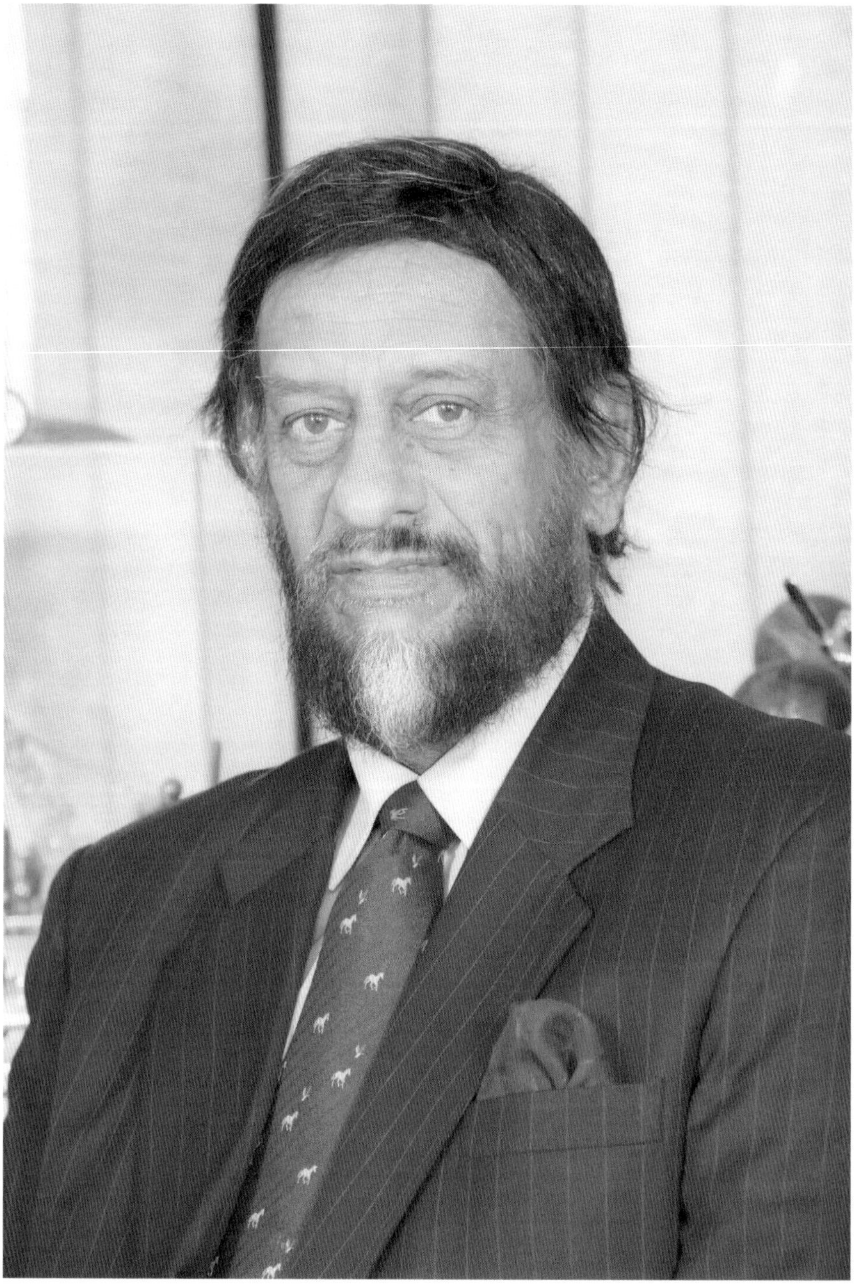

**Dr. Rajendra Pachauri**
Public land-grant college North Carolina State has made numerous contributions to national and international research. The winner of the 2007 Nobel Peace Prize, Pachauri (1940–present) received both his master's and doctoral degrees from NC State. As chairman of the Intergovernmental Panel on Climate Change, he shared the Nobel Prize with former vice president Al Gore "for their efforts to build up and disseminate greater knowledge about man-made climate change, and to lay the foundations for the measures that are needed to counteract such change." Pachauri's work currently focuses on the negative effects of climate change, especially in third-world countries. (Courtesy of Dr. Pachauri.)

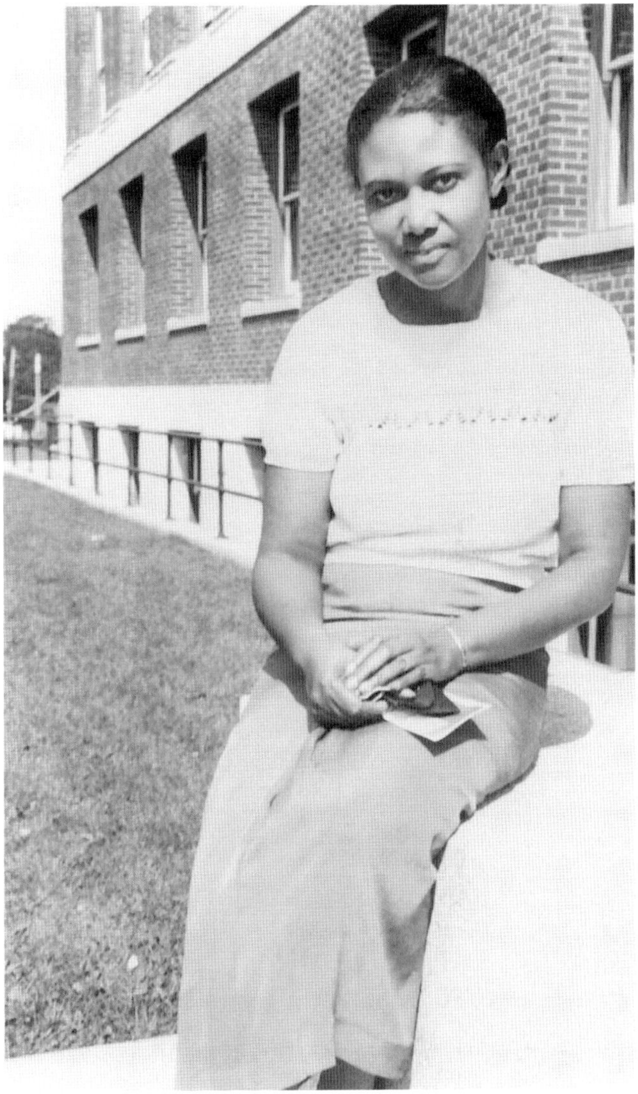

**Dr. Roger Arliner Young**
Young (1899–1964) saw many successes over her career, but her contributions have remained hidden in the shadows of history. When she was 25 years old, she beat out another leading researcher to publish her article "On the Excretory Apparatus in the Paramecium" in the September 12, 1924, issue of *Science* magazine, making her the first black woman in her field to do so.

Young took her first science course in her fifth year at Howard University, receiving a C in introductory zoology. Prof. Ernest Everett Just encouraged Young to continue in zoology and took her on as his personal research assistant. He helped get her paper published, saw her earn her master's degree from Chicago University, and spent the summers with her researching at the Marine Biological Laboratory in Woods Hole, Massachusetts. She taught at Howard, and when Just went out of town, he left her in charge of the biology department.

The stress caused by this responsibility, combined with their deteriorating personal relationship, led to Young failing her first doctoral entry exams. Just started becoming publicly antagonistic, calling her teaching "far below standards" and saying he had "no respect" for her as a person. She countered, claiming he deliberately distracted her from her work and denied her access to lab equipment; nevertheless, Howard fired Young in 1936. Young reconnected with a fellow Woods Hole researcher to get back on track and earn her degree from Pennsylvania, making her the first black woman to earn a zoology doctorate, but issues from her mental breakdown would follow her for the rest of her life.

Young took over the biology department at Shaw University in 1942. She joined civil rights advocates on campus, including burgeoning labor activists. Young traveled with "Operation Dixie" to help the tobacco workers of Eastern North Carolina, mostly black and female, unionize. On a Raleigh-to-Williamston bus in July 1946, she refused to give up her seat for a white rider. The bus was forced to stop in Nashville, North Carolina, where she was questioned and possibly arrested, nine years before Rosa Parks took the same stand in Montgomery, Alabama.

Unfortunately, Young's story did not end as triumphantly as Parks's. She moved on to several short-term positions at schools in Texas, Mississippi, and Louisiana. Her mother died in 1953, escalating her mental instability and leading to her institutionalization. She died poor and alone two years after her release. (Courtesy of the Marine Biological Laboratory Archives.)

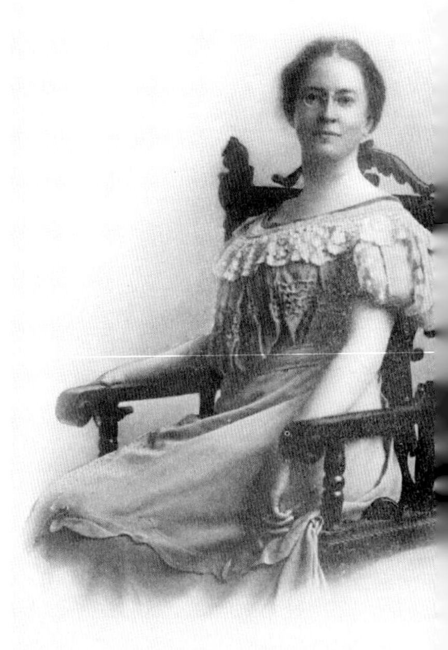

### Dr. Elizabeth Delia Dixon-Carroll

In 1895, Dixon-Carroll (1872–1934) graduated from the Women's Medical College of New York, which is now Cornell University. In 1899, Baptist Female University, now Meredith College, hired her as their resident physician. She joined the Raleigh Academy of Medicine and married a dentist, Dr. Norwood Carroll. Against convention, she kept her maiden name, Dixon. The couple built a joint practice while she continued her work at Meredith. (Courtesy of Meredith College Archives.)

### William Oliver Smith

Smith served as a first lieutenant with the 318th Machine-Gun Battalion, 81st Division, during World War I. On November 9, 1918, near Haudiomont, France, Smith led his platoon in an attack. The next day, the enemy launched a counterattack, and Smith, under heavy fire, held his position for an hour. He was wounded three times, eventually running out of ammunition and being taken prisoner. He received the Distinguished Service Cross. Smith's Wildcat Division is remembered with this memorial on the capitol grounds. (Authors' collection.)

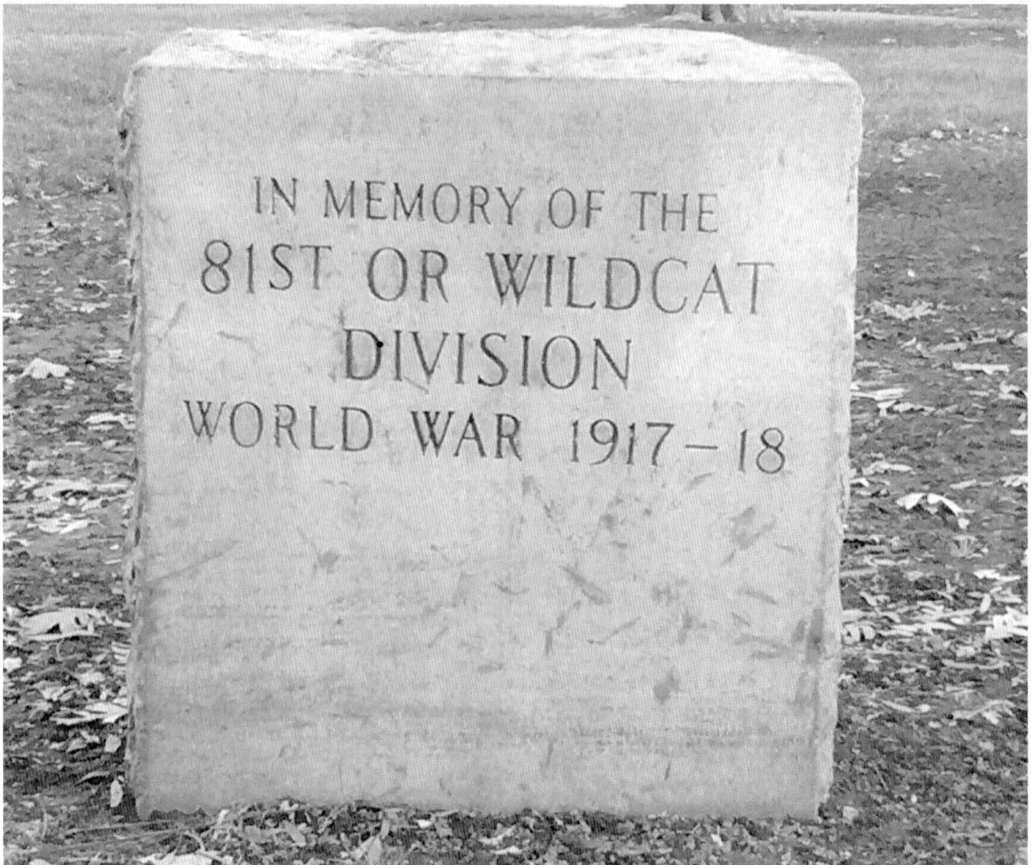

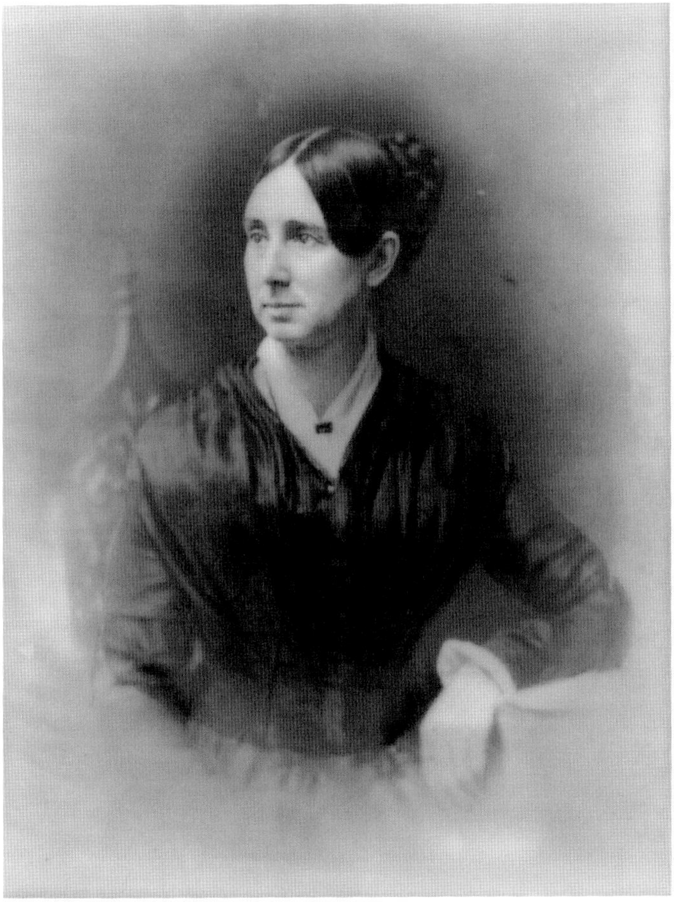

**Dorothea Dix**
In 1848, Dix (1802–1887), "America's apostle of humanitarianism," came to Raleigh as part of her crusade begun in 1841 to better the lives of the mentally ill. She had made such an impact by the time of her arrival in Raleigh that North Carolina and Delaware were the only two states in the country without hospitals specifically for their citizens with mental illness. While in Raleigh, she stayed at the Mansion House hotel, directly across the street from the courthouse and jail, and observed the conditions within the city. Because North Carolina had no facilities specifically for its citizens who struggled with mental health issues, cities often resorted to jailing them to keep them off the streets. Dix visited neighborhoods all over the city and gathered evidence of people "in more or less suffering and exposed states, according to the ability of their friends to provide for them" across Wake County. She presented her stories to the general assembly to plea for $100,000 for mental health reform and a state hospital for their care.

Her efforts met resistance until she befriended Louisa Dobbin, wife of Representative James Dobbin, who was staying at the Mansion House as well. Dix cared for Louisa when she became fatally ill, and, as she lay dying, Louisa requested her husband champion the cause of the hospital to repay Dix's kindness. Five days after Louisa's death, James gave a speech described as "one of the most touchingly beautiful efforts that we have ever heard" by one of the bill's original opponents. A week later, the law passed, creating the State Hospital for the Insane. The hill on which it was to be built was christened Dix Hill. With help from Dix and Raleigh residents Charles Hinton and George Mordecai, it opened in 1856 with 11 patients, five from Wake County, and was named after Dix's grandfather, Dr. Elijah Dix. The hospital itself was not renamed the Dorothea Dix Hospital until a century later, and it closed in 2012, ironically due to underfunded mental health reforms. (Courtesy of RCM.)

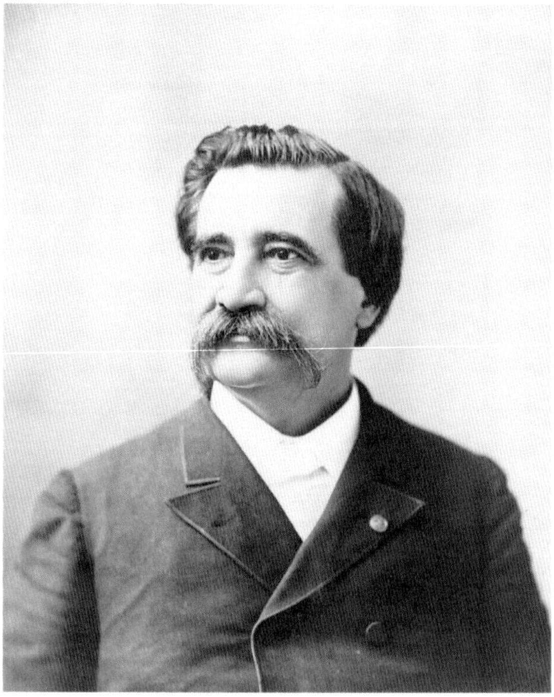

**Gen. John A. Logan**

Logan arrived in Raleigh in April 1865 at the head of the US 15th Army Corps, accompanying Gen. William T. Sherman on his march through the South in pursuit of the Confederate general Joseph E. Johnston, located in and around the capital city. Fearing the same destruction that Sherman had brought to the cities of Atlanta and Columbia, Raleigh's city leaders met Sherman outside the city and successfully pled for preservation.

Johnston's generals moved west out of Raleigh to evade the Federal army and tried to evacuate wounded men and supplies at nearby railroad depots. On April 13, fighting erupted on Raleigh's outskirts, the combat continuing until the armies reached the town of Morrisville. After the Confederates barely escaped the station, uncoupling their supply cars in order to move faster, Gen. Judson Kilpatrick, leader of the advancing cavalry, wrote to Sherman that he had "fought over nearly every foot of ground from Raleigh to this point" through "barricades of the strongest character."

Mere days before the conclusion of this battle, Grant accepted the surrender of Lee in Virginia. Trapped between armies, Johnston telegraphed Sherman in Raleigh, wishing "to enter into the needful arrangements to terminate the existing war." Logan camped his men on the lands of John Devereaux and Moses Mordecai, but had his headquarters in Morrisville. As negotiations began on April 17, Sherman received a telegram of Pres. Abraham Lincoln's death. He tried to keep the assassination from the troops until after his meeting with Johnston, so that "a fate worse than that of Columbia would [not] befall" Raleigh, but Logan recognized the possibility for violence was still strong and set out immediately for the city.

An angry mob of about 2,000 of his own troops met him at the edge of Raleigh. Logan used all of his influence and tried to order them back to camp, with no luck. Eventually, Logan ordered two artillery pieces to fire on the men if they did not obey, and the mob finally dispersed. Logan rose to general after joining the Army during the Mexican War in 1846 as a volunteer, and enjoyed great respect from both his men and his peers. His quick thinking and level head saved Raleigh from destruction.

The capital city still does not remember Sherman fondly, but Logan became an unlikely Civil War hero for Raleigh. He is also credited with starting what is now known as Memorial Day. (Courtesy of Library of Congress.)

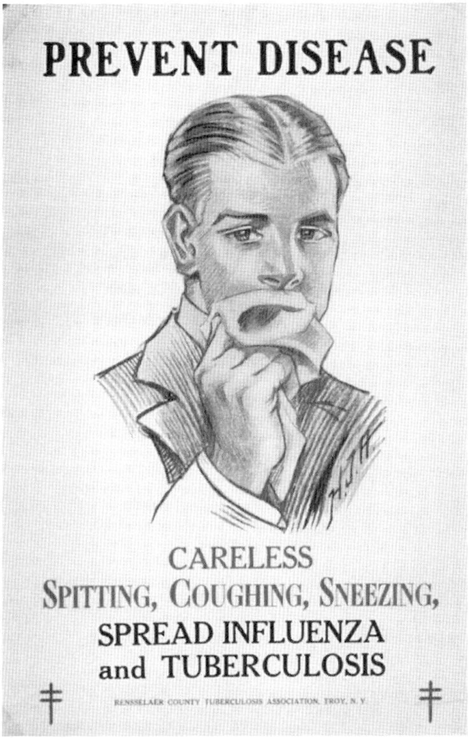


**Lucy Riddick and Eliza Page**
During the outbreak of Spanish influenza in 1917–1919, many people made a difference through nursing and other relief efforts. Two of these were Lucy Riddick and Eliza Page. The local Red Cross recruited Raleigh citizens to help nurse the sick. Riddick and Page were among 200 who rose to the occasion, caring for students at North Carolina State. Their heroic actions resulted in the women succumbing to the deadly disease themselves. (Courtesy of archive.org.)

**Dr. Benjamin Kilgore**
The Wake County Public Health Service called for all publicly distributed milk to be pasteurized in an attempt to cull the outbreak of Spanish influenza in 1919. Dr. Kilgore responded by setting up the first pasteurization plant at the North Carolina State Agricultural Experiment Station in 1919, and then establishing his own dairy, Pine State Creamery. (Courtesy of OR.)

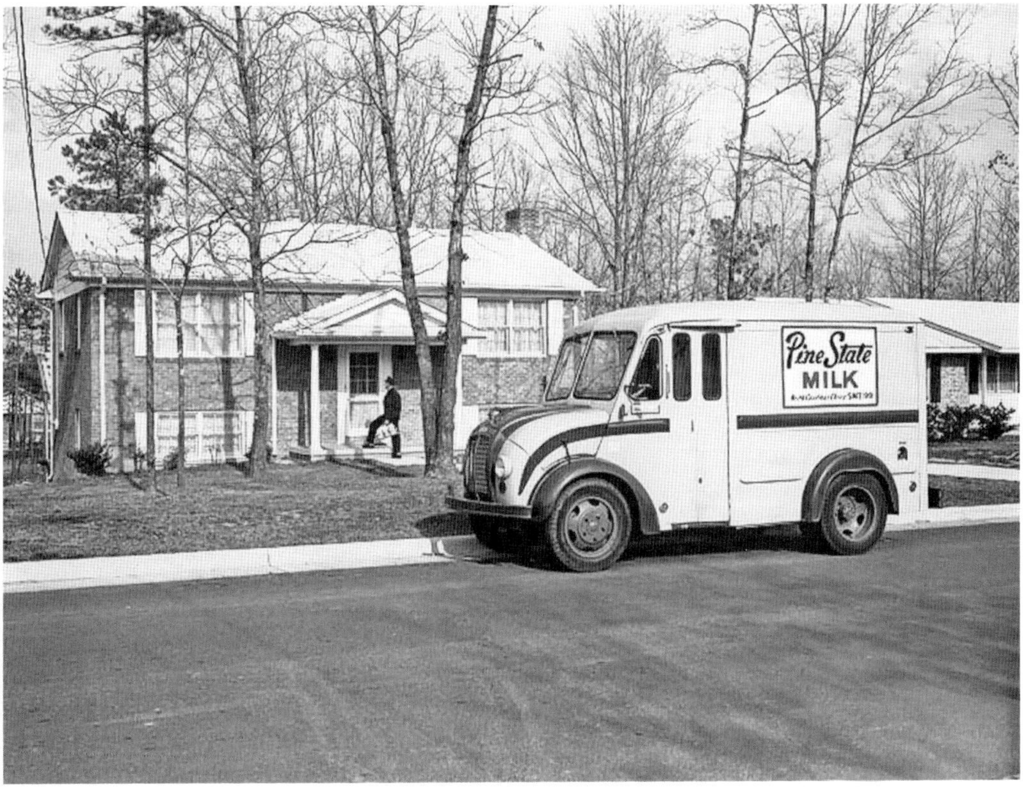

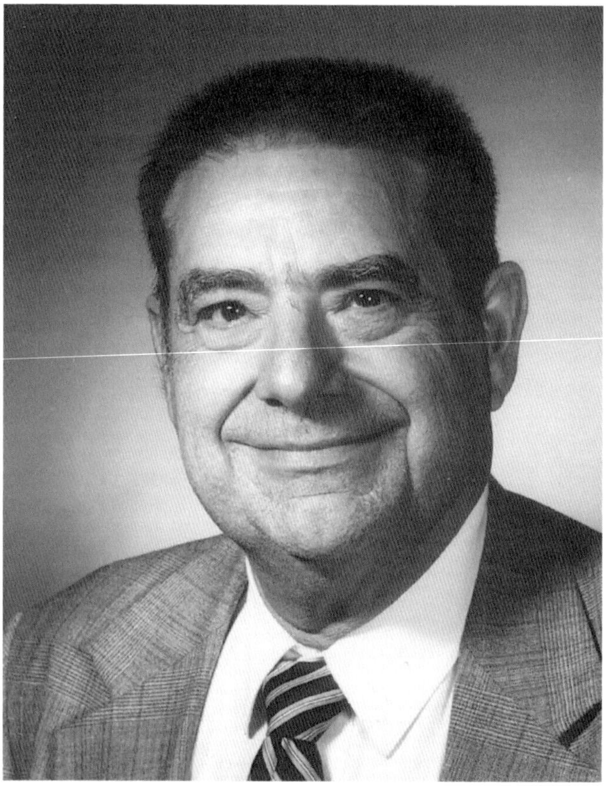

### Dr. Donald Bitzer

Bitzer (1934–present), electrical engineer, computer scientist, and Distinguished University Research Professor at North Carolina State, co-invented the Emmy Award–winning flat plasma television display screen in 1964 so that students whose research required staring at screens for hours could save their eyes from a flickering display. In addition to his many other awards, he is the namesake of the Donald L. Bitzer Creativity Award, the aim of which is to "recognize and encourage creativity in undergraduate computer science students." (Courtesy of Dr. Donald Bitzer.)

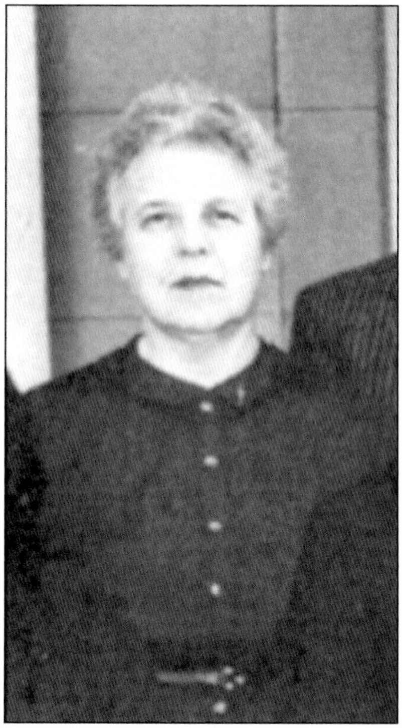

### Dr. Nell Hirschberg

Dr. Hirschberg worked on the home front during World War II, receiving a Red Cross Award for her work. She earned her PhD and became a bacteriologist with the North Carolina State Board of Hygiene, also teaching bacteriology at North Carolina Central University. Hirschberg was also involved in music. The Nell Hirschberg Cello Chair commemorates her at the North Carolina Symphony. (Courtesy of North Carolina Central University Archives.)

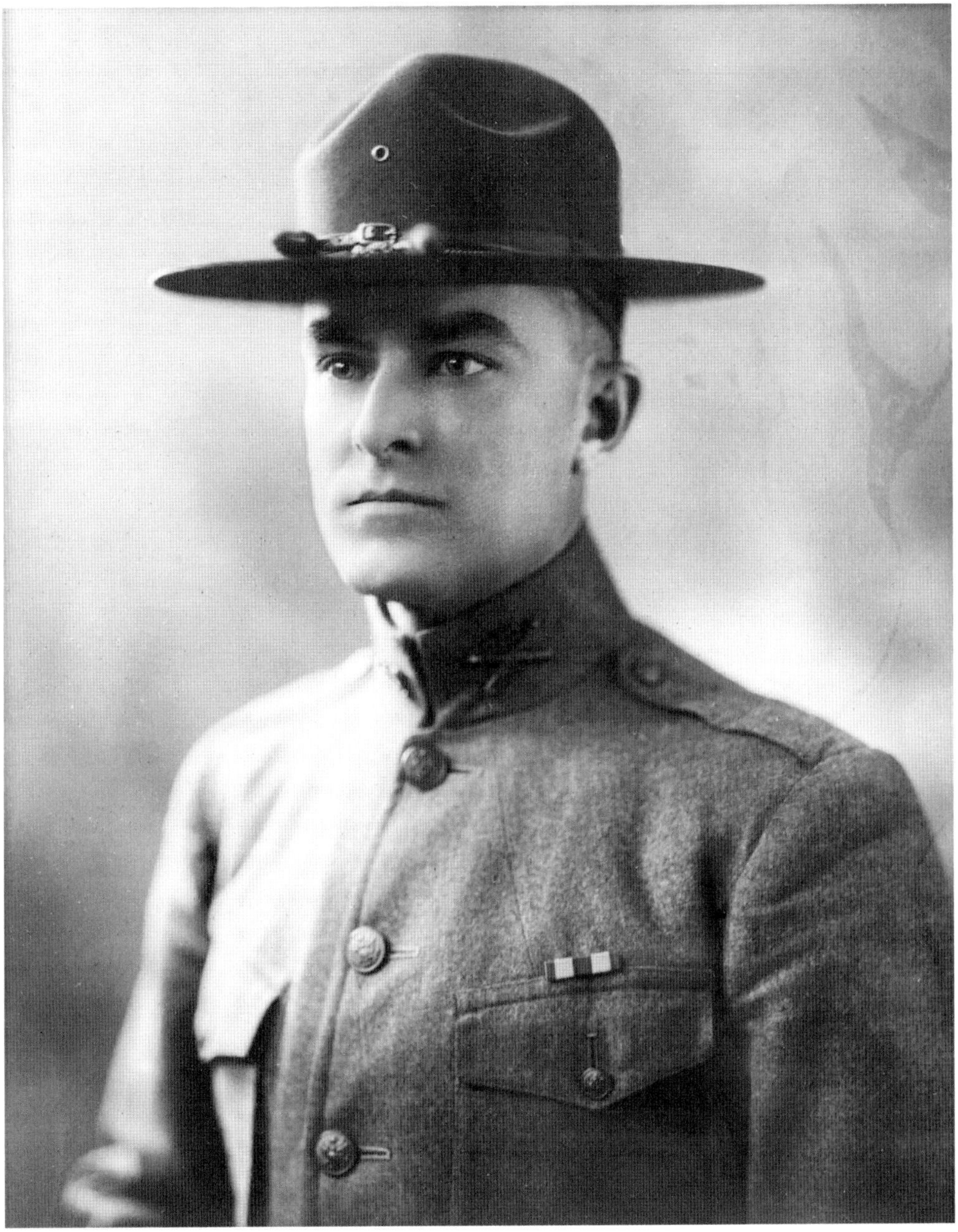

John C.S. Lumsden

Lieutenant Lumsden of Raleigh served as an observer in the 12th Aero Squadron during World War I. On July 28, 1918, his squadron was attacked over Chateau-Thierry, France, by eight German planes. On at least three occasions during that fight, Lumsden turned his gun from protecting himself in order to keep the Germans from the plane that was performing the observation mission. Lumsden took down one enemy plane and disabled another with his efforts. However, in fearlessly exposing himself to save his comrades and their mission, Lumsden was struck by a bullet in the head and perished.

The French government awarded him the Croix de Guerre, and the Aero Club of America awarded him the Honor of Merit bronze tablet. (Courtesy of SANC.)

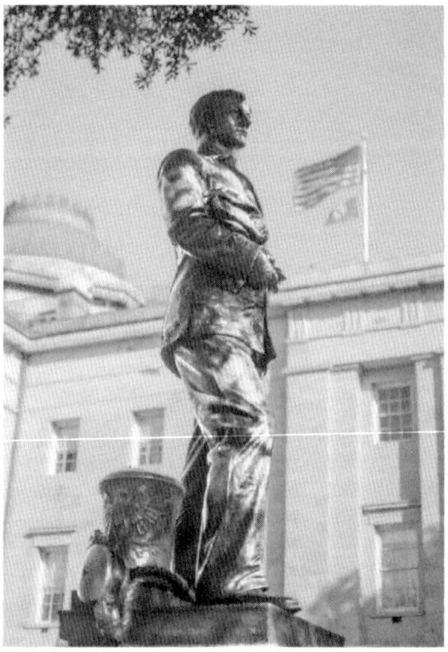

**Ens. Worth Bagley**
Bagley (1874–1898) died on board the torpedo ship USS *Winslow* from shots fired on shore at Cardenas, Cuba, making him the first and only American naval officer killed during the Spanish-American War. His death moved Raleigh. The state held a military funeral on the capitol grounds and erected the statue shown here. Ensign Bagley's brother-in-law Josephus Daniels wrote a book memorializing him, and a small town outside Raleigh renamed itself Cardenas, after the place of his death. (Courtesy of Dmitri Medvedev.)

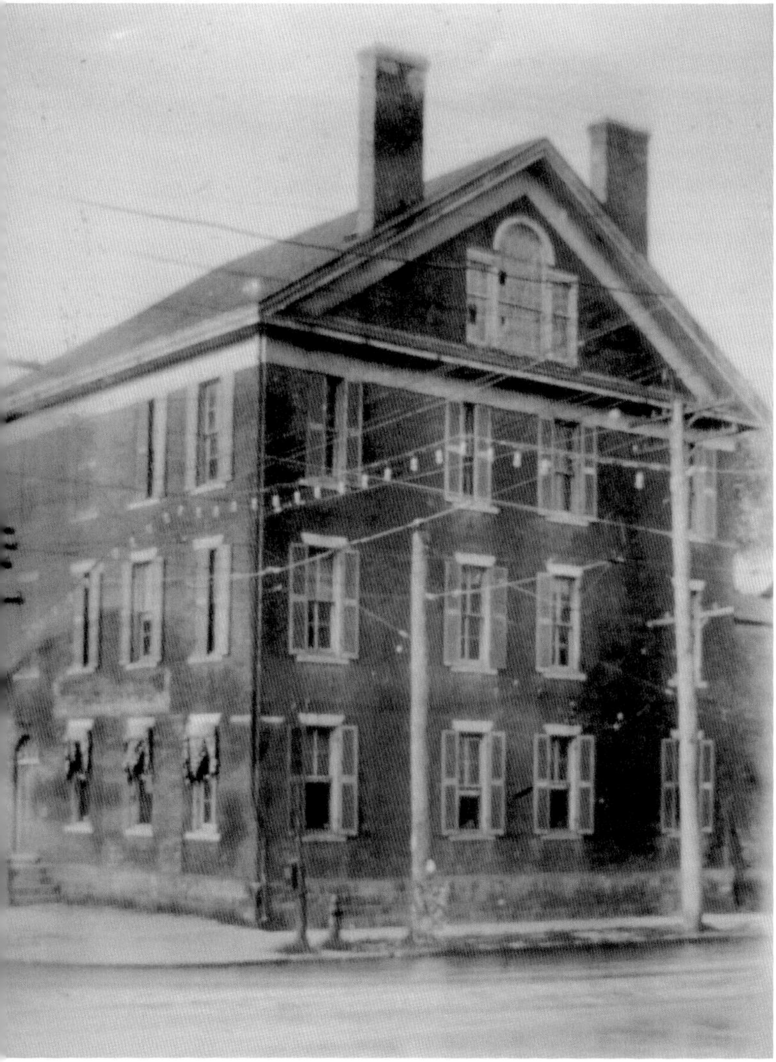

**Dr. Fabius Haywood**
Haywood (1803–1880) had his home and office, pictured here later in the century, on Fayetteville Street in the 1840s. In 1848, he was among the first physicians in the state to use ether or chloroform during surgery, doing so about a year after anesthesia was first demonstrated in Massachusetts. While many people found this action radical, it helped pave the way for future medical improvements. (Courtesy of OR.)

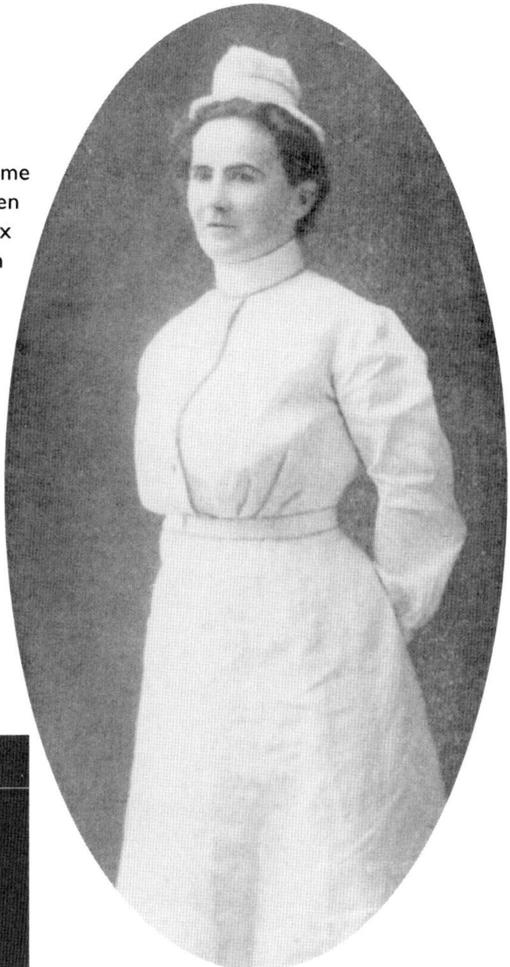

**Mary Lewis Wyche**
While in her 30s, Wyche (1858–1936) studied to become a nurse. She was hired as the first head nurse when Rex Hospital opened in 1894. She organized the Rex Hospital Nursing School, the first in the state, which opened with four students. In addition, Wyche began the Raleigh Nurse's Association in 1901 and the State Nurse's Association in 1902. She pushed the North Carolina legislature to establish a board of examiners for nurses. (Authors' collection.)

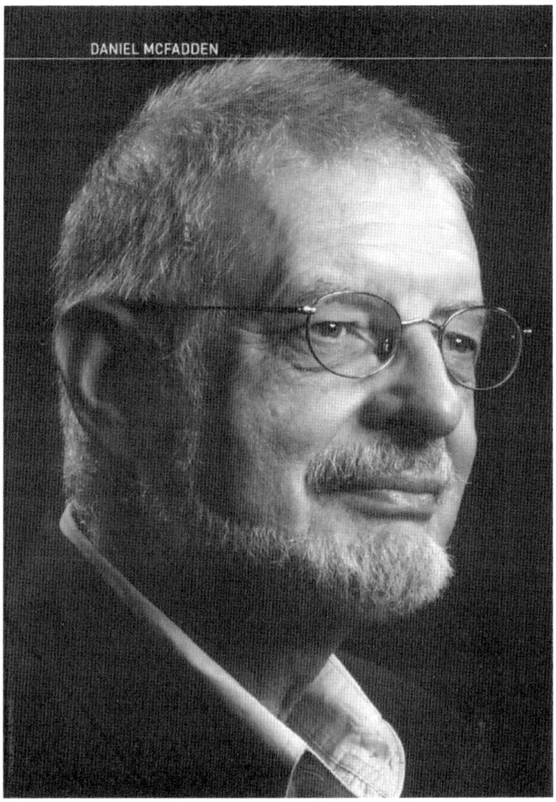


**Dr. Daniel McFadden**
McFadden (1937–present) grew up in Raleigh and went on to study at the University of Minnesota. He is a leader in the study of health policy analysis. In 2000, he was awarded the Nobel Prize in Economics for the development of theory and methods for analyzing selective samples. McFadden has won several other awards for his work in the years since, and continues to research and educate. (Courtesy of Dr. Daniel McFadden.)

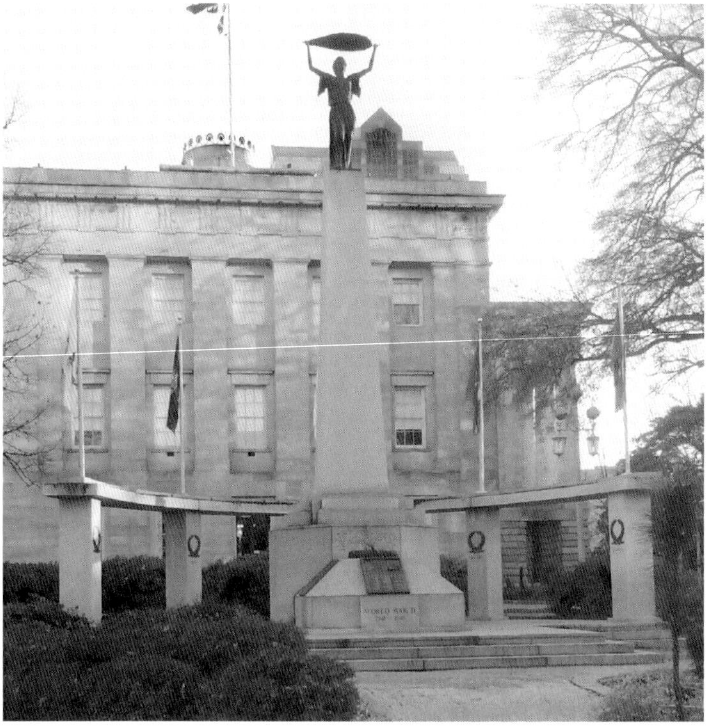

**Cpl. Irvin B. Mayer**
Mayer served in Company C, First Battalion, 23rd Marines. Wounded in action twice in July 1944 during the Tinian campaign, Mayer both times returned to duty the same day. He received a Purple Heart for his wounds on July 4, and a Gold Star for his wounds on July 11. On February 19, 1945, he was fatally wounded at Iwo Jima and received the Silver Star. He and other North Carolina veterans are remembered with this monument on the north side of the state capitol. (Authors' collection.)

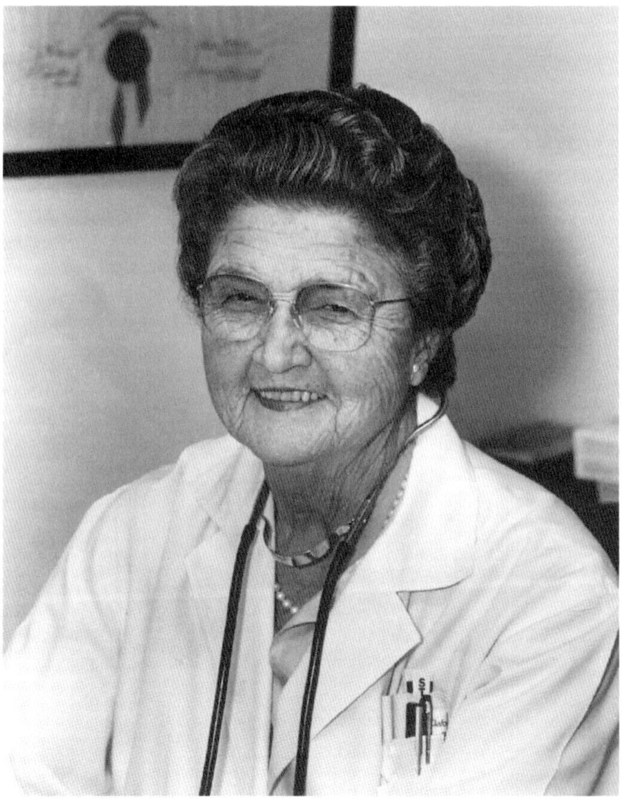

**Dr. Annie Louise Wilkerson**
Wilkerson (1914–2005) was inspired by her father to become a doctor. After completing school, she went to Rex Hospital. She was told she would not receive an internship because she was a woman, but she nonetheless applied and was accepted. After her residency, Wilkerson worked at her father's practice while continuing at Rex and at St. Agnes Hospital. She opened an OB/GYN practice, making her the first woman in Raleigh with that specialty. (Courtesy of RCM.)

# CHAPTER THREE

# For the People

Because all work and no play can make any city dull, it is natural that some residents of any town will turn their efforts to entertaining and pleasing their neighbors. From the first anthology of North Carolina poetry published by Mary Bayard Devereux Clarke in 1854, to the all-star play of current major league baseball player Josh Hamilton, the people of Raleigh know the value of entertaining both others and themselves.

Bigger than baseball in Raleigh, though, is college basketball, and the intense rivalries on "Tobacco Road" between North Carolina State, the University of North Carolina, and Duke all began in 1946 with the arrival of Everett Case as coach of NC State's Wolfpack. He encouraged North Carolina athletes to practice basketball instead of football, and the move paid off. Case led NC State to nine straight conference championships, creating a national name for the team in the process. Another legendary coach, Jim Valvano, won a thrilling national championship with the team in 1983, but left a greater legacy with his foundation to find a cure for cancer, created as a result of his own battle with the disease.

Raleigh also has had its fair share of stars of the stage and screen. American Idol singer Clay Aiken grew up in Raleigh. Family success stories include actor Ira David Wood III, his son Ira David IV, and daughter Evan Rachel, who all grew up in Raleigh.

Many artists early in Raleigh's history had to overcome racial obstacles, however. George Moses Horton, an enslaved man born at the turn of the 19th century, published the first book by an African American in the South in 1829 and used the proceeds of his very popular works in an unsuccessful attempt to buy his freedom.

The methods of entertainment have changed over time, and Raleigh's public performances have mirrored its stages of growth as a city. You can tell a lot about a town by how its citizens entertain themselves and what they find worth paying for. Raleigh's current commitment to the arts demonstrates its ongoing evolution as a community.

### David Thompson

Thompson (1954–present) led the Wolfpack to its first NCAA championship in 1974, defeating reigning champion UCLA. He was named Most Outstanding Player of the tournament. Thompson's NBA career started strong but was derailed by injuries and substance abuse. After recovering, Thompson wrote a book about his life and finished his degree at NC State. Only his number 44 has ever been retired by NC State. (Courtesy of Athletics Photographs, 1893–2003 (UA023.004), ua023_004-003-am0012-000-007, Special Collections Research Center, North Carolina State University Libraries.)

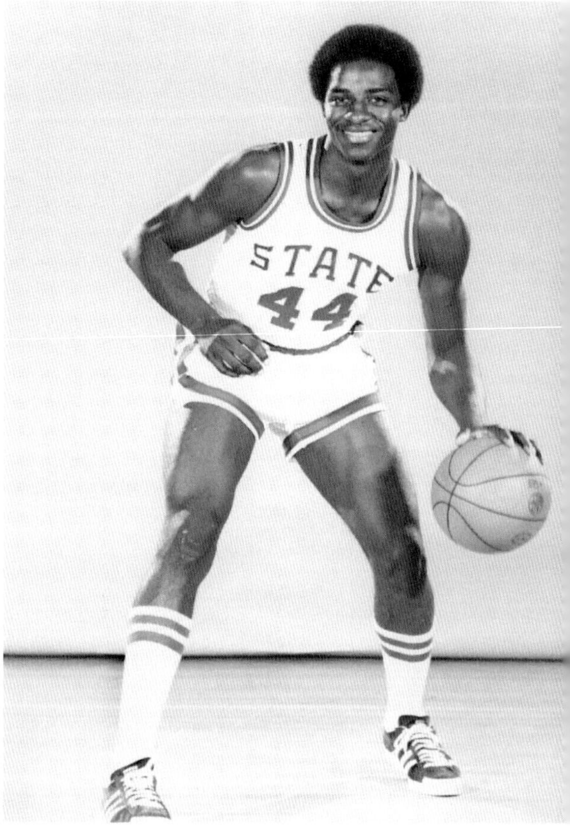


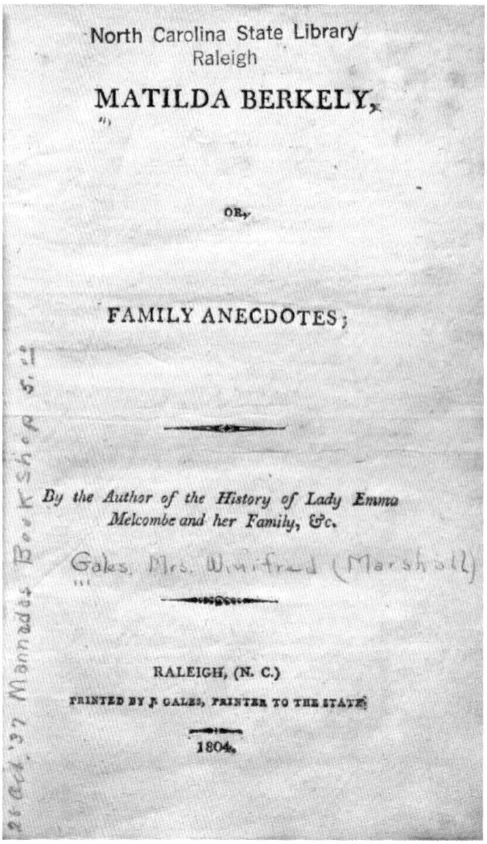



MATILDA BERKELY,

OR,

FAMILY ANECDOTES;

*By the Author of the History of Lady Emma Melcombe and her Family, &c.*

Gales, Mrs. Winifred (Marshall)

RALEIGH, (N. C.)

PRINTED BY J. GALES, PRINTER TO THE STATE.

1804.

### Winifred Marshall Gales

Gales (1761–1839), a novelist and poet, moved to Raleigh in 1799. She wrote *Matilda Berkely: or, Family Anecdotes*, and had it published by her husband, Joseph Gales on the Raleigh *Register* press in 1803. All of her previous works had been published in London. This was the first book published by a Raleigh resident, and the first volume of fiction printed in Raleigh. Gales and her husband moved to Washington in 1833. (Courtesy of the North Carolina State Library.)

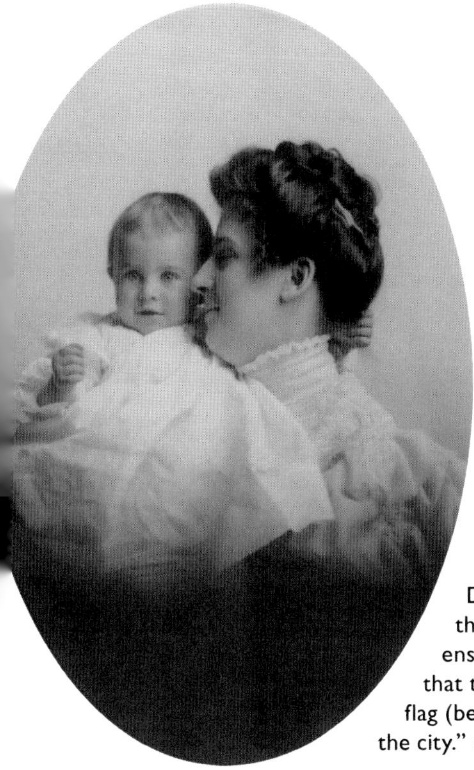

### Kate Denson

During the Battle of Manila Bay in the Spanish-American War, the USS *Raleigh* captured a Spanish vessel, the *Riena Christina*, and sent one of her quick-firing guns to Raleigh, the ship's namesake, to use for celebrations. In return, the board of aldermen decided to create an ensign for the ship. After reviewing local artists, they selected Denson (1877–1952), a former St. Mary's student, as the designer. On July 7, 1899, they drew up a contract with her. Denson, seen in the photograph to the left with a baby, finished in December and presented the flag to the board. Unfortunately, the ship had been decommissioned four months prior, so the ensign was cast aside and forgotten. It was not until the 1960s that the city manager found the old piece of fabric in a box. The flag (below) was voted by the city council as the "authentic flag of the city." (Courtesy of RCM.)

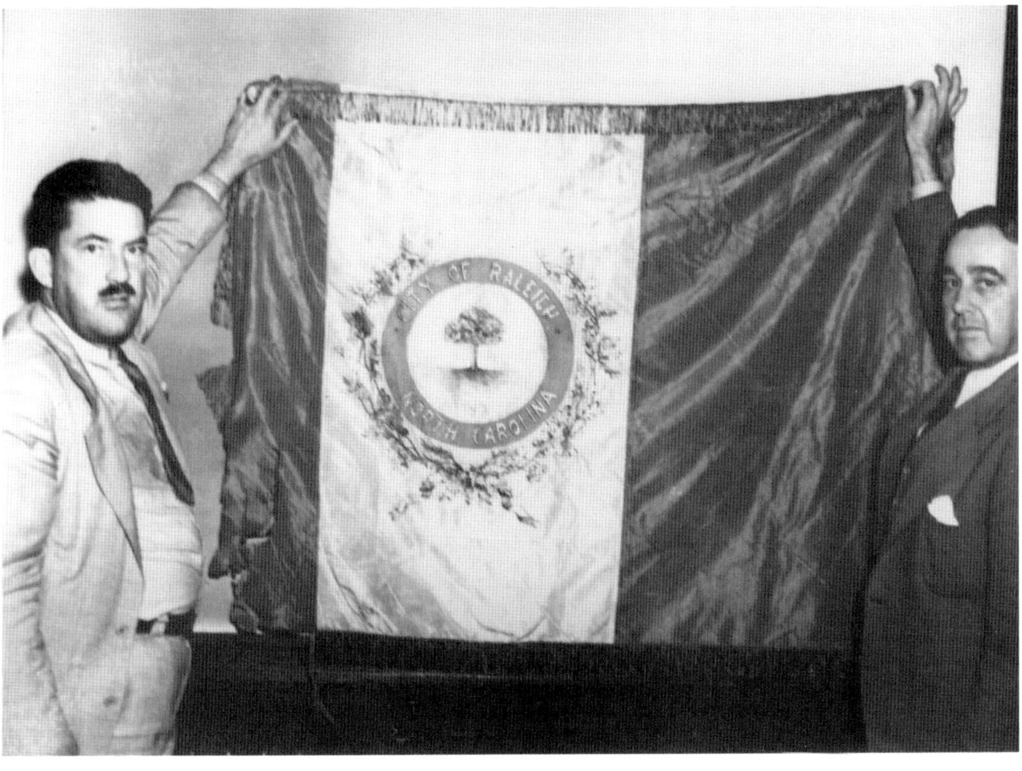

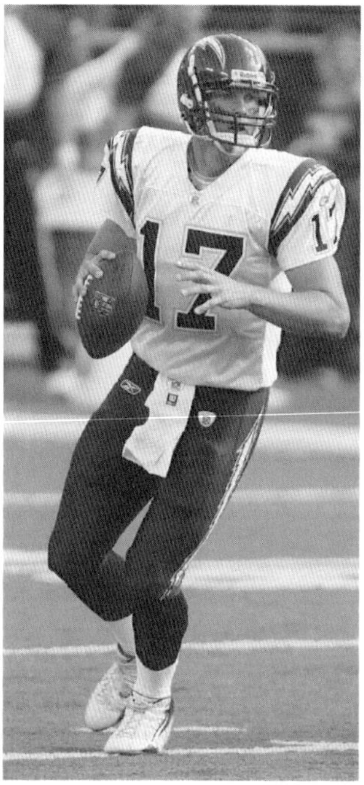

**Phillip Rivers**

Record-setting quarterback Rivers (1981–present) starred at North Carolina State before establishing his career in the NFL. He has been selected to the Pro Bowl four times with the San Diego Chargers and finished as a finalist for the 2012 Walter Payton NFL Man of the Year Award, given for both on- and off-the-field excellence. (Photograph by Keith Allison.)

**Ann Preston Bridgers**

Raleigh playwright Bridgers was active in the formation of the Raleigh Little Theatre during the 1930s. She served as a liaison between the Raleigh Little Theatre and the Federal Theatre Project, which was a New Deal organization developed under the administration of Pres. Franklin D. Roosevelt. With federal support and through the efforts of citizens like Bridgers, the Raleigh Little Theatre thrives to this day. (Courtesy of Raleigh Little Theatre.)

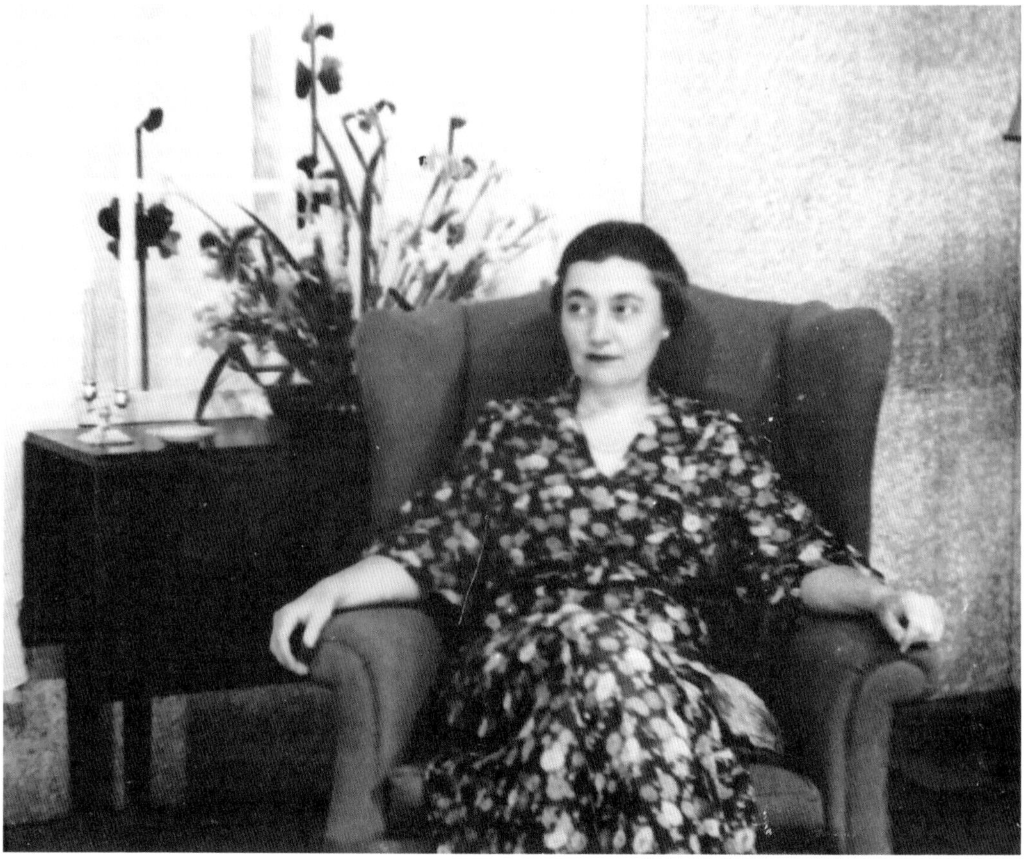

### Marshall Wyatt

Raleigh native Wyatt (1950–present) was managing an art gallery in San Francisco in the 1980s when an intriguing find at a record swap led him across the country to the Appalachian Mountains and eventually back home. The old 78 rpm disc was a recording by Frank Blevins, a fiddler from Ashe County, North Carolina, and his band, the Tar Heel Rattlers. Unable to shake his curiosity about their sound, Wyatt took a shot in the dark, picked up the phone, and called information. The local operator found a listing for a Frank Blevins living in Ashe County, and when the man answered, Wyatt thought he had found his man! It turned out to be Blevins's son, but his father was in fact still alive and living nearby.

This sparked an integral chain of events for Wyatt's future, including multiple cross-country flights to meet Blevins and other old-timers discovered through interviews. Wyatt discovered new records and kept pictures and research from his conversations, and rather than see them disappear again into history, Wyatt turned them into a record of his own, *Music from the Lost Provinces*. The releases from Wyatt's label, Old Hat Records, can hardly be called just albums. In addition to the consummately curated track list, each one comes with beautiful historical images and meticulously researched liner notes that would be more at home in a binder or a book.

His efforts have not gone unnoticed, despite his unassuming style. The Grammy Award–winning group the Carolina Chocolate Drops cites his second album, featuring Depression-era African American fiddlers, as inspiration for their formation, and his 2007 release, *Good for What Ails You: Music of the Medicine Shows 1926–1937*, was nominated for two Grammys. For Wyatt, the creation of each album is as much about his interest in and enjoyment of the music as it is any accompanying commercial or critical success. He has released albums of music from cotton mills and violin players, as well as collections based around whimsical subjects, such as barbecue and chickens, each one as carefully crafted as the last.

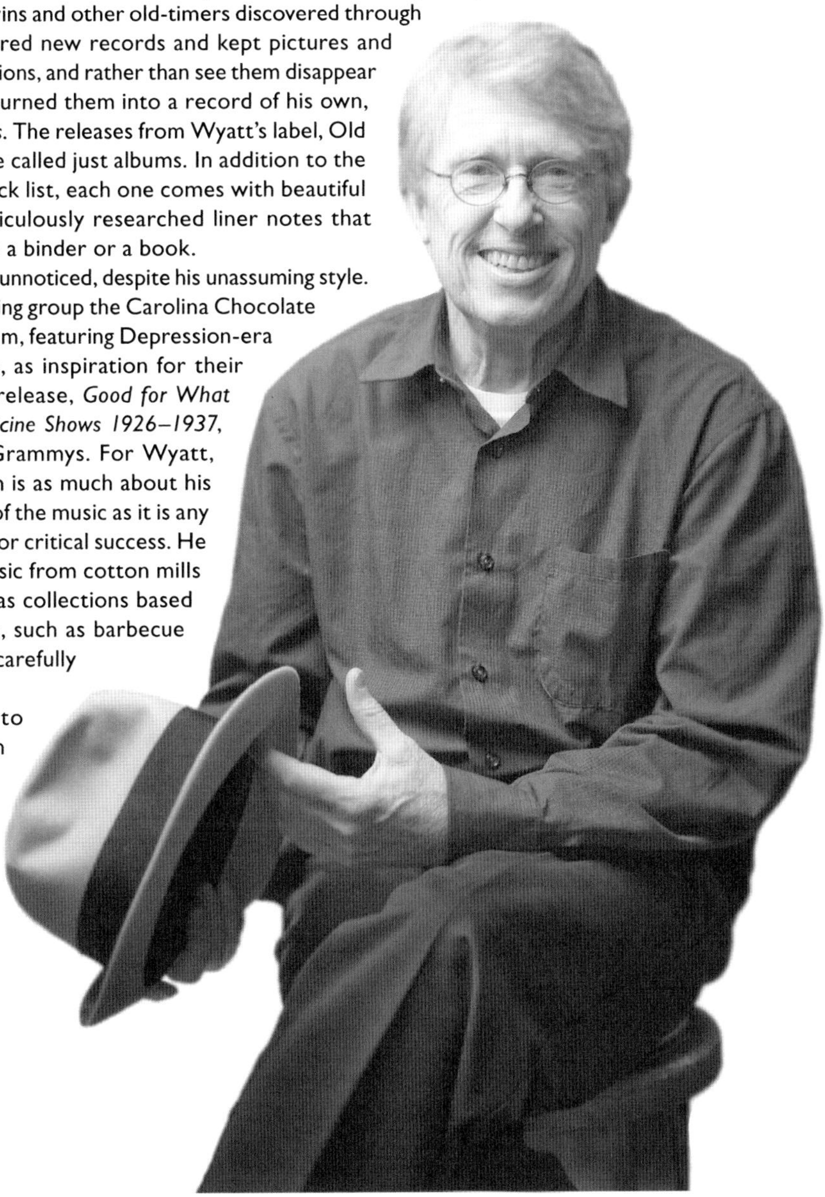

Wyatt has deep ties to Raleigh. He is the son of Edgar M. Wyatt of Wyatt-Quarles Seed Company and a great-nephew of former prison superintendent Col. William J. Hicks. (Courtesy of Marshall Wyatt.)

### Jim Valvano

North Carolina State basketball coach "Jimmy V" (1946–1993) led the underdog "Cardiac Pack" to a national championship in 1983. Shortly after he was diagnosed with bone cancer, he gave an inspiring speech about perseverance, urging "don't give up . . . don't ever give up." After he passed away, he left behind the V Foundation, which works with organizations and researchers all over the world to fund the search for a cure for cancer. (Courtesy of Basketball (Men's): Coaches (UA023.004.024), 0002846, Special Collections Research Center, North Carolina State University Libraries.)

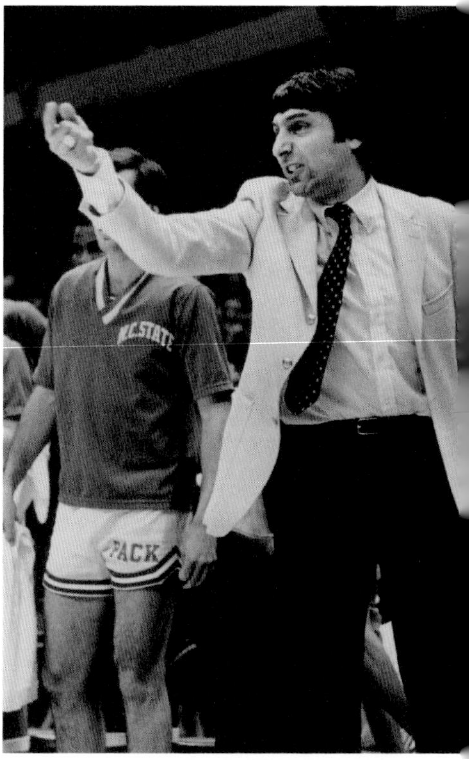

### Clay Aiken

Aiken (1978–present) shot to national attention in 2003 as the runner-up in the second season of the singing show *American Idol*, but his neighbors in Raleigh already knew about his talented vocals from choirs and local musical theater productions. Aiken's debut album, *Measure of a Man*, went multi-platinum. He is especially active in support of the National Inclusion Project for children with disabilities and for gay rights. (Photograph by Judy Butler.)

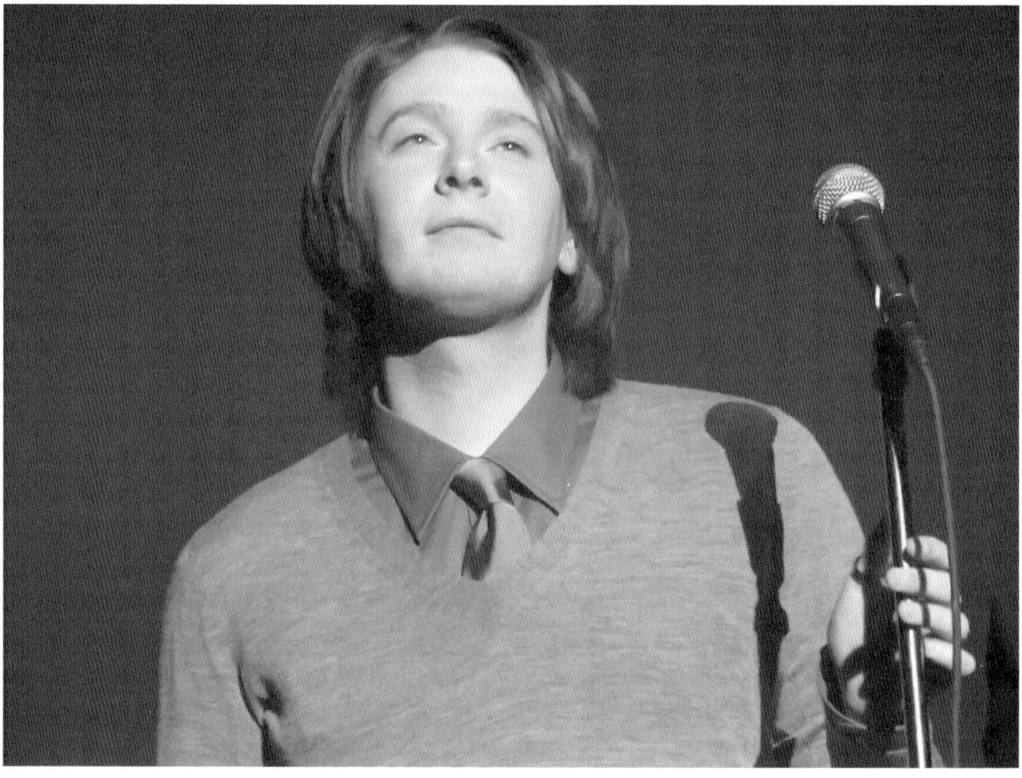

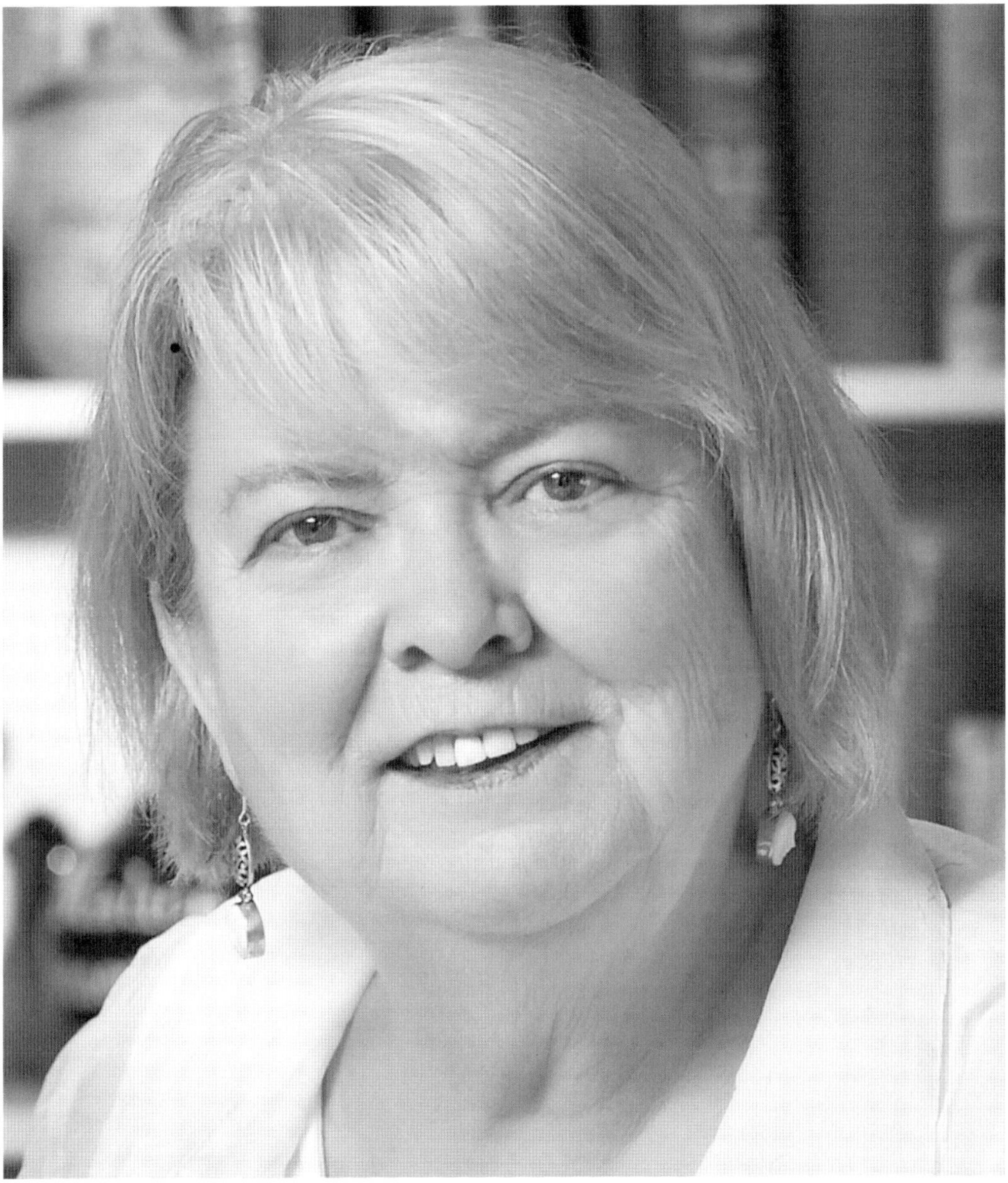

**Margaret Maron**
Maron grew up just south of Raleigh in a farming family that has lived in the area for centuries. As a young adult, Maron left North Carolina and explored the world. She soon discovered a passion for writing and, through diligence and determination, developed it into a talent and a skill. In 1981, she published her first mystery novel. While her early books centered on characters based in New York City, she has written with a distinctly local flavor for most of her work. Her mystery novels are set in a fictional county outside of Raleigh and are based on Maron's own experiences in North Carolina. To date, she has written 26 novels and two collections of short stories. Today, she lives in a house that has been in her family for generations, along with her husband, Joe. She has won several major mystery-writing awards and continues to write about her experiences through the mysteries of Deborah Knott. (Courtesy of Margaret Maron.)

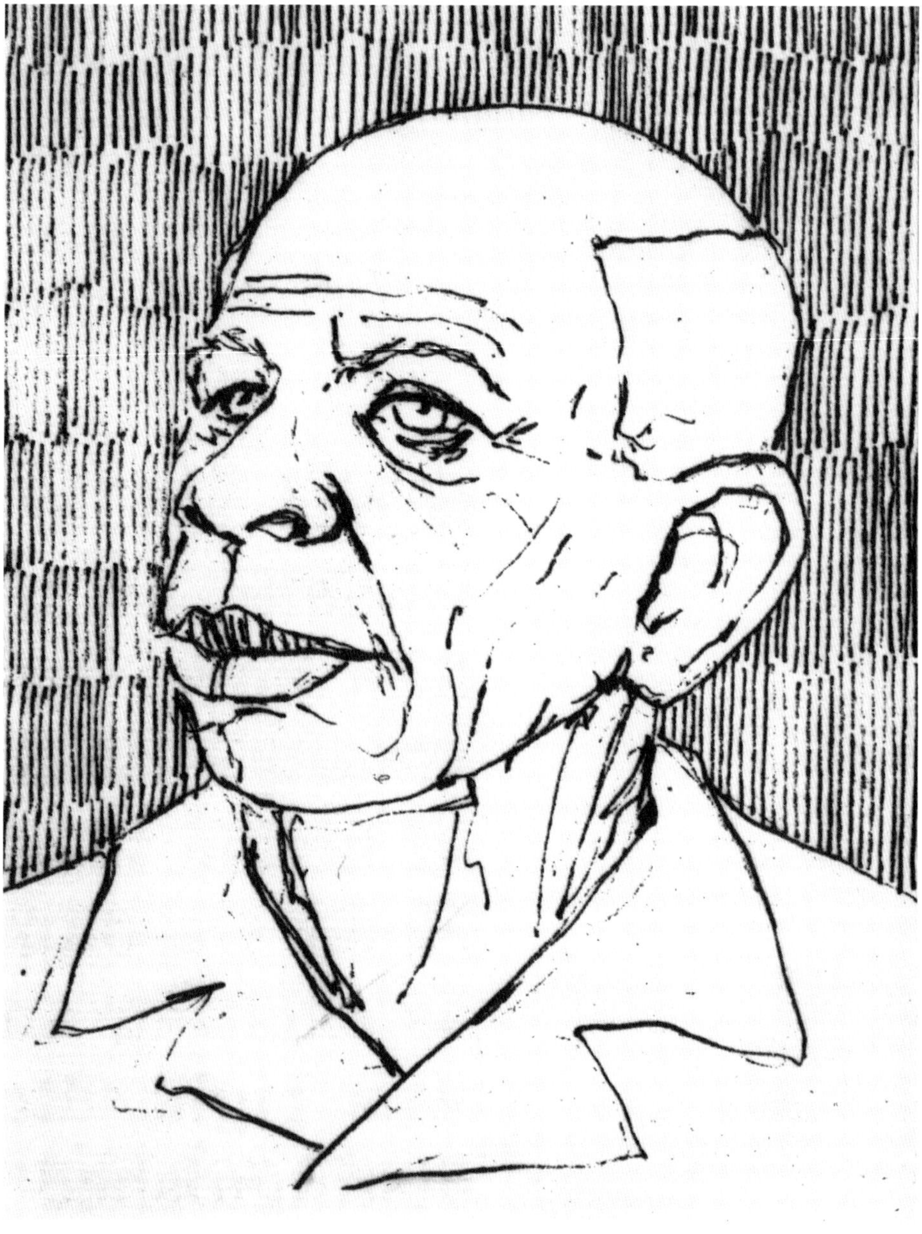

**George Moses Horton**

Horton (1797–1884), a slave on a Chatham County plantation, published the first book by an African American in the South in July 1829. Raleigh *Register* editor Joseph Gales had previously featured some of Horton's work in his paper and encouraged the publication as part of Horton's ultimately unsuccessful effort to purchase his freedom. *The Hope of Liberty* was a collection of poems and one of at least two other books Horton was able to see into publication, many of which included moving attacks on slavery. Horton began composing poems in his head as a teenager. He first earned money from his art when students at the University of North Carolina paid him to recite as they transcribed his words, likely making him the state's first professional poet. In 2006, the University of North Carolina named its newest building the George Moses Horton Residence Hall. (Courtesy of SANC.)

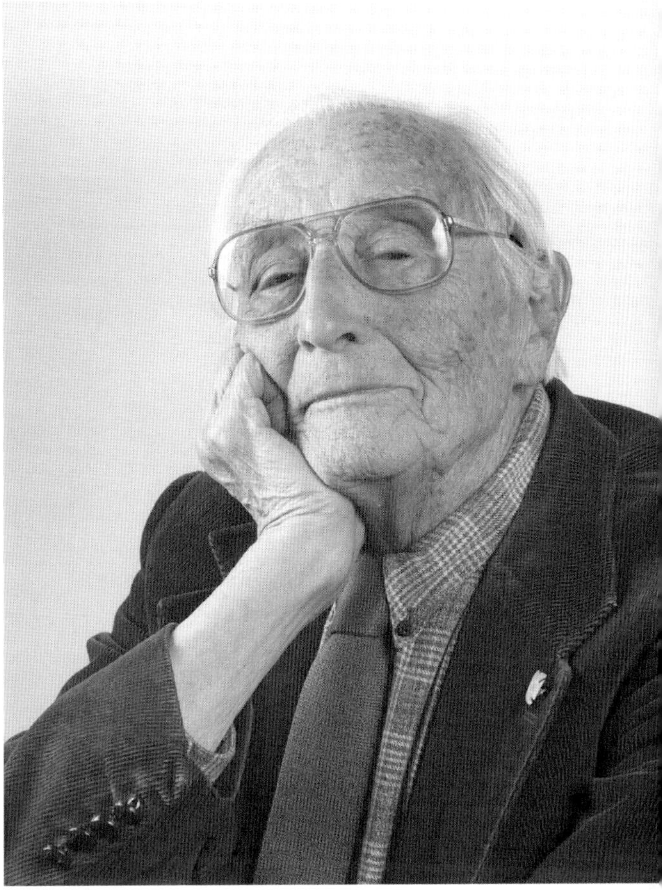

**Dr. Abram Kanof**
Kanof (1903–1998), who arrived in the United States after fleeing a pogrom against Jews in Russia, developed his interest in Jewish history while on the board of the Jewish Museum of New York. Upon retirement, he and his wife moved to Raleigh. Using many objects they had collected, the couple created the Judaic Art Gallery at the North Carolina Museum of Art in 1983, one of only two collections of Judaica in an American art museum. (Courtesy of North Carolina Museum of Art.)

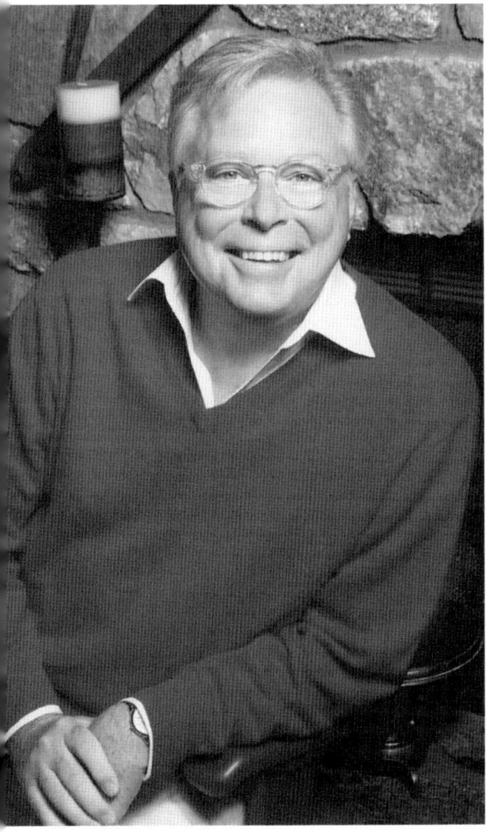

**Ira David Wood III**
Wood (1947–present) is probably most recognized as Scrooge, the headlining character of his renowned 1974 adaptation of *A Christmas Carol.* As executive director of Theatre in the Park, located in Pullen Park, he has shaped Raleigh's arts landscape by making the stage accessible while growing it to international acclaim. Two of his children also became actors after getting their start at Theatre in the Park, Evan Rachel Wood and Ira David Wood IV. (Courtesy of Theatre in the Park.)

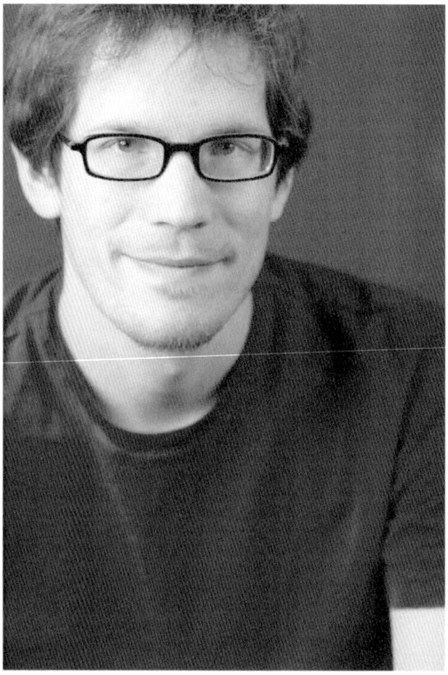

**Ian Finley**
Finley moved to Raleigh in 2004 to serve as director of education at Burning Coal Theatre Company. His scripts often involve local historic sites, incorporated through the "Our History" play series, which has dramatized the history of over 75 different people, places, and events in Raleigh. In 2012, Finley was named the Piedmont Laureate. (Courtesy of Ian Finley.)

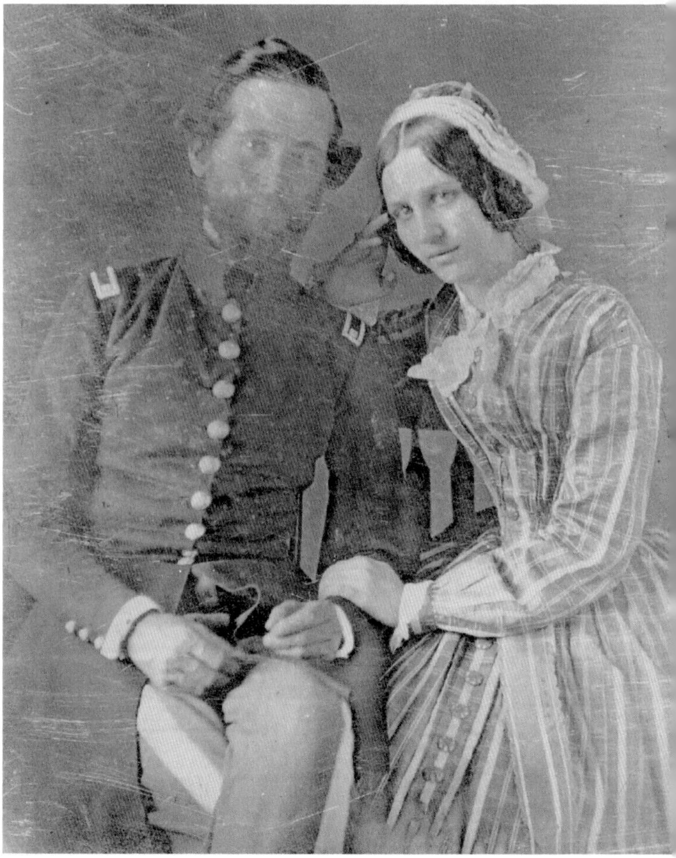

**Mary Bayard Devereux Clarke**
Clarke (1827–1886) was one of Raleigh's earliest distinguished poets. She authored North Carolina's first anthology of poetry, *Wood Notes, or Carolina Carol* in 1854, which contained works by 60 poets from across the state. She included works by local Raleigh authors as well as a few poems of her own. During the Civil War, she wrote for the weekly regional newspaper the *Mercury*, which was "devoted to Polite Southern Literature." She is pictured here with her husband. (Courtesy of SANC.)

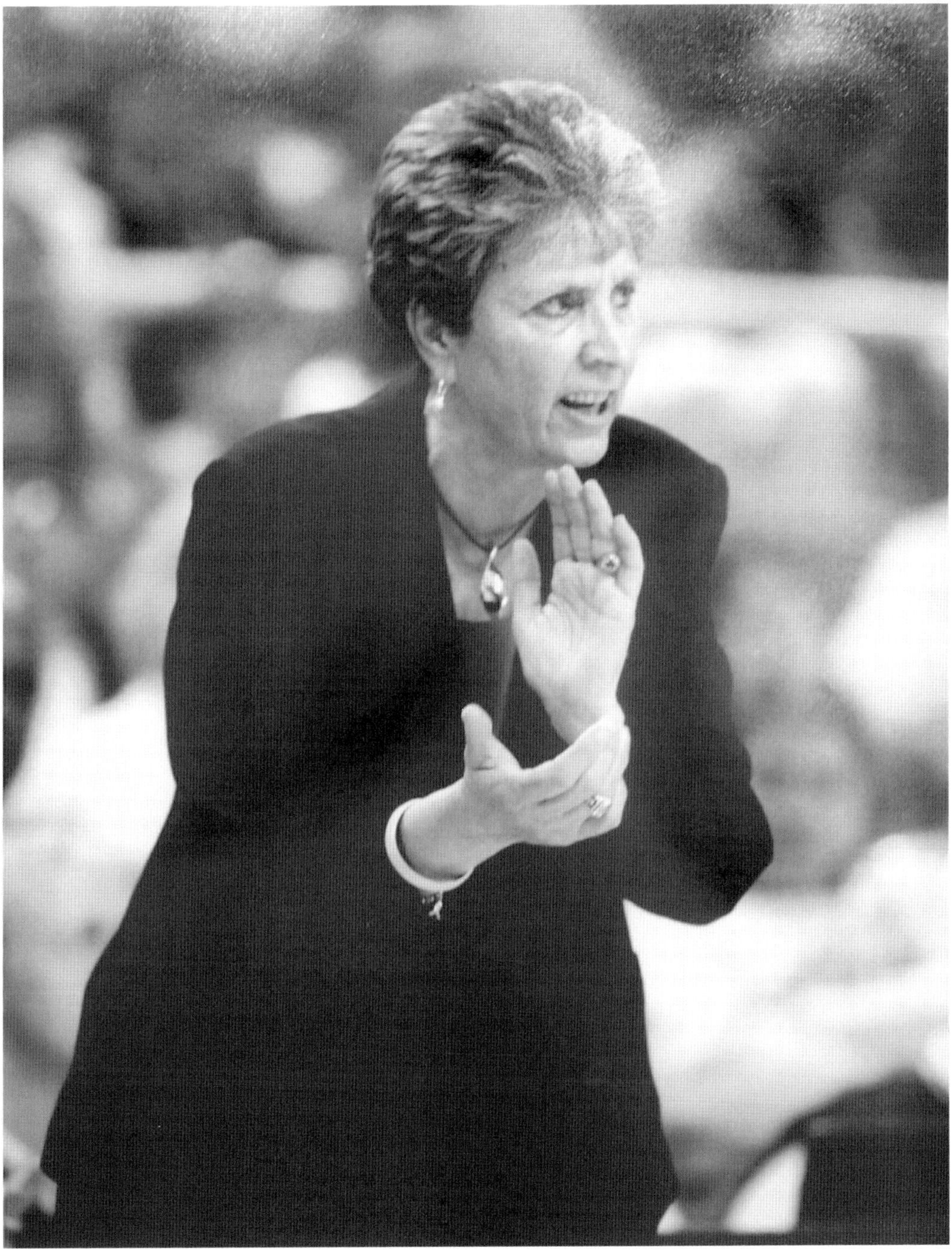

**Kay Yow**

Coach Yow (1942–2009) was the face of the North Carolina State basketball team for over 30 years before finally succumbing to breast cancer. She had over 700 career wins, coached the 1988 women's Olympic team to a gold medal, and was inducted into the Naismith Memorial Basketball Hall of Fame. Like fellow NC State coach Jim Valvano, she used her fight against cancer to bring awareness to the search for a cure. (Courtesy of RCM.)

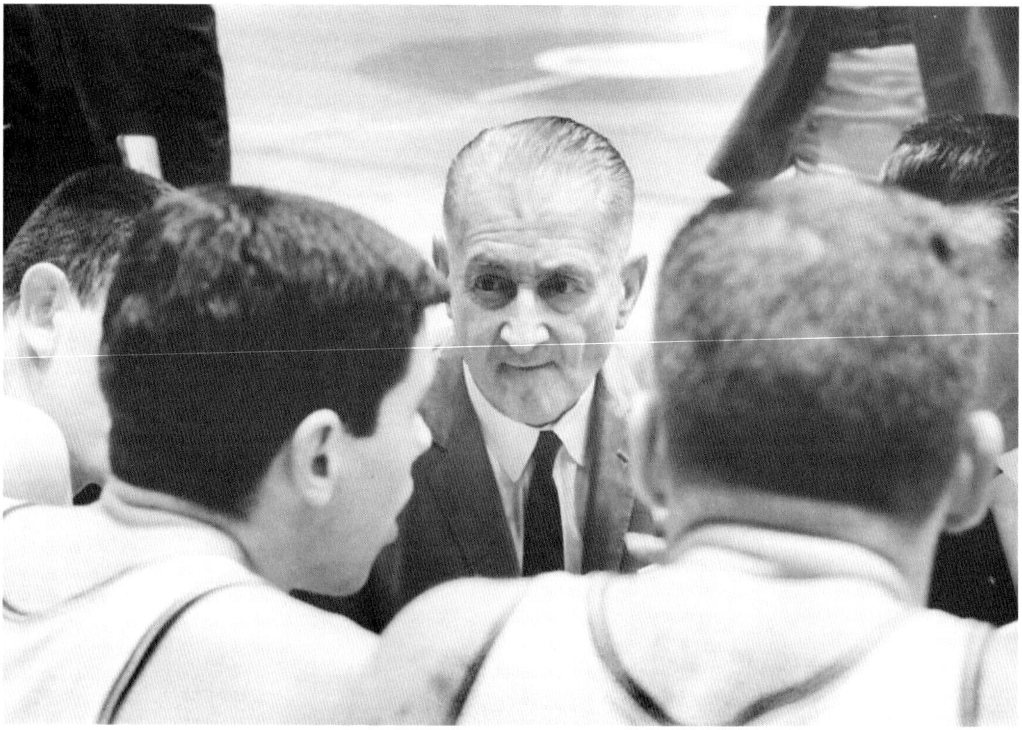

**Everett Case**

Tobacco Road, ACC basketball, cutting down the net after a big win, jerseys with numbers, announcing starting players, pep bands at games—these and many other innovations that shaped what college basketball is today all directly resulted from the influence of one man: Everett Case (1900–1966). In North Carolina, Case is known best as the legendary coach of the North Carolina State Wolfpack.

He arrived in Raleigh in 1946, already possessing a special legacy for his coaching success in Indiana's high school league. There, he amassed one of the best coaching records of all time over 23 years, mostly with one school, and became one of only five coaches to ever win four Indiana state championships. He came to NC State after leaving the Navy, where he spent most of World War II as athletic director of naval flight schools in California and Indiana.

High schools in North Carolina, preferring football, did not take basketball as seriously as did the Hoosiers. But Case personally traveled from the coast to the mountains, recruiting both current and future players, and encouraging the schools to build better gyms.

With a record that still stands as the best in school history, including nine straight conference championships, Case's Wolfpack teams challenged neighboring schools Duke, Wake Forest, and North Carolina to improve their teams as well just to keep pace. He won three ACC Coach of the Year awards, and NC State created and hosted the Dixie Classic, a holiday tournament including the local colleges. He spent several years serving probation for various recruiting and point-shaving scandals, but his players and his school remember him fondly.

Case retired in 1965 after being diagnosed with inoperable cancer, but after the team won the 1965 ACC Championship, they brought him on the court in a wheelchair so he could cut down the last strand of the net. He left most of his money to his former players and to scholarship funds at NC State and his Indiana high school after his death, and he requested that he be buried in Raleigh, facing North Carolina Highway 70, so that he could "wave" to future Wolfpack teams heading down the road to play Duke or UNC. (Courtesy of RCM.)

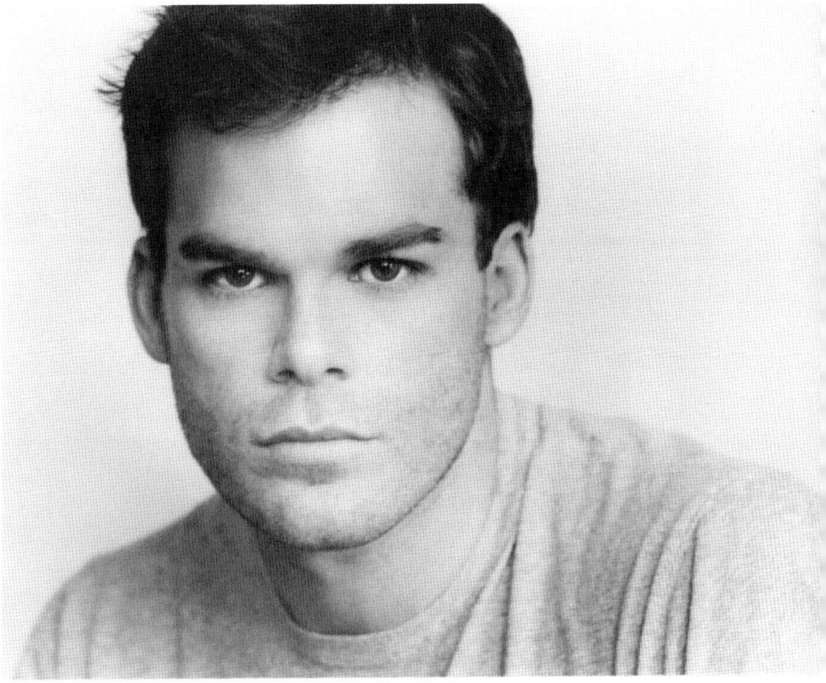

**Michael C. Hall**
Hall (1971–present) is a popular actor, known for his starring role in Showtime's *Dexter*. Hall was born in Raleigh and attended Ravenscroft School. It was there that his passion for acting began. He starred in school productions and sang in the boys' choir. After attending college to become a lawyer, Hall switched to professional acting. (Courtesy of Ravenscroft.)

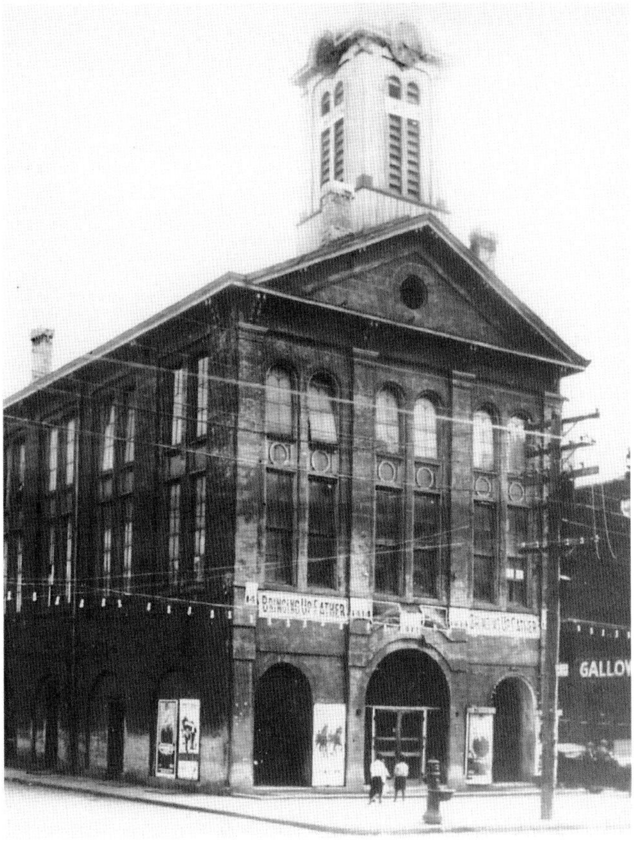


**The Haywood Brothers Minstrels**
The Haywood Brothers Minstrels were organized and managed by Sherwood Upchurch, who promoted local entertainment in Raleigh. Members included Richard Hayes and John and George Haywood. All of the members were African American and natives of Raleigh, and the group toured the south for several years at the end of the 19th century, including playing at Metropolitan Hall in Raleigh, shown here. (Courtesy of RCM.)

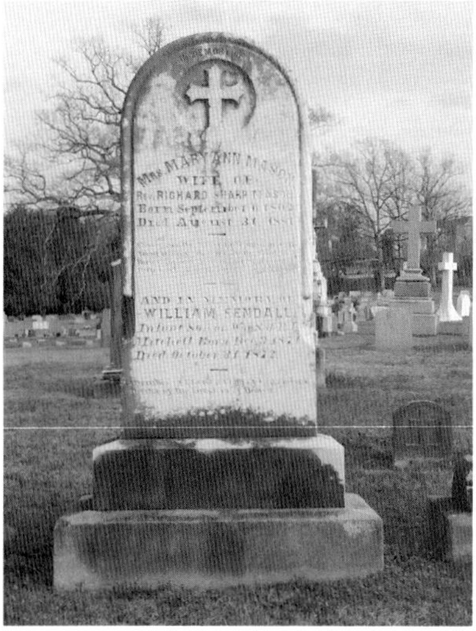

## Mary Ann Bryan Mason

Mason (1802–1881) wrote the first children's book by a native North Carolinian in 1859, *A Wreath from the Woods of North Carolina*, which she illustrated herself with drawings of native wildflowers. She published a novel set in Raleigh as well as a housekeeping book, and she was a painter, sculptor, and musician. Her self-taught cameo-making skills won her first prize at the 1854 state fair. (Authors' collection.)

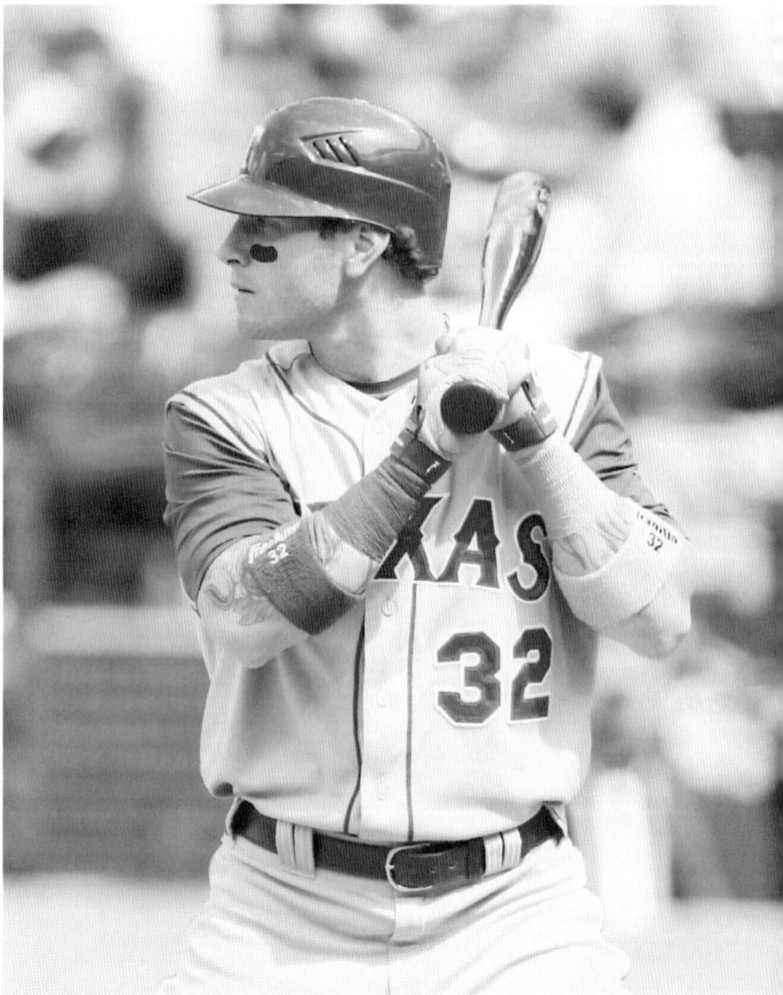


## Josh Hamilton

Hamilton (1981–present) first caught the eye of baseball fans and scouts at Athens Drive High School in Raleigh. Selected as the first pick of the 1999 MLB draft, Hamilton battled personal demons and addiction for years before finally making his major-league debut in 2007. Since then, he has made multiple All-Star teams and in 2010 won the American League MVP award. He has appeared in two World Series with the Texas Rangers. (Photograph by Keith Allison.)

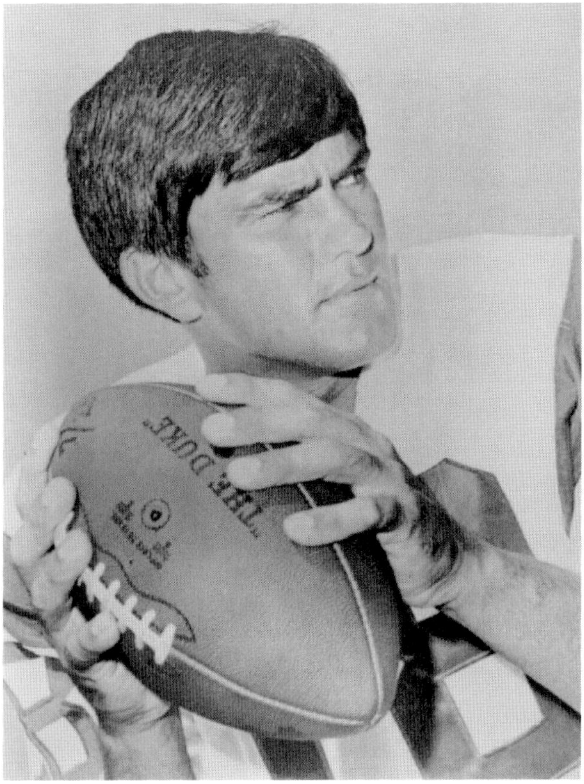

**Roman Gabriel**
Gabriel (1940–present) starred at quarterback for the North Carolina State Wolfpack football team in the mid-20th century, where he was a two-time All-American and set team passing records in almost every category. The Los Angeles Rams picked him in the first round of the 1962 NFL draft, and he continued his stellar career through the 1970s, winning the NFL MVP award in 1969. (Courtesy of SANC.)

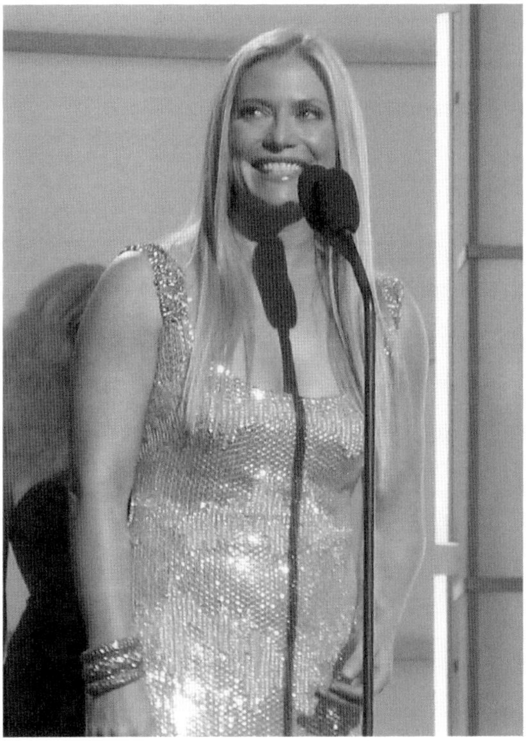

**Emily Procter**
Procter (1968–present) was raised in Raleigh, where she attended Ravenscroft School. She went on to study journalism and dance at East Carolina University. Following graduation, she was employed as a television weather anchor in Greenville before she made it to the big leagues. She is best known for her television roles as Calleigh Duquesne in *CSI: Miami* and as Ainsley Hayes in *The West Wing.* (Photograph by Vanessa Ip.)

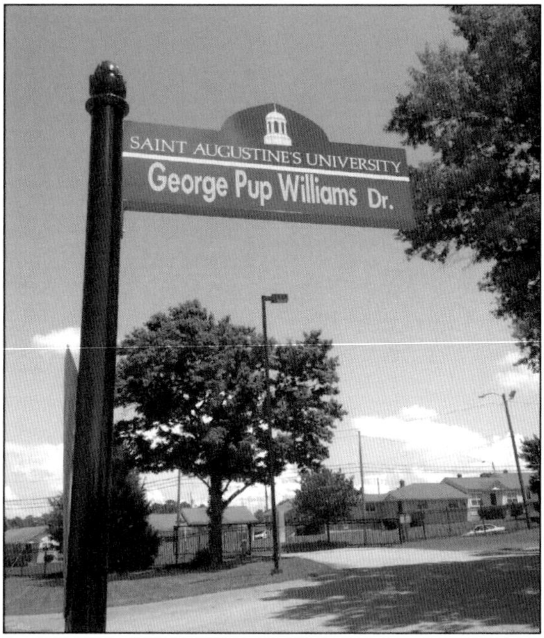


### George Williams

As track and field coach and athletic director at St. Augustine's University since 1976, "Pup" Williams has won 31 national championships and over 100 Coach of the Year awards, all while keeping his student-athletes' graduation rates over 95 percent. Williams has coached at the 1996 and 2004 Olympics, and 32 of his pupils have competed in the Olympic games. A street on campus (pictured here) is named after him, and in 2011, St. Augustine's opened the George Williams Athletic Complex in his honor. (Authors' collection.)

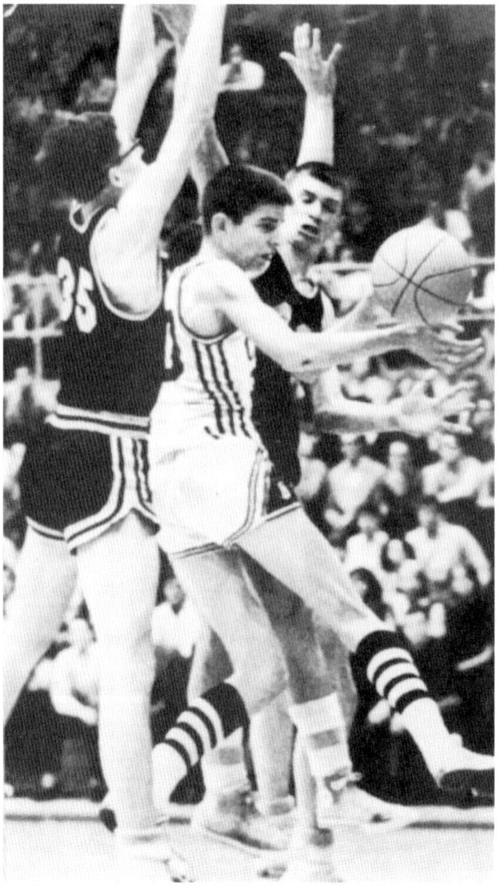

### Pete Maravich

"Pistol Pete" (1947–1988) was a sharp-shooting basketball star known for his showmanship and fearless play. His father was a college coach who recruited Pete to play for him at Louisiana State University. He was a five-time NBA All-Star and remains the all-time leading NCAA Division I scorer, with 3,667 points. Maravich moved to Raleigh, where he starred at Needham Broughton High School, when his father became assistant coach at North Carolina State under Everett Case. (Courtesy of Broughton High School.)

# CHAPTER FOUR

# Educating the Future

Today, Raleigh is one of the most academically blessed areas of the United States, but the city has not always held that distinction. Prior to 1804, Raleigh did not even have an organized school. In that year, the Raleigh Academy opened its doors on Burke Square, leading the way for future amazing schools and inspiring educators to call Raleigh home. In the early 19th century, Raleigh was home to two inspiring schools that were centuries ahead of their time. In 1808, John Chavis opened an integrated school that taught both white and black students, and, while his school was eventually shut down because of this, he brought a better education to a generation and encouraged many disadvantaged students to reach for more. In 1844, the North Carolina School for the Deaf, Dumb, and Blind opened in downtown. It was home to the first publication in the United States to be printed by the deaf and for the deaf.

Raleigh is home to two private schools that opened their doors in the mid-19th century: St. Mary's was opened under the leadership of Rev. Aldert Smedes in 1842, and Ravenscroft in 1868. Both of these schools have contributed excellent educators and student-citizens to the community since then.

By the late 19th century, many institutes of higher learning were opening their doors in Raleigh, including North Carolina State University, St. Augustine's University, William Peace University, Shaw University, and Meredith College. The late 19th century also saw the public school system take off in Raleigh. It would eventually merge with the Wake County school system to form the current district.

Today, Raleigh's leading schools and universities attract students from around the world to study under the many brilliant educators here. This chapter will explore some of the many men and women who helped to shape the landscape of Raleigh's education system and fought for improvements and equality in the schools.

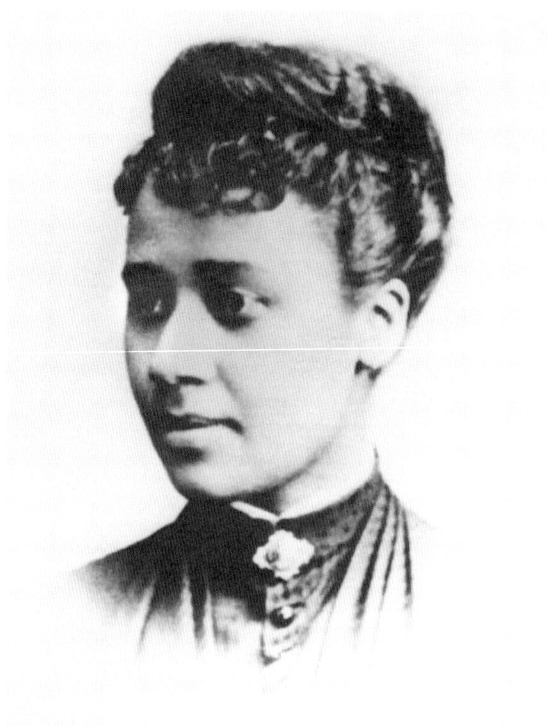

**Anna Julia Cooper**

Cooper (1858–1964) was born next to the North Carolina state capitol, but under state law, she was enslaved as the property of one of Raleigh's white citizens. She benefited, however, from her mother's literacy, which was passed on to Anna and her siblings, despite existing laws against slaves reading and writing. Therefore, Cooper's dreams of becoming a teacher one day had a head start.

After the Civil War, schools and colleges for African Americans began opening across the South. Cooper was nine years old in 1867 when St. Augustine's Normal School and College opened in Raleigh and selected her as part of their inaugural class to train as teachers. She spent the next 14 years studying Latin, Greek, and advanced mathematics in the more-demanding "men's courses" and helping tutor other students. While at school, she married George Cooper, her Greek teacher, although he died two years later.

Cooper searched for a higher education than St. Augustine's could offer, and Oberlin College in Ohio accepted her at a sophomore standing in 1881 to pursue a bachelor's degree. Oberlin admitted men and women of all races, and Cooper once again excelled at the highest levels. A year after graduating with a degree in mathematics, St. Augustine's offered her the chance to teach mathematics, Latin, and Greek in Raleigh.

Back in her hometown, Cooper dove into community leadership, establishing a Sunday school group and joining the North Carolina Teachers' Association. She was seemingly planning a long life in Raleigh. Oberlin granted her a master's degree in mathematics based on her teaching at St. Augustine's, but later that same year, 1887, Cooper accepted a position teaching Latin and math at Washington High School in Washington, DC, an academically challenging school for African Americans. She retired from Washington in 1930, but over the intervening 43 years, she embarked on a pioneering course, writing and speaking about African American and women's rights. Her most famous book, *A Voice from the South by a Black Woman of the South*, helped earn her status as the first black feminist. She cofounded the Colored Woman's League of Washington, DC, and became just the fourth African American woman to receive a PhD, from the Sorbonne in Paris.

Cooper died at age 105, just before Pres. Lyndon Johnson signed the Civil Rights Act of 1964 into law. Her memorial service was held in the chapel at St. Augustine's. (Courtesy of RCM.)

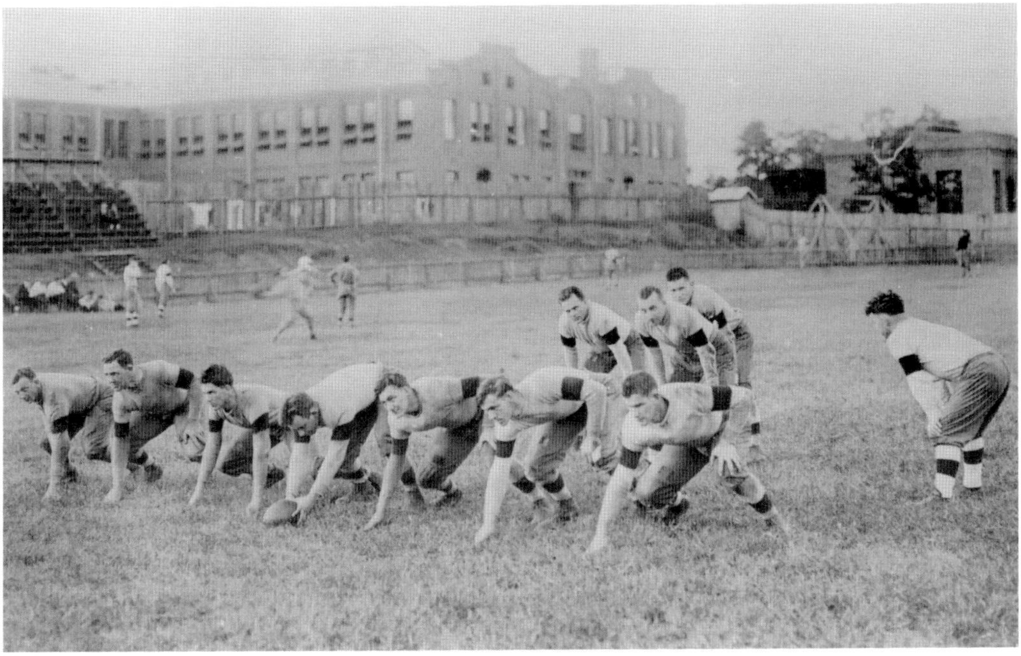

**Wallace C. Riddick**
Variously professor, dean, and president of North Carolina State from 1892 to 1937, Riddick (1864–1942) oversaw the nascent stages of the school's growth into North Carolina's largest university. After the school's restructuring in 1923, he transferred positions, from president to dean of the new School of Engineering, and 15 years later, he admitted local Katharine Stinson as the first woman in the engineering program. Riddick also coached the school's first football team. The 1914 NC State team is pictured here on Riddick Field. (Courtesy of Athletics Photographs, 1893–2003 (UA023.004), ua023_004-005-am0049-000-002, Special Collections Research Center, North Carolina State University Libraries.)

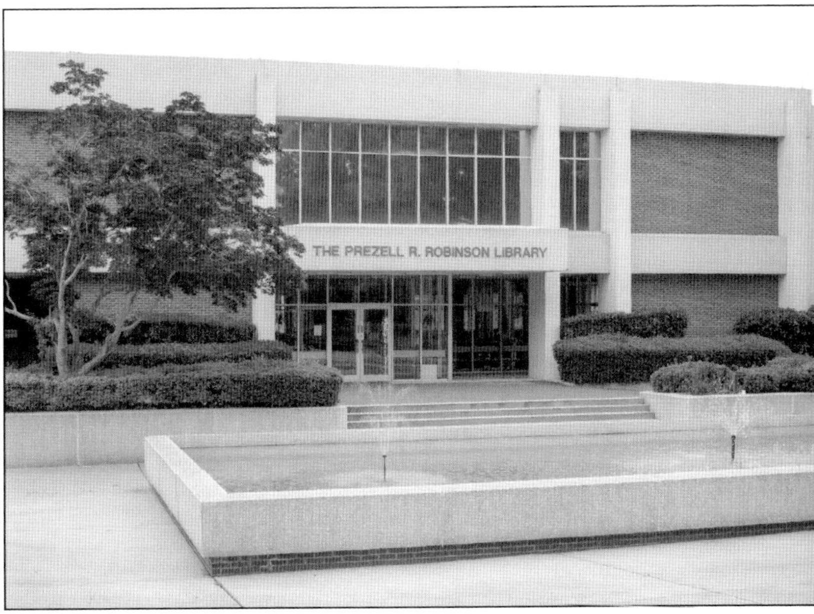


**Dr. Prezell R. Robinson**
Robinson (1923–present) retired from St. Augustine's in 1995 after serving as president for 30 years. He had first arrived at the school to earn his bachelor's degree in economics and social science after World War II. A master's and doctorate from Cornell University in the 1950s and a Fulbright Fellowship to India subsequently brought him back to St. Augustine's in 1956 as dean and sociology professor. He has been at the school ever since. (Courtesy of Dmitri Medvedev.)

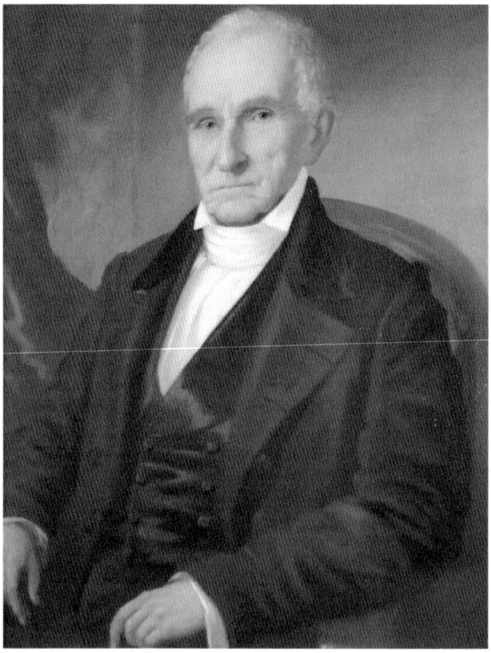

**William Peace**

Peace, a local businessman and citizen of Raleigh, opened a general merchandise store in 1798 and served as a lieutenant in a volunteer corps during the War of 1812. He is best remembered for donating the land and $10,000 for the establishment of Peace Institute (now William Peace University), a school for women, which opened in 1872, seven years after Peace passed away. (Courtesy of William Peace University.)

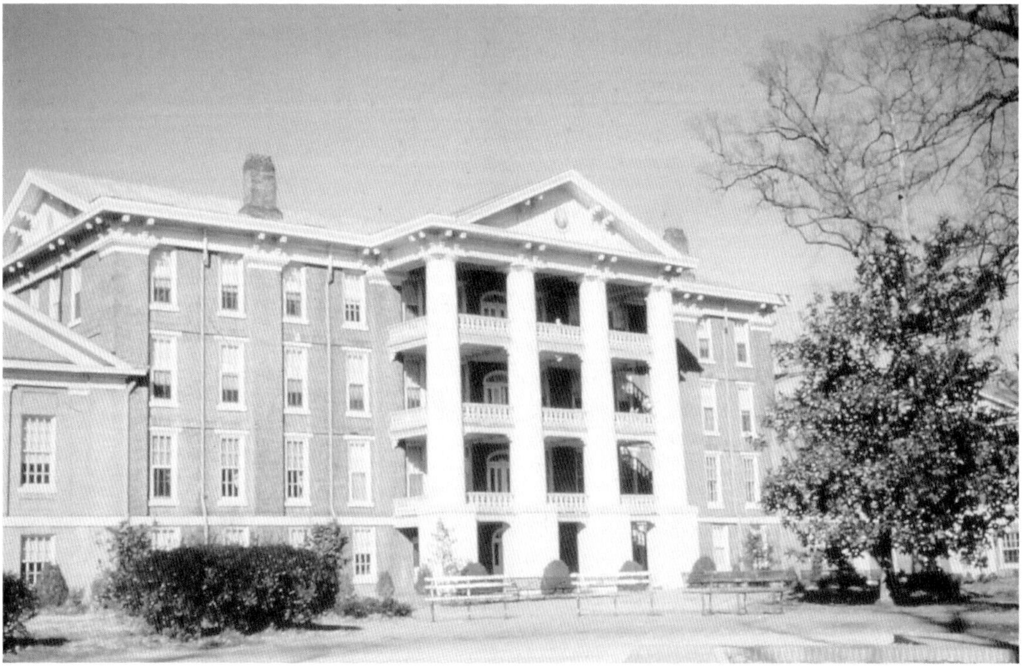

**Robert Burwell**

Reverend Burwell (1802–1895), first principal of Peace Institute in 1872, ran the all-girls school with the help of his son, John, and his second wife, Frances, who was lady principal and a former student. Peace offered primary, preparatory, and collegiate courses, with subjects ranging from mathematics to music, and, from 1879 to 1889, what were likely the South's first kindergarten classes. The school, shown here, still operates in Raleigh, offering coeducational enrollment as of 2012. (Courtesy of OR.)

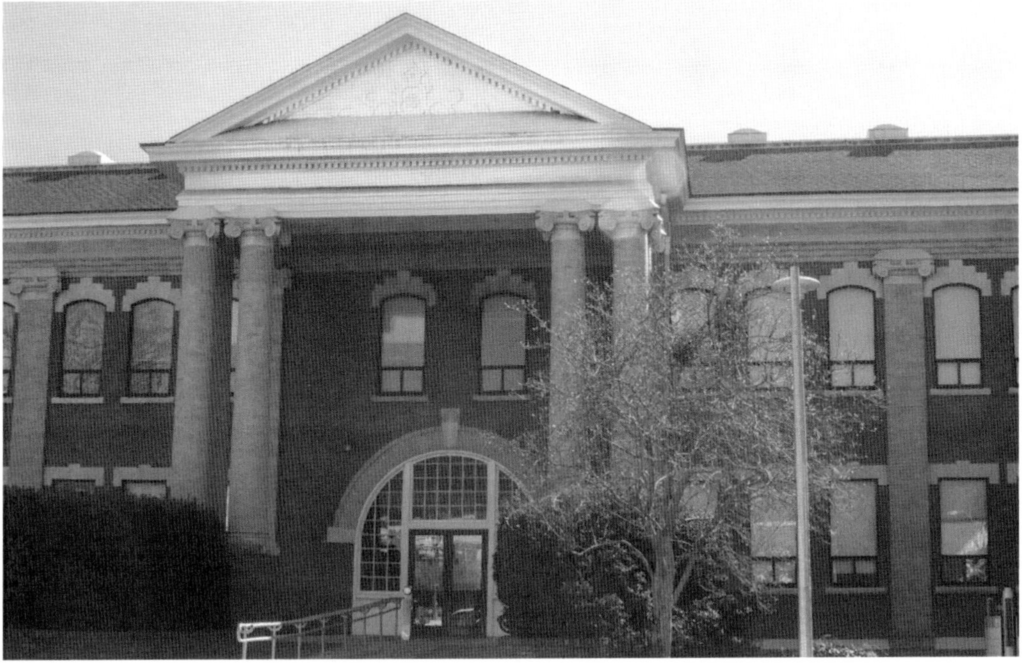

**Ed Carson, Manuel Crockett, Irwin Holmes, and Walter Holmes**

North Carolina State's first African American undergraduates, Ed Carson, Irwin Crockett, Irwin Holmes, and Walter Holmes, enrolled in 1956. The governor did not stand in the doorway to block them, as Alabama's did several years later. But the students did not have an entirely friendly welcome, either. Irwin Holmes co-captained the tennis team, but soccer player Walter Holmes could not play in enough games to officially letter because so many teams refused to play against him. Winston Hall, pictured here, is where all four attended engineering classes. (Authors' collection.)

**Kemp Battle**

The main legacy of Kemp Battle (1831–1919) is as the longtime president of the University of North Carolina following the Civil War. He also lived in Raleigh, where he founded Citizens National Bank in 1871 and the North Carolina State Life Insurance Company in 1872. The latter was the only successful locally based life insurance company in Raleigh until the 20th century. (Courtesy of RCM.)

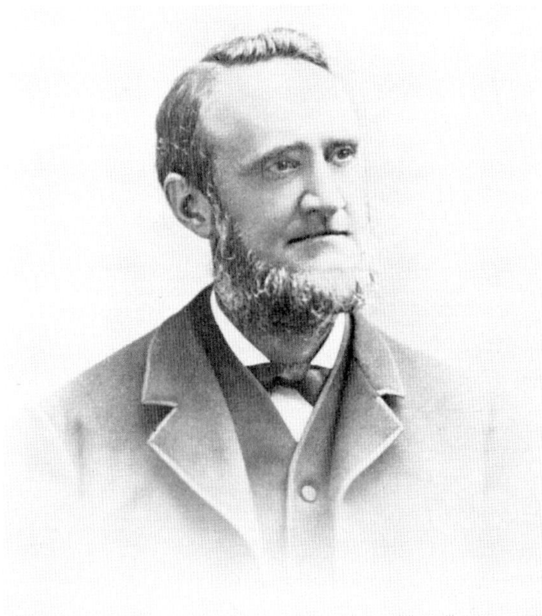

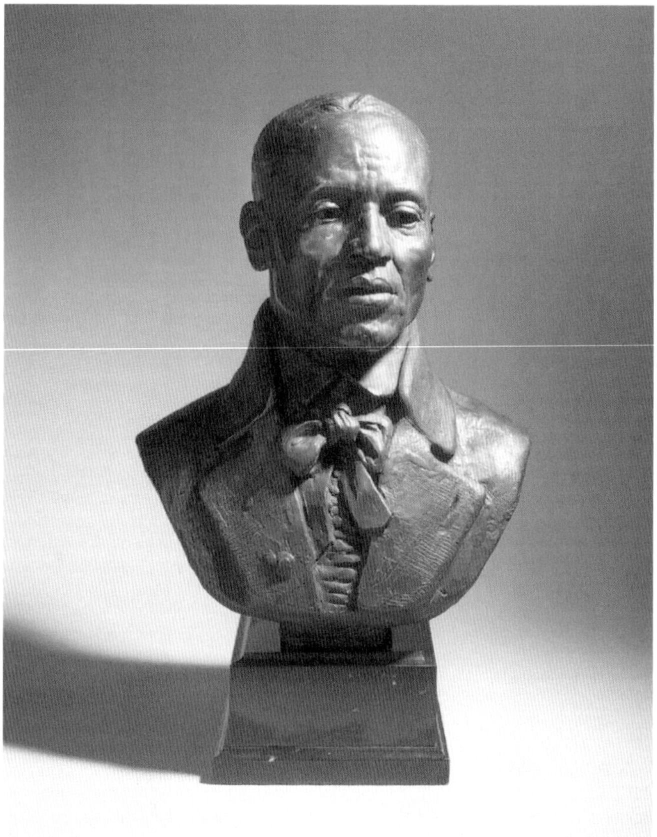

## John Chavis

Reverend Chavis (1763–1838) was born in North Carolina in 1763, but little is known about his early life. It is likely that he served an indentured servitude and received an education. During the American Revolution, he fought for three years with the 5th Virginia Regiment. Following the war, he married, had a child, attended Princeton University, and lived for some time in New Jersey. Returning to Virginia, Chavis found work as a private tutor for a family. Seeking further educational opportunities in 1795, he attended the Liberty Hall Academy, which is now known as Washington and Lee University. He graduated in 1800 with a degree in theology and was granted a license to preach, which he did fervently for the next seven years, serving as a missionary for the general assembly of the Presbyterian Church to slaves in Maryland, Virginia, and North Carolina. In 1807, he returned to his home state and settled in the new state capital, Raleigh, to preach. A year later, he opened up a classical school that was different than most at the time—he taught white and black children together. The school was successful, but some of his white students' families opposed the integrated classrooms, so Chavis segregated the children. The school continued; white pupils were taught during the day, and black students in the evening. Chavis would maintain lifelong friendships with many of his students, including Sen. Willie P. Mangum, despite their political differences. The school was very successful until the early 1830s. In response to the Nat Turner Rebellion of 1831, in which Turner, an educated slave and preacher, led a bloody rebellion against whites in Virginia, laws were passed that crippled Chavis's school. The first, in 1831, made it illegal to teach free black children, and the second, in 1832, barred African Americans, free or enslaved, from preaching. Chavis lamented the institution of slavery, but also criticized the abolitionist movement, believing it often hindered their cause rather than promoting good works. Chavis died in 1838. While the records are unclear, many believe that he suffered a violent death at the hands of white supremacists. (Courtesy of RCM; sculpture by Richard Weaver.)

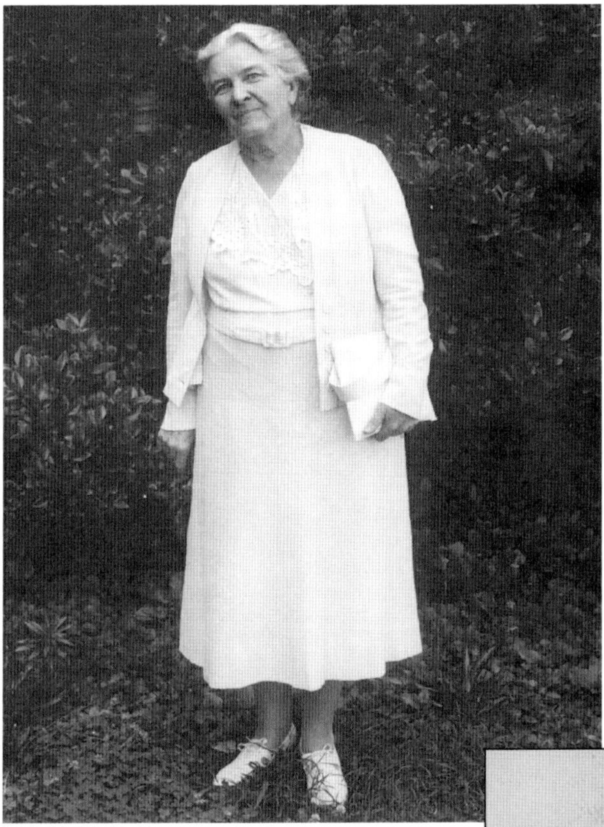

**Jane Simpson McKimmon**
After serving as the state director of the women's division of the Farmer's Institute, McKimmon (1867–1957) was the first North Carolina State Home Demonstration agent in 1911. Her agents traveled the state and taught homemaking skills to rural women. The program developed standardized canning and increased efficiency in home food production. During World War I, McKimmon was director of home economics for the food program. (Courtesy of People: administrators, faculty, and staff, m(UA023.024), 0009036, Special Collection Research Center, North Carolina State University Libraries.)

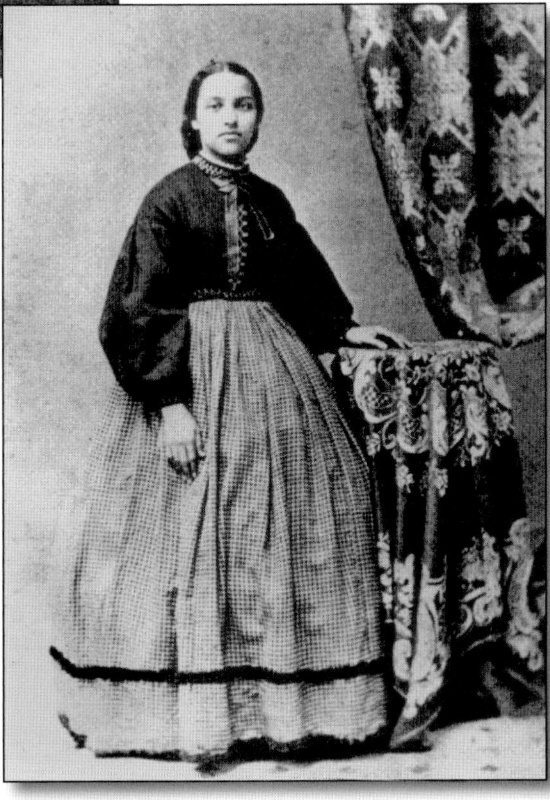

**Mary Jane Patterson**
Patterson (1840–1894), a Raleigh native, moved to Ohio in 1856 and enrolled in Oberlin College, the only school that would accept black women with equal standing to their classmates. She graduated with a bachelor of arts degree in 1862, becoming the first African American woman to obtain that honor. Patterson went on to be the principal at the first public high school for African Americans in the country. (Courtesy of Oberlin College Archives.)

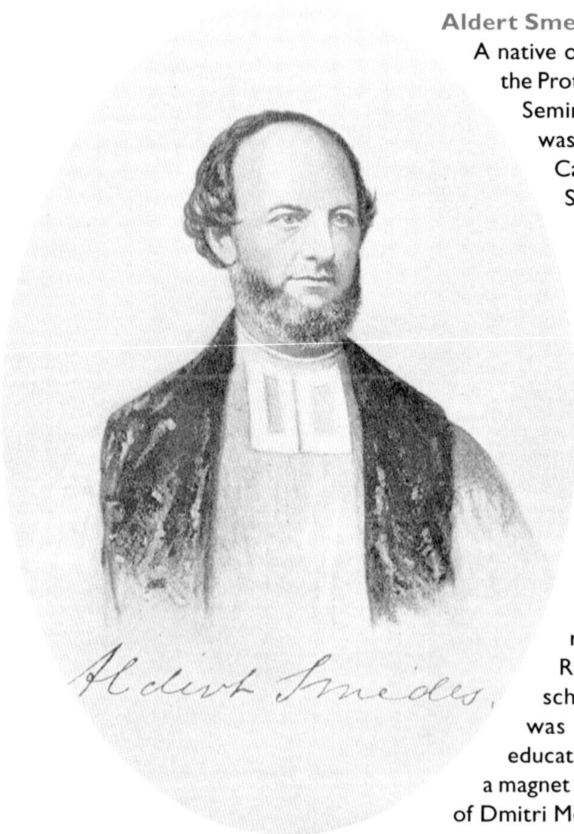


### Aldert Smedes

A native of New York, Smedes (1810–1877) studied at the Protestant Episcopal Church's General Theological Seminary. In 1841, Smedes met Bishop Ives, who was running the former Episcopal School of North Carolina. Smedes seized the opportunity to open St. Mary's School, a school for young, upper-class women. He hoped to transform society through influencing his students, making them educated, elite Christian women. (Courtesy of St. Mary's School.)

### Frederick J. Carnage Jr.

The Raleigh City School Board's first African American member in 1949, Carnage (1895–1988) used his position to advocate for civil rights, integration, and, most importantly, Raleigh's children. When a new junior high school was proposed by the board in 1963, it was named after Carnage to honor his work in education. Fred J. Carnage Middle School is currently a magnet school located in southeast Raleigh. (Courtesy of Dmitri Medvedev.)

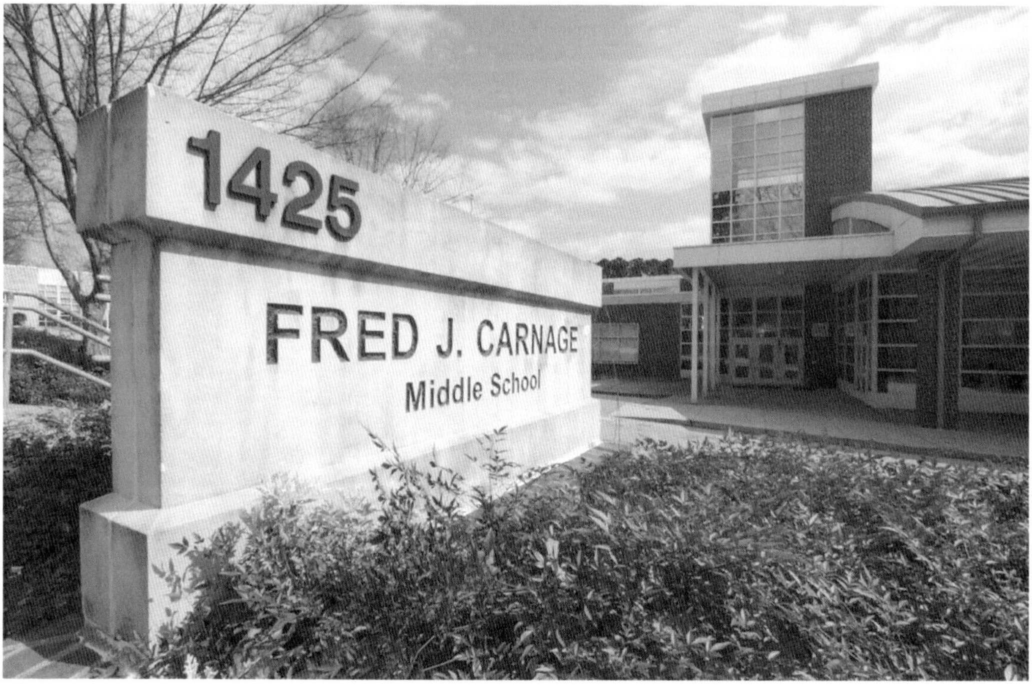

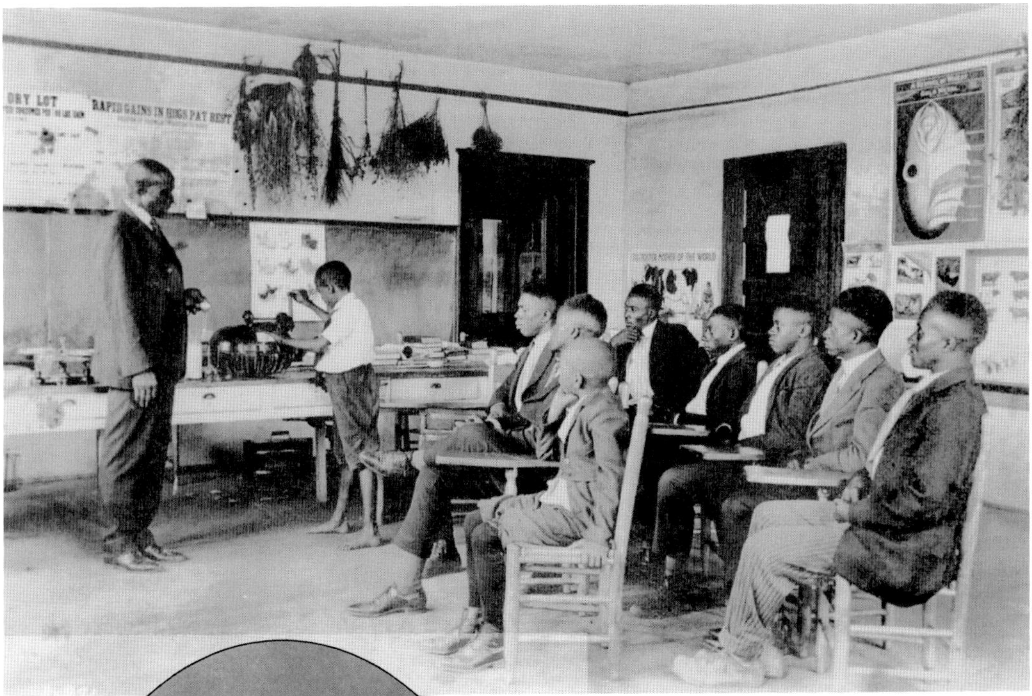

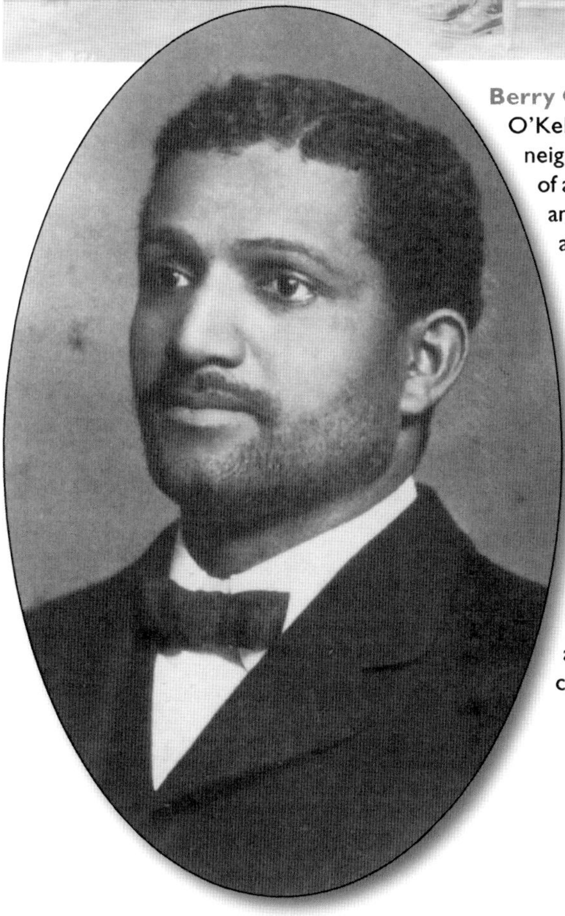

**Berry O'Kelly**

O'Kelly lived in and helped establish the Method neighborhood in Raleigh. O'Kelly was part owner of a general store in 1889, when his partner moved and he bought him out. The successful businessman also raised cattle, operated a cotton gin, and owned a gristmill in Method. In 1890, O'Kelly petitioned to get the Method post office established at his store, and he became Wake County's only African American postmaster. In addition to his successful business ventures, O'Kelly was passionate about improving education in Method. In 1916, he opened the Berry O'Kelly Training School, seen above. In 1919, the school became North Carolina's first fully accredited rural high school open to African American students and Wake County's first public high school for African Americans. O'Kelly's work helped to make Method a vibrant and progressive community in the early 20th century. (Courtesy of RCM.)

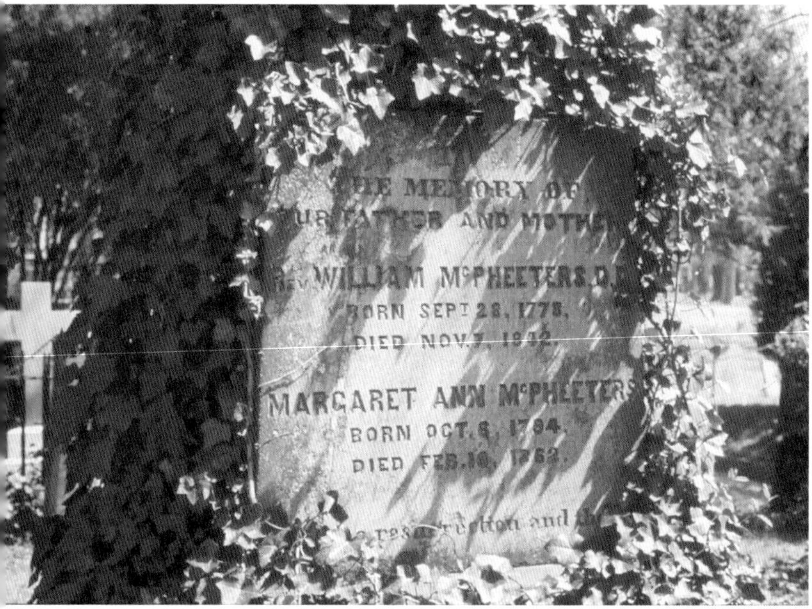

### William McPheeters

Raleigh appointed Reverend McPheeters (d. 1842) "pastor of the city" in 1810, the same year he succeeded Rev. William L. Turner as principal of Raleigh Academy. McPheeters founded the First Presbyterian Church in 1816 and, under his guidance, Raleigh Academy reached the peak of its success and reputation, increasing its enrollment and including female and scholarship students for the first time. (Courtesy of OR.)

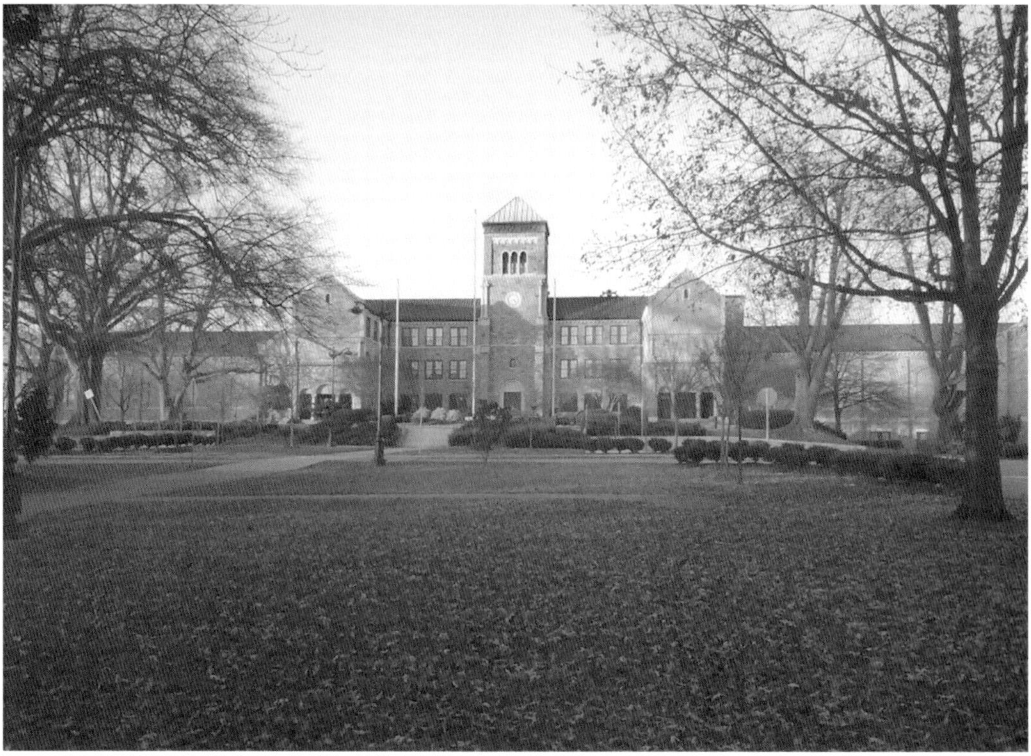

### Needham B. Broughton

Broughton owned a successful local printing company and was active in local politics. He served on the board of agriculture and as a state senator in 1901–1902. However, he is best remembered for his work promoting Wake County public schools. Needham B. Broughton High School, pictured here, was named in his honor and remains open today. (Authors' collection.)

# CHAPTER FIVE

# Social Crusaders

Where would society be without social crusaders, those brave souls who have come in and stood up for the rights of minorities and the opposed, from fighting for the freedom of slaves in the antebellum South, to fighting for the preservation of Raleigh's historic sites today. Social crusaders encourage reform and rights for all of Raleigh's citizens, no matter the opposition against them.

Lunsford Lane was a freed slave in Raleigh. After experiencing trials and tribulations at the hands of slave owners and white supremacists, Lane went on to become a notable speaker for the abolitionist movement and traveled the country encouraging manumission. He may have passed John Rex on the streets of Raleigh in the 1830s. Rex sought to improve the health of those around him, willing his money to establish the first public hospital in Raleigh. Richard Pullen donated land to establish a space for recreational enjoyment, known as Pullen Park, just a few years later.

In the 20th century, Raleigh was home to many people who fought for civil rights. Ella Baker, a former Shaw University student, organized a series of meetings on campus that led to the creation of the Student Non-Violent Coordinating Committee (SNCC). Meanwhile, Raleigh high school student Joe Holt and his family worked to desegregate the Raleigh public school system, while countless others worked in the educational, social, and legal realms to demand justice for all.

Recently, Raleigh has been home to a number of intrepid women in the preservation field, such as Vallie Henderson, a champion for Historic Oakwood, and Beth Crabtree, who dreamed of a place where Raleigh's history could be preserved.

No matter their cause, citizens of Raleigh have been fighting to improve the city since it was established.

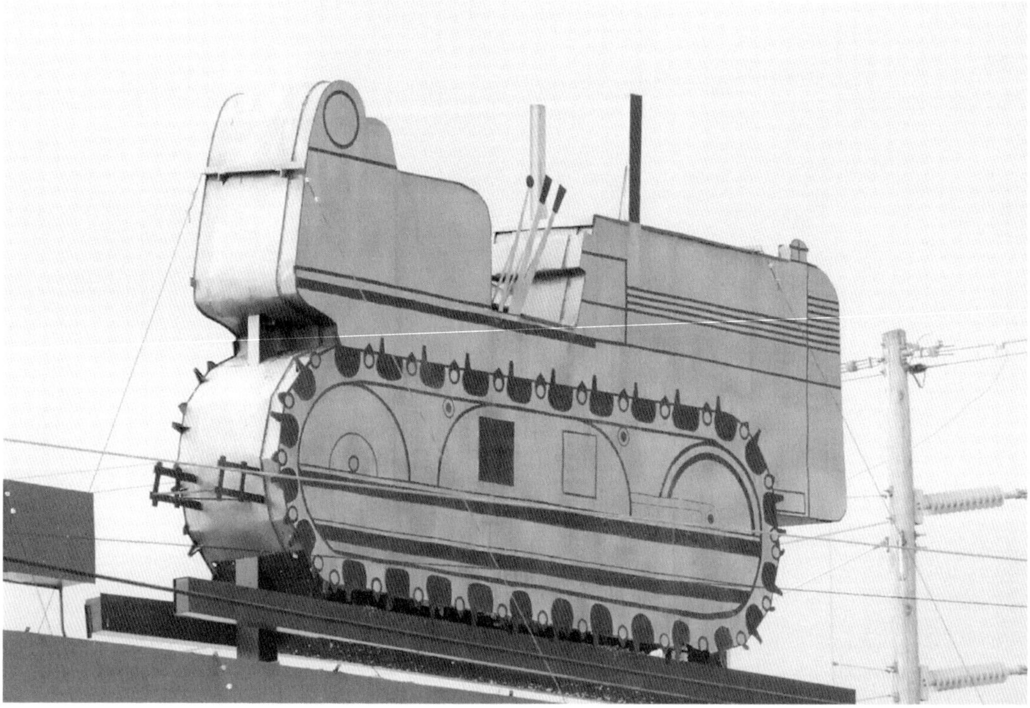

### A.E. Finley

Finley (1895–1986) started the North Carolina Equipment Company in Raleigh in 1931 and built it into the largest equipment distributorship in the country by 1951. The company's sign is pictured here. With his wife, Marian, he established the A.E. Finley Foundation to give to area universities, hospitals, children's groups, and the arts. An avid golfer, Finley helped open the Raleigh Golf Association to provide a public course for families unable to afford country club dues. He also supported local YMCAs. (Courtesy of Dmitri Medvedev.)

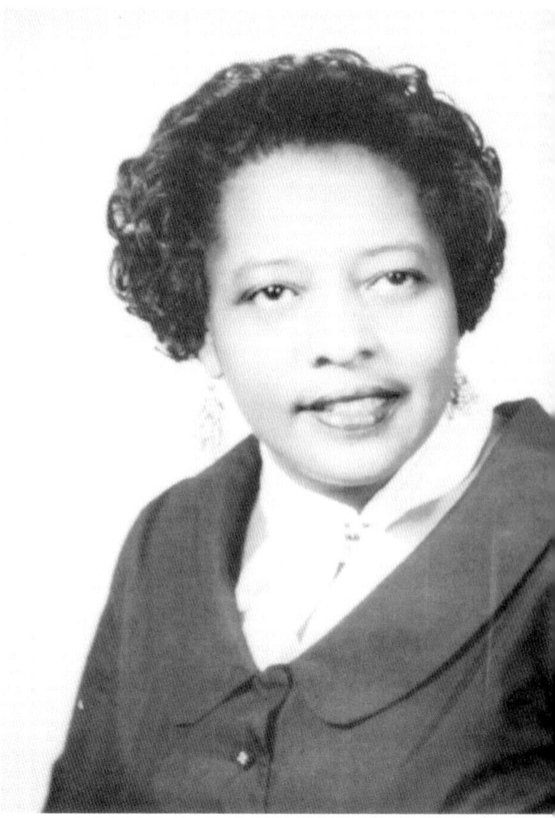

### Elizabeth Cofield

A Raleigh educator and civil rights activist, Cofield (1920–2009) worked as a professor of education and personnel administrator at Shaw University, and was the first African American elected to the Raleigh Board of Education. Cofield was also the first African American woman elected to the Wake County Board of Commissioners. (Courtesy of RCM.)

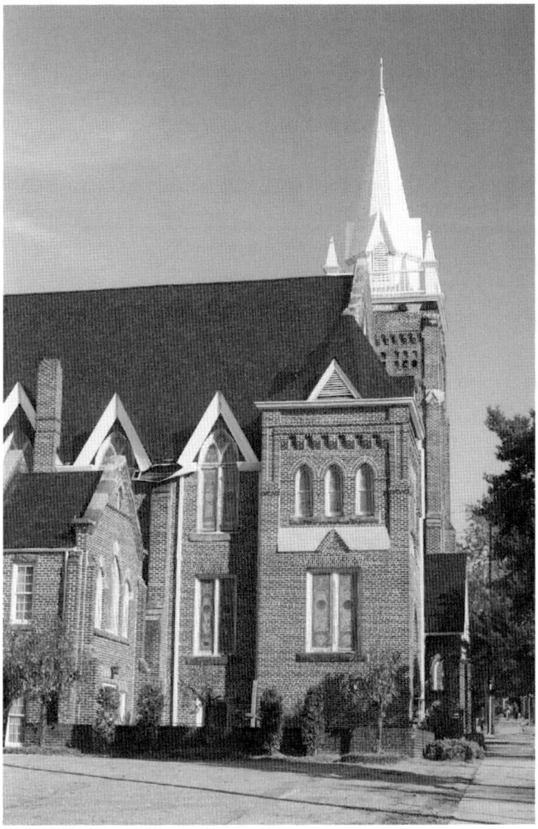

**R.W.H. Leak**

The pastor of St. Paul's Church (shown here), Reverend Leak first joined white supremacist Josephus Daniels to fight for prohibition in 1886, then continued supporting the Democrats, backing Jim Crow laws and literacy tests, seemingly due to a personal feud with opposition leader James H. Young. Not until a decade later, when he realized the inadequacies in voting, school funding, and political representation for African Americans, did Leak fight against the "lily white" ruling party. (Courtesy of Dmitri Medvedev.)

**R. Stanhope Pullen**

Pullen used the gains from his astute business sense to help create three major Raleigh landmarks. He saved Peace Institute from bankruptcy in 1872, donated the original 60 acres for North Carolina State in 1887, and donated an adjacent 80 acres later that year to the city of Raleigh for the future Pullen Park, named in his honor. His home is pictured here. (Authors' collection.)

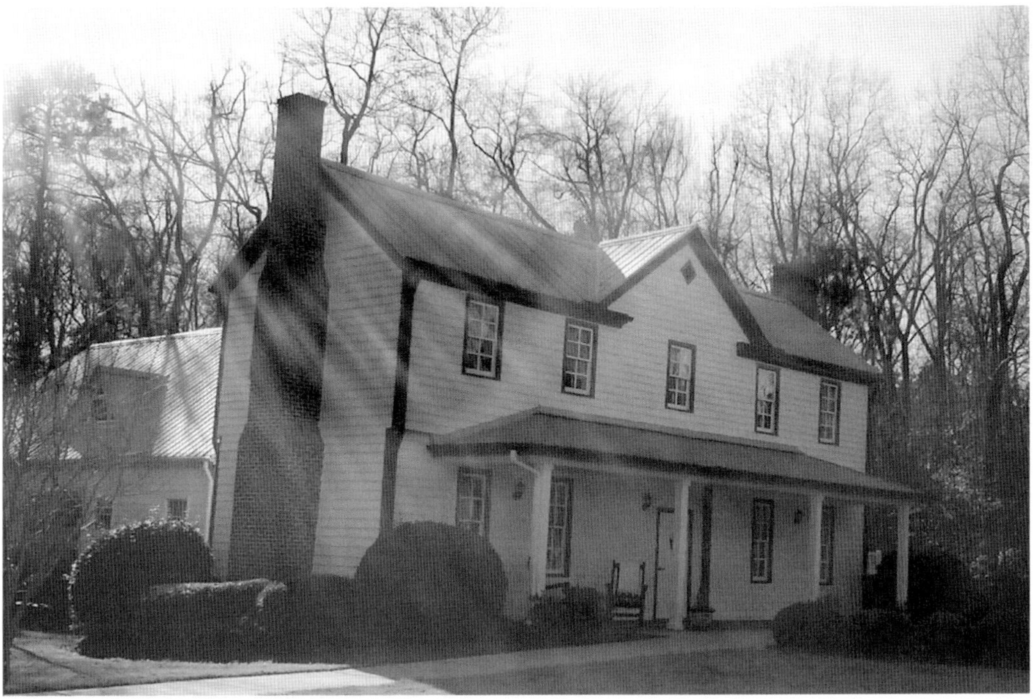

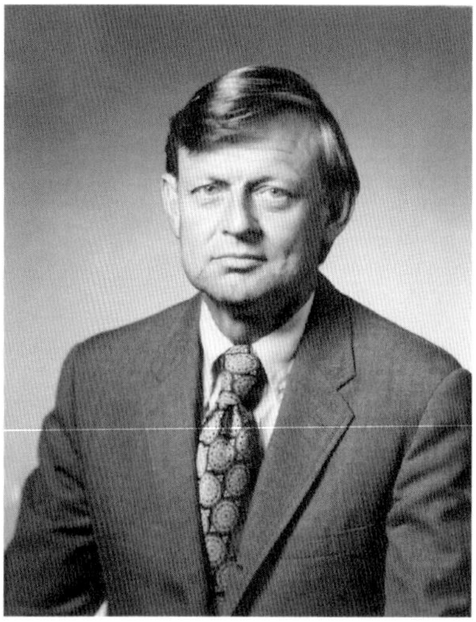

## Cyrus and Carolyn King

In the 1950s and 1960s, activism for integration was the main social cause of Cyrus and Carolyn King, especially the desegregation of local parks and schools. As the years went on, the Kings have worked for the rights of the LGBT community, for the abolishment of the death penalty, and to end war. Since the early 1980s, the Kings have been a fixture in downtown Raleigh every week for the Fayetteville Street First Wednesday Peace Vigil. (Courtesy of RCM.)

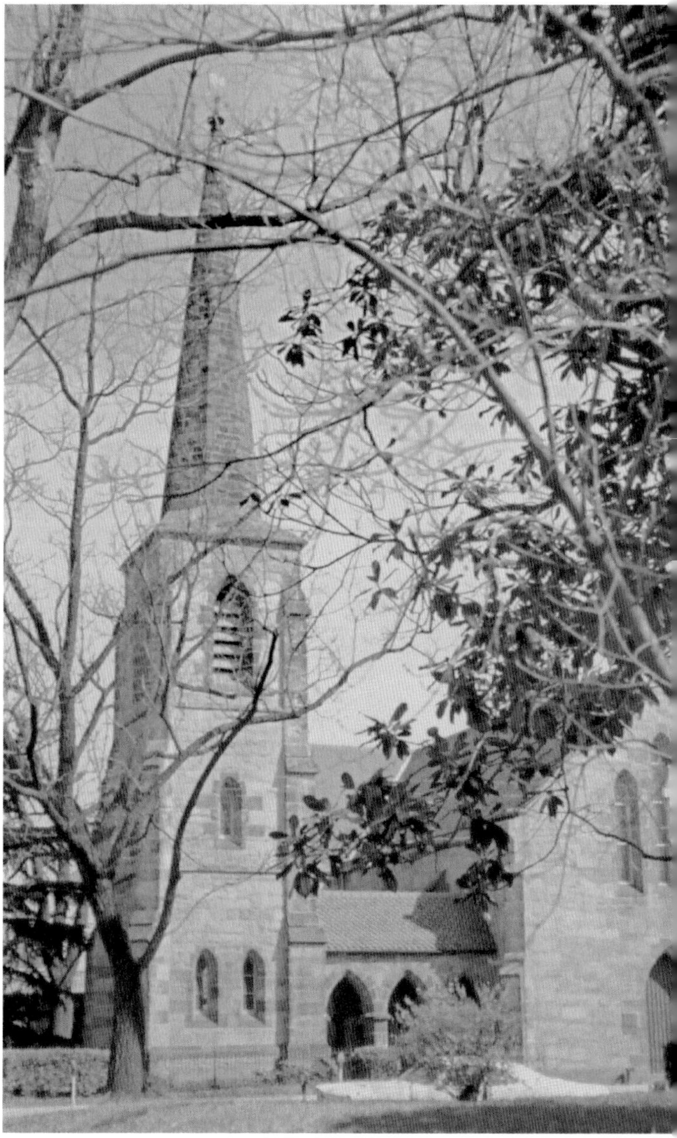

## Mary Sumner and Thomas Blount

Despite spending much of their lives elsewhere, both Mary Sumner Blount (1777–1822) and her husband, Thomas, impacted Raleigh's early landscape. Thomas fought for the United States in the Revolutionary War, was elected a representative to Congress, and served on the commission to design the new capital of Raleigh. For this last work, a street was named after him. After her husband's death, Mary left money in her will to build what became Christ Episcopal Church, pictured here. It is one of Raleigh's oldest congregations. (Courtesy of OR.)



70

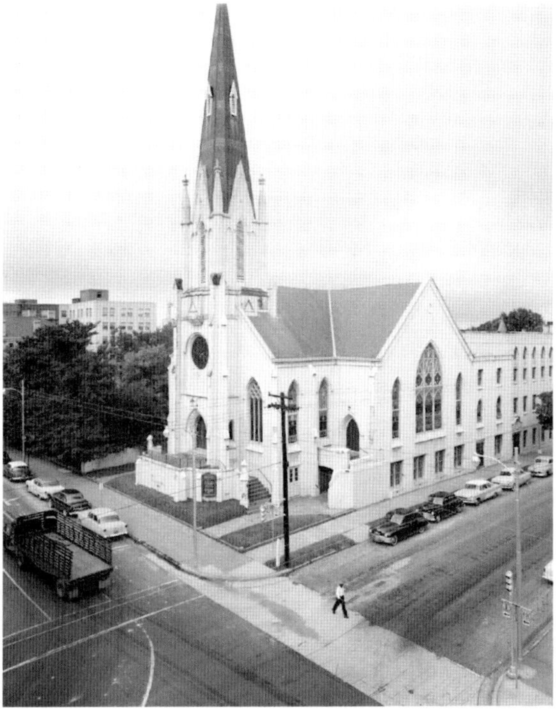

### Sallie Towles, Sarah Lewis, Virginia Swepson, and Anna Justice

In 1874, Towles, Lewis, Swepson, and Justice were elected the first female deacons of Raleigh's First Baptist Church, pictured here. Their election ushered in a new age of church governance at a time when churches dominated the landscape in Raleigh. The election also led to the current policy requiring an equal number of male and female deacons. (Courtesy of OR.)

### John Rex

John Rex was a wealthy plantation owner in Wake County. In his will of 1839, he provided for "the erection and endowment of an infirmary or hospital for the sick and afflicted poor of the city of Raleigh." This laid the grounds for the first public hospital in Raleigh (shown here). The institution opened in 1894, 55 years after Rex's death. (Courtesy of RCM.)

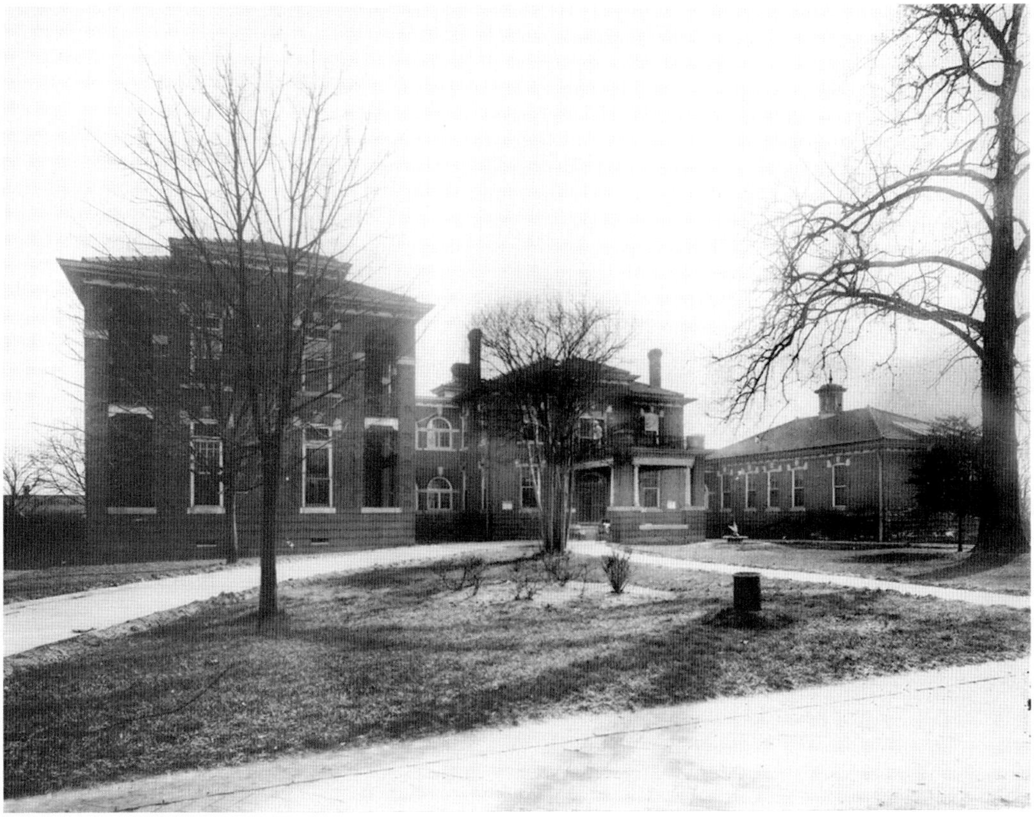

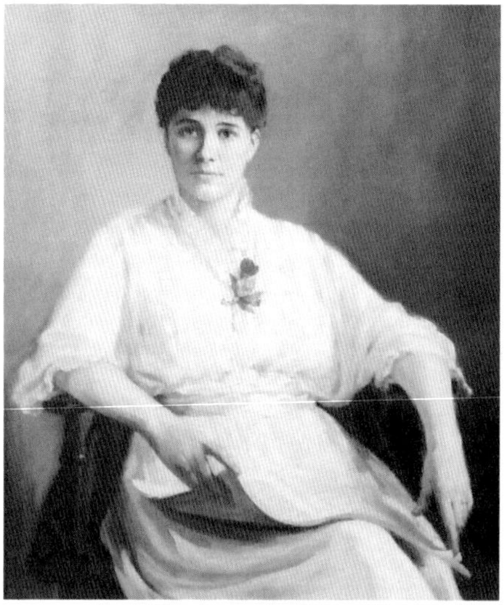

**Olivia Raney**
Richard Raney was a successful businessman who served on the chamber of commerce. In February 1896, the chamber started working on the establishment of a public library. In May, Raney's wife, Olivia, passed away. Richard invested his fortune in the establishment of the library, a cause Olivia strongly supported. The Olivia Raney Library, which opened in 1901, was Wake County's first public library. (Courtesy of OR.)

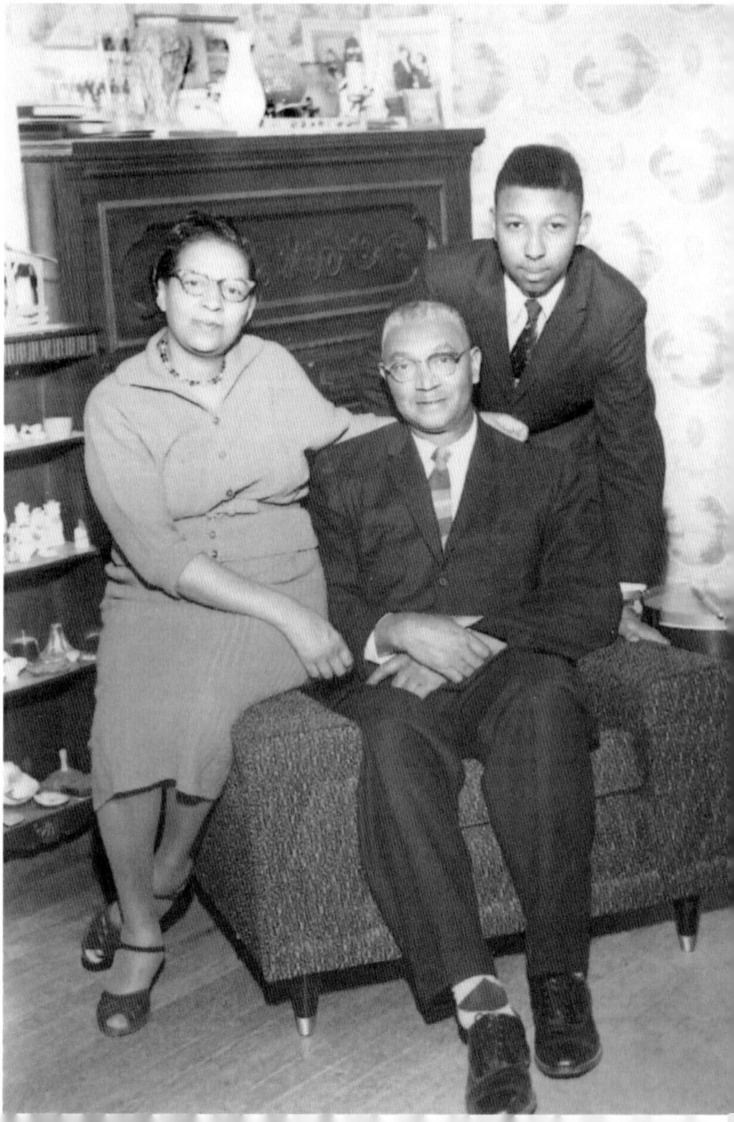

**Joseph Holt Jr.**
Holt was the first student to try to integrate the Raleigh schools. In 1956, his family attempted to enroll him at Daniels Junior High School, but were denied. The following year, they applied at Broughton High School, but were once again denied. This continued each year of school until his graduation. The family suffered persecution for their efforts, including Joe's father losing his job. Holt was never accepted to a white school. (Courtesy of RCM.)

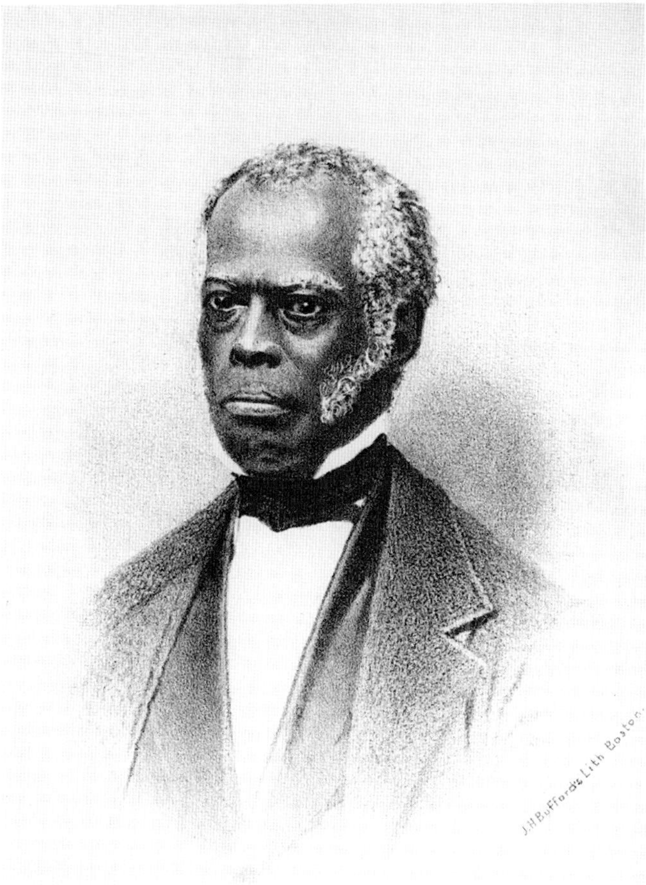

**Lunsford Lane**
Lane (1803–1879) was born a slave in the Sherwood Haywood household in 1803. As the only child of their house servants, Lunsford also worked in their home. As a man, he learned from his father how to manufacture smoking tobacco, and was able to improve on the flavor. His tobacco quickly became popular among legislators in Raleigh. He was able to earn enough money through the sale of tobacco and homemade pipes, in addition to taking odd jobs and hiring out his time, to purchase his freedom. He then saved enough money to open his own tobacco store in downtown Raleigh, which became very successful. Lane also started working as a janitor in the office of Gov. Edward Dudley's private secretary. By 1840, Lane was able to buy a house and lot in Raleigh, and had plans to buy his wife and six children, who were still held in slavery. However, in the tumultuous 1840s, Lunsford Lane's success was not popular with many whites in the area. Soon, they forced him to leave Raleigh, his property, and his family. They used a legal technicality to force him out—that Lane's freedom had been granted in another state (the fact of which is not clear), and that no free slave from another state could stay in North Carolina. Lane traveled to the North and met up with the abolitionist movement in Boston. He was hassled once again, accused of being a runaway slave, but with the help of his new friends, Lane was cleared of the charges and able to raise the rest of the money to purchase his family. He traveled back to Raleigh in the spring of 1842 with plans to purchase his family and return North. An angry mob was waiting for Lane, though. They tarred and feathered him, but with the help of friends and some luck, Lunsford was able to escape. His family, including his mother, freed by his former owner, left North Carolina by train. Once safe, Lunsford published his account and started traveling and lecturing. He became a leader and inspiration in the abolitionist movement. (Courtesy of RCM.)

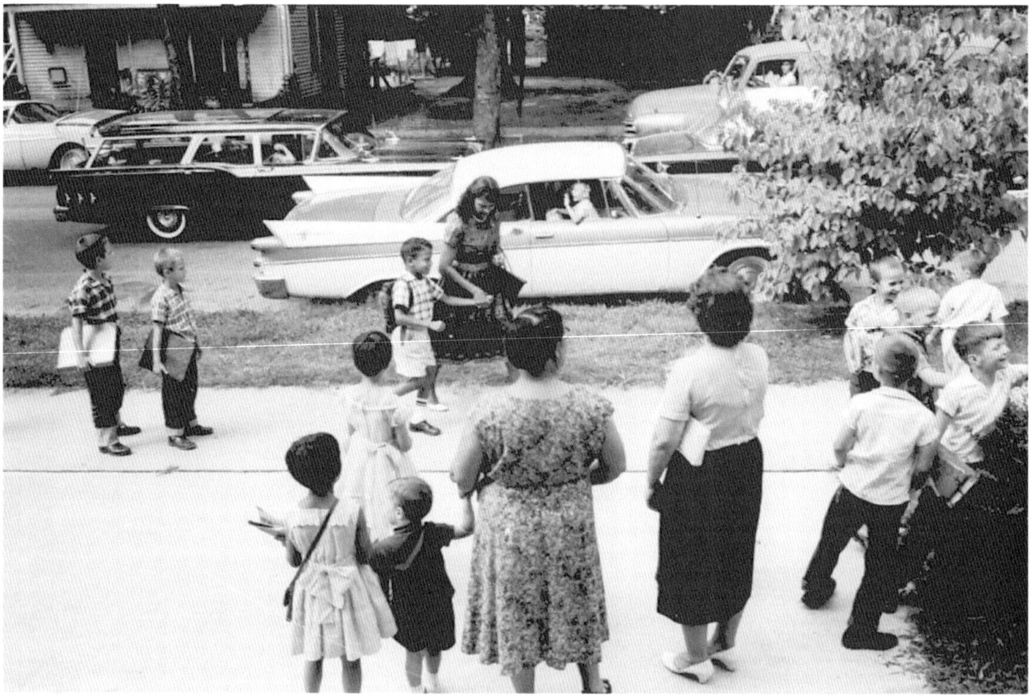

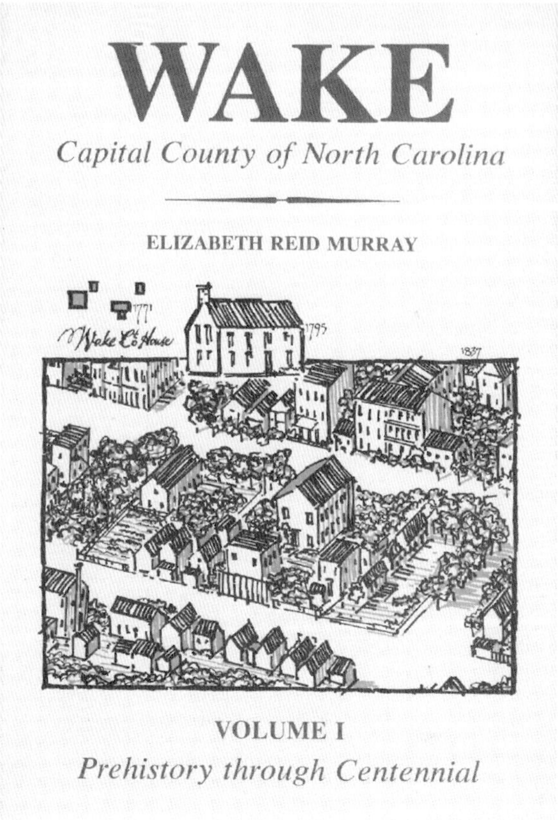


**William Campbell**
Campbell (1953–present) was born during the height of the civil rights movement. In 1960, seven-year-old William was the first African American to integrate a white school in Raleigh. He is shown here being walked to his first day of class. William would grow up to become a noted politician, serving as the mayor of Atlanta, Georgia, from 1994 to 2002. (Courtesy of RCM.)

**Elizabeth Reid Murray**
Murray is known for her promotion of Raleigh's libraries, historic sites, and preservation. She is the author of *From Raleigh's Past* and *Wake: Capital County of North Carolina, Volumes I and II*. She has collected Wake County artifacts and memorabilia over several decades, and they are available to local researchers at the Olivia Raney Local History Library. (Authors' collection.)

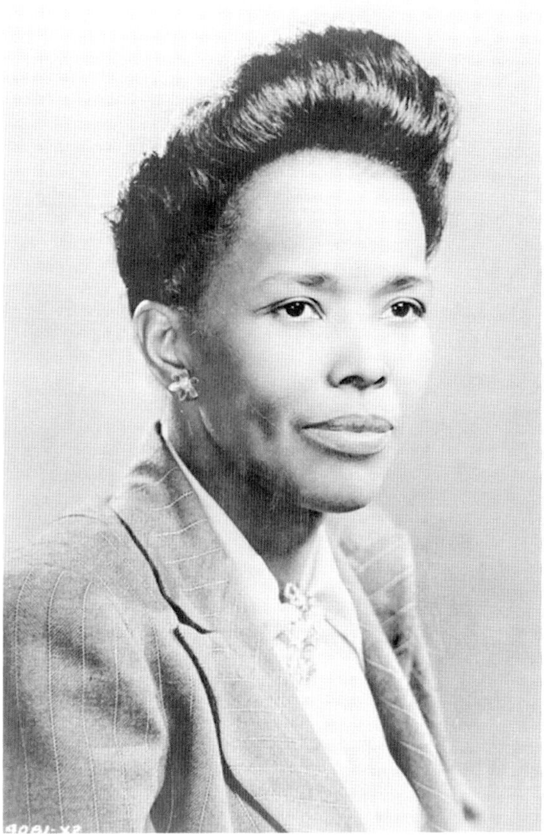

**Ella Baker**

Baker (1903–1986) moved to North Carolina when she was nine. She attended Shaw University, then moved to New York City, where she became involved in politics, working for the NAACP, the SCLC, the SCEF, and the WPA. In 1960, she held a series of meetings at Shaw University. From these meetings was formed the Student Non-Violent Coordinating Committee, which organized voter registration drives, sit-ins, freedom rides, and more. (Courtesy of RCM.)

**Henry Martin Tupper**

Reverend Tupper (1831–1893) founded Shaw University in 1865, the first college for African Americans established after the Civil War. Tupper, a Baptist minister, came to Raleigh with the Freedmen's Bureau, and his first Bible study classes at the old Guion Hotel are credited as the start of the university. He was Shaw's first president until his death in 1893, and he built the first dormitory in the country solely for black women, Estey Hall, pictured here, in 1874. (Courtesy of OR.)

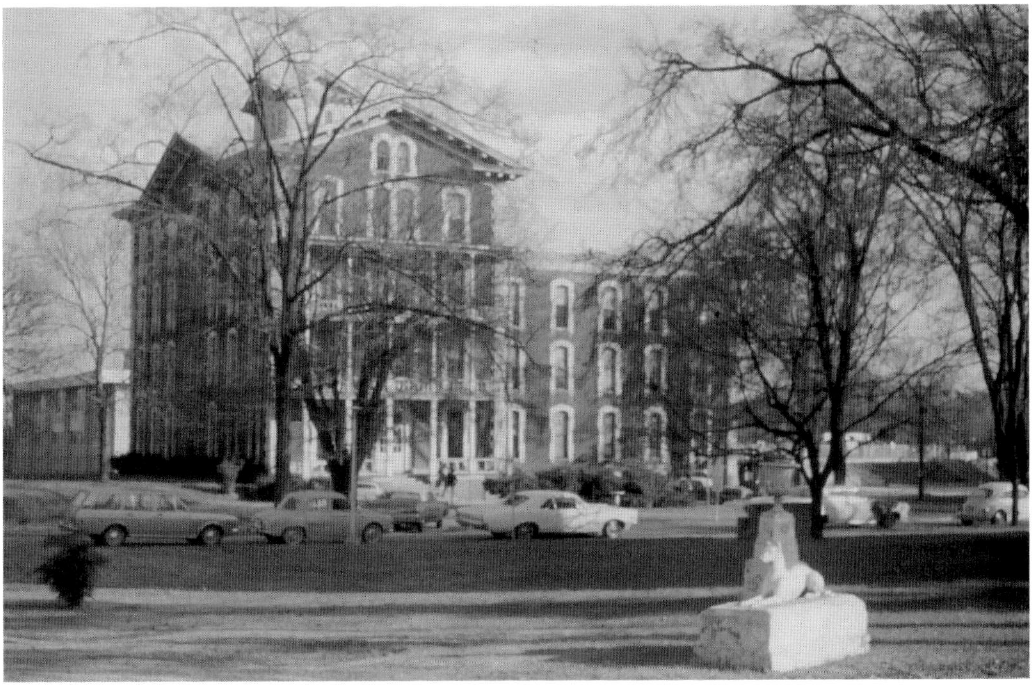

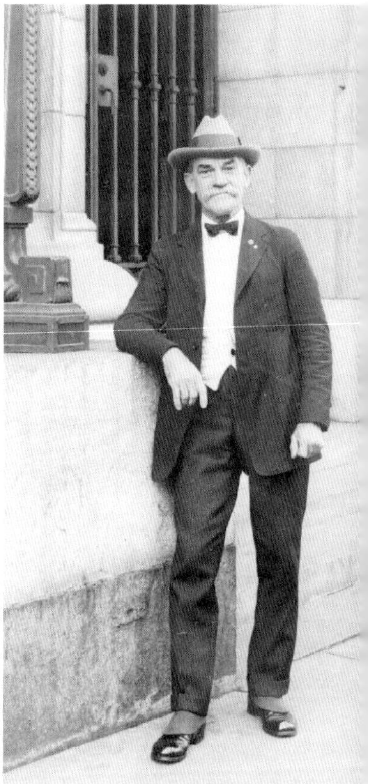

## Fred Olds

Olds (1853–1935) settled in Raleigh in the 1870s to work in the insurance business. He served as secretary for the chamber of commerce, and soon became interested in newspaper work, obtaining a position as a reporter with the Raleigh *News*. Later, he became editor at *The News and Observer*. He served on the staff of Gov. Zebulon Vance, in the National Guard, and in the State Guard. Among all of Olds's achievements, he is best remembered for his dedication to the preservation of North Carolina history. He strove to acquire the history of the everyday person, collecting deeds, family papers, and other documents of North Carolina families, which have been donated to the state. Olds also published history books and helped share history with students and other youths. (Courtesy of University of North Carolina Library at Chapel Hill.)

## Helen Elias

Elias (1867–1954), daughter of Michael and Regina Grausman, was a charter and active member of the Woman's Club of Raleigh. She helped form the Hebrew Benevolent Association and the first Parent-Teachers Association in Raleigh. During World War I, she helped found the Wake County chapter of the Red Cross, and the Victory Farming Program. She was part of the Flu Epidemic Relief during the Spanish influenza outbreak, and organized a nonsegregated visiting nurse service. The Raleigh chapter of the American Red Cross is pictured here during World War I. (Courtesy of RCM.)

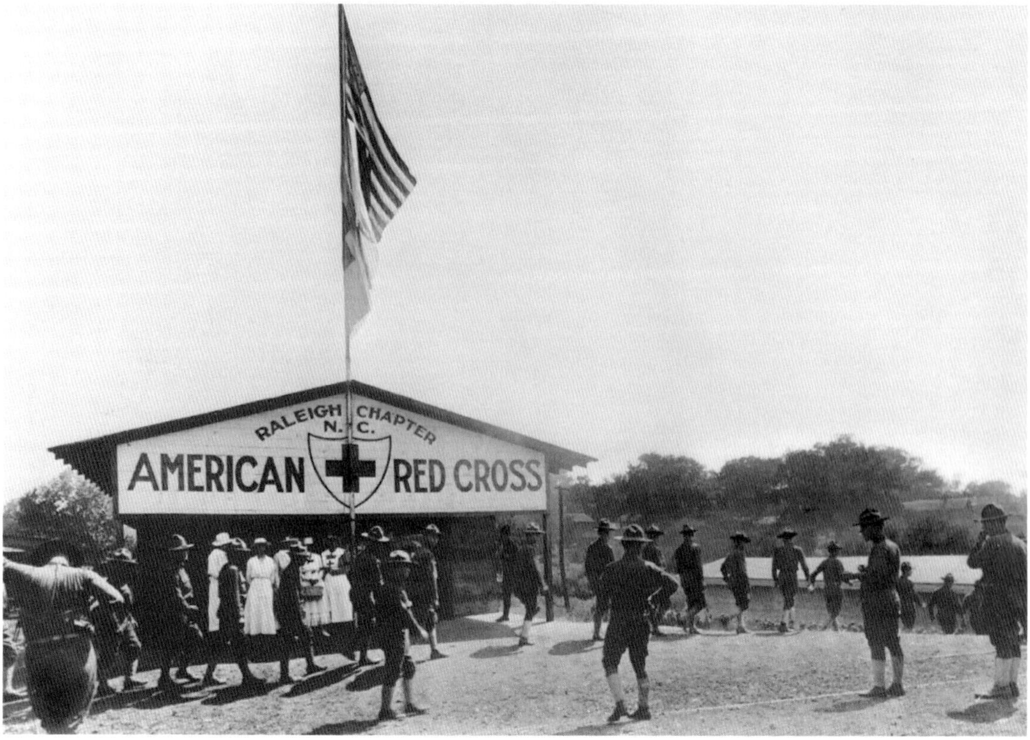

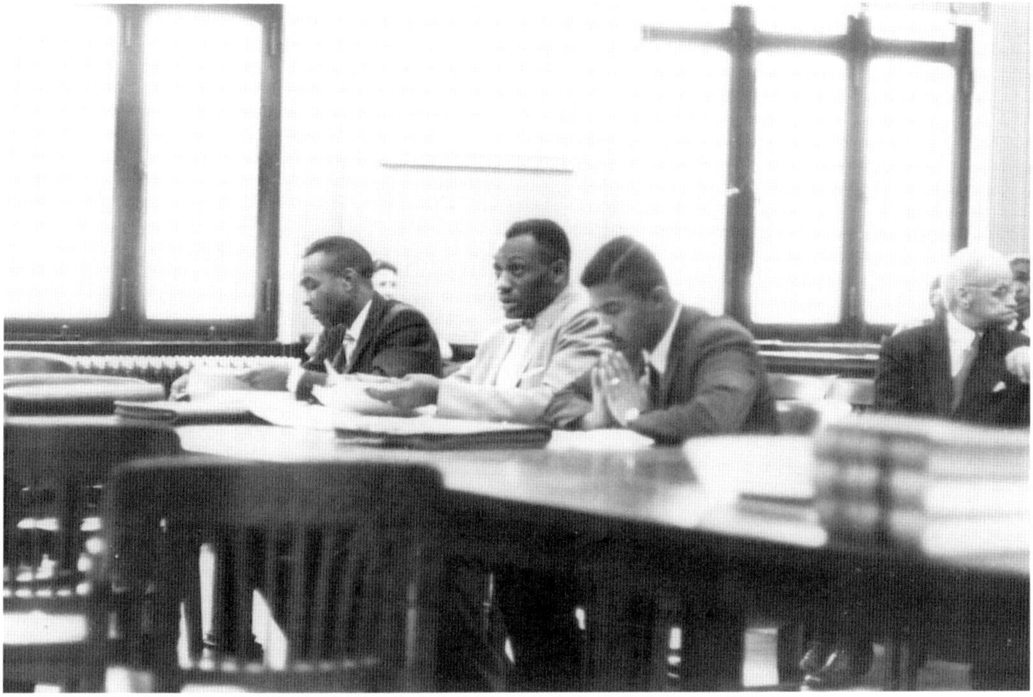

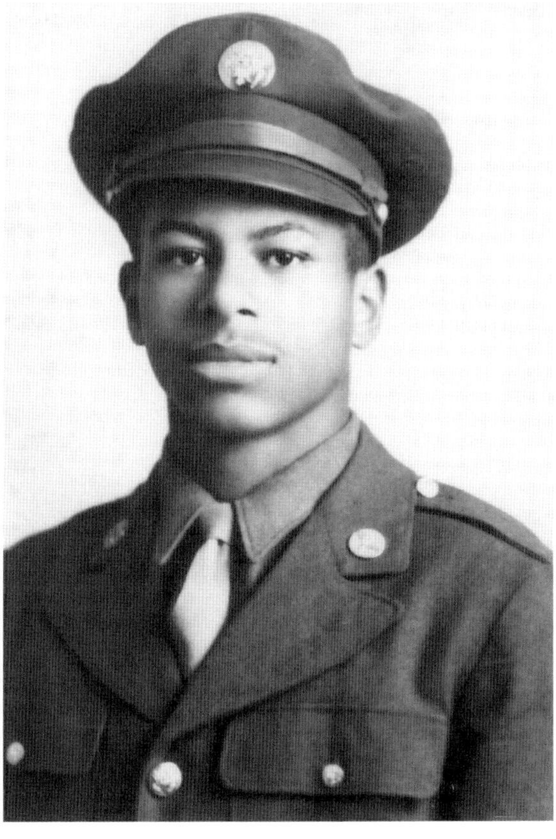

**Herman Taylor and Samuel Mitchell**
The Taylor and Mitchell Law Firm was established in 1952. The firm was known across the state for its handling of civil rights cases. Among others, they represented the Holt family in its suit against the Raleigh City School Board. Taylor and Mitchell designed the school integration theories that were successful in Raleigh. (Courtesy of RCM.)

**Harold and Lucille Webb**
Harold served as a Tuskegee Airman and was a force for school integration. He was the first African American state personnel director and the deputy state superintendent of public instruction. In 2007, he received the Congressional Gold Medal. Lucille served on the Wake County Board of Health. The Kellogg Foundation had her lead their Community Based Public Health Initiative, and she is heralded by the Centers for Disease Control and Prevention. (Courtesy of RCM.)

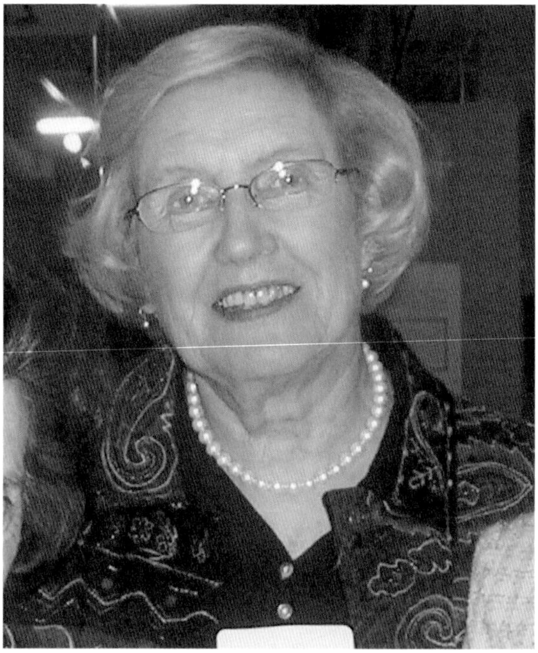

## Mary Cates

Beth Crabtree was a Raleigh historian who started the idea for the Raleigh City Museum. After her death, Mary Cates, a civic leader and five-term Raleigh city councilor, carried on Crabtree's dream. In 1990, Cates brought together advocates to create the Raleigh City Museum, whose mission was "To Preserve Raleigh's Past for the Future." It was the "only home for artifacts of the city and its people." (Courtesy of RCM.)

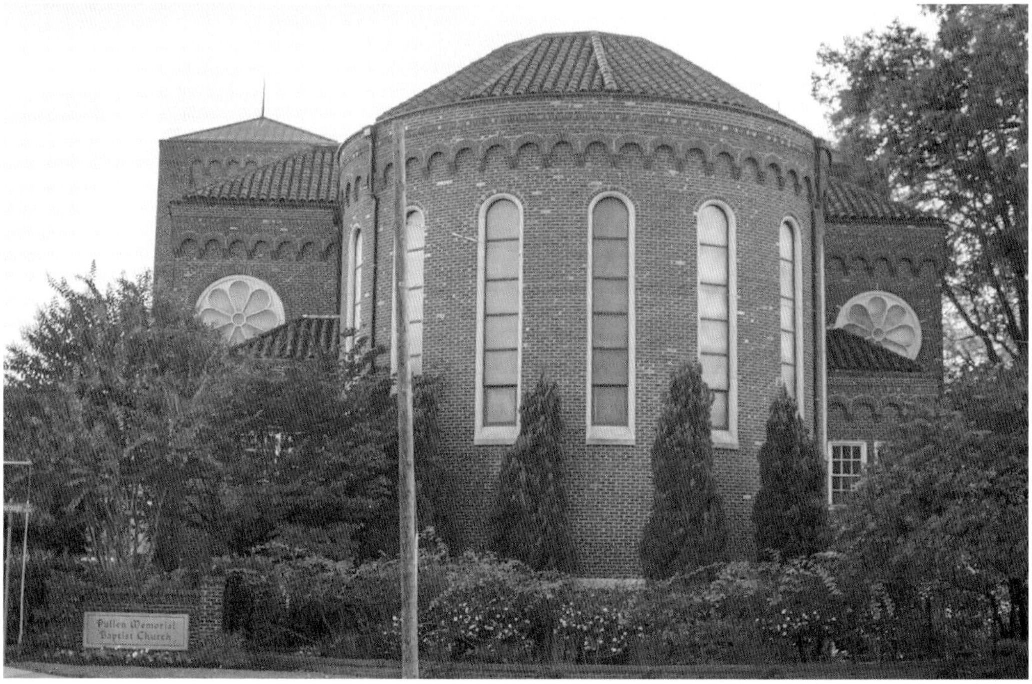


## William Wallace Finlator

Reverend Finlator (1913–2006), pastor at Pullen Memorial Baptist Church on Hillsborough Street (pictured here) during the tumultuous years of 1956–1982, used his pulpit to advocate for civil rights, the end of segregation, labor unions, economic justice, equal access to education, and world peace. Receiving responses ranging from death threats to state and national awards, Finlator continued to urge his congregation to confront the issues of the day with a progressive mind and open heart. (Courtesy of RCM.)

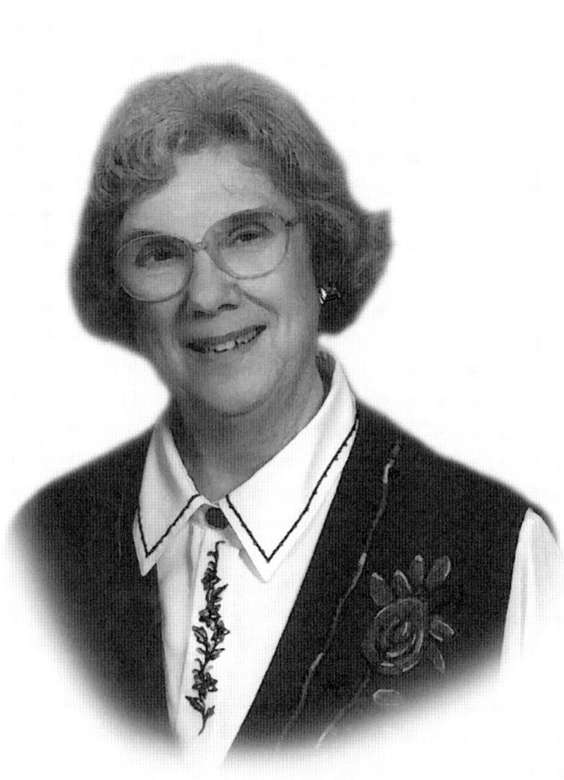

**Sarah Denny Williamson**
Williamson (1928–2013) moved to Raleigh because her father served on the state supreme court. She grew to love the city and became involved with preservation efforts. Williamson served on the Raleigh Historic Sites Commission, as the director of Preservation North Carolina, and on the Attorney General's Committee on Historic Preservation Legislation. She won three awards for her preservation work, including the Sir Walter Award. (Courtesy of Raleigh Hall of Fame.)

**Vallie Lewis Henderson**
Henderson (1907–1998) was a voice for the Oakwood community for 60 years. She moved there in 1935 and founded the Oakwood Garden Club in 1950. In 1970, Vallie organized opposition to a freeway that would have cut through the historic homes. She helped get Oakwood listed as Raleigh's first historic district and formed the Society for the Preservation of Historic Oakwood. (Authors' collection.)

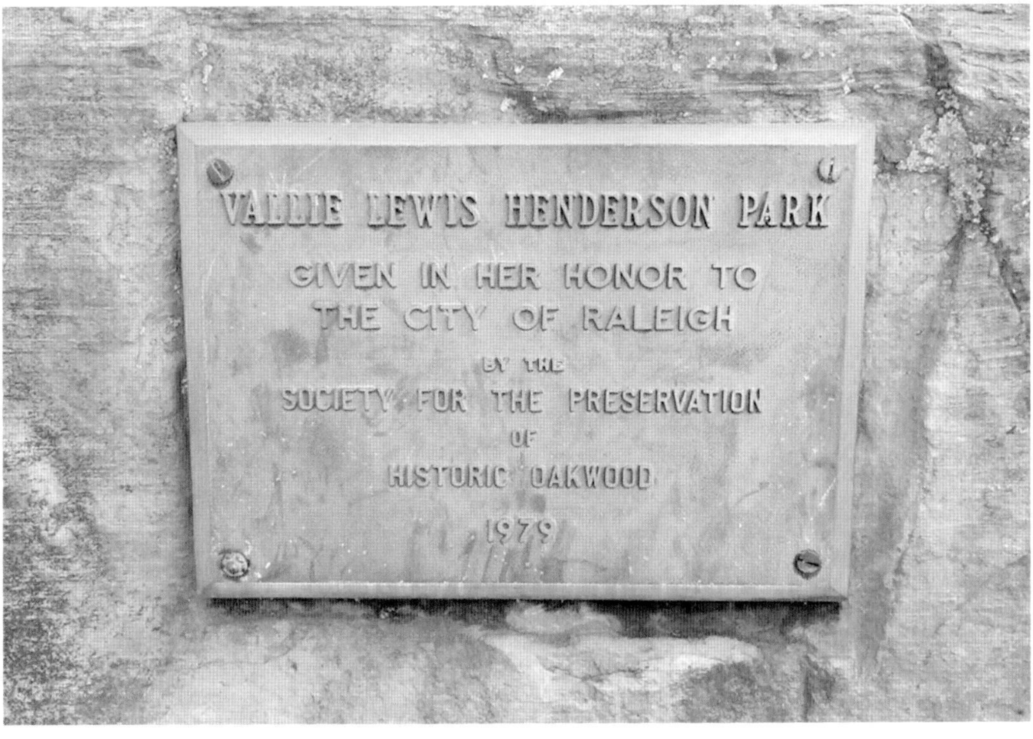

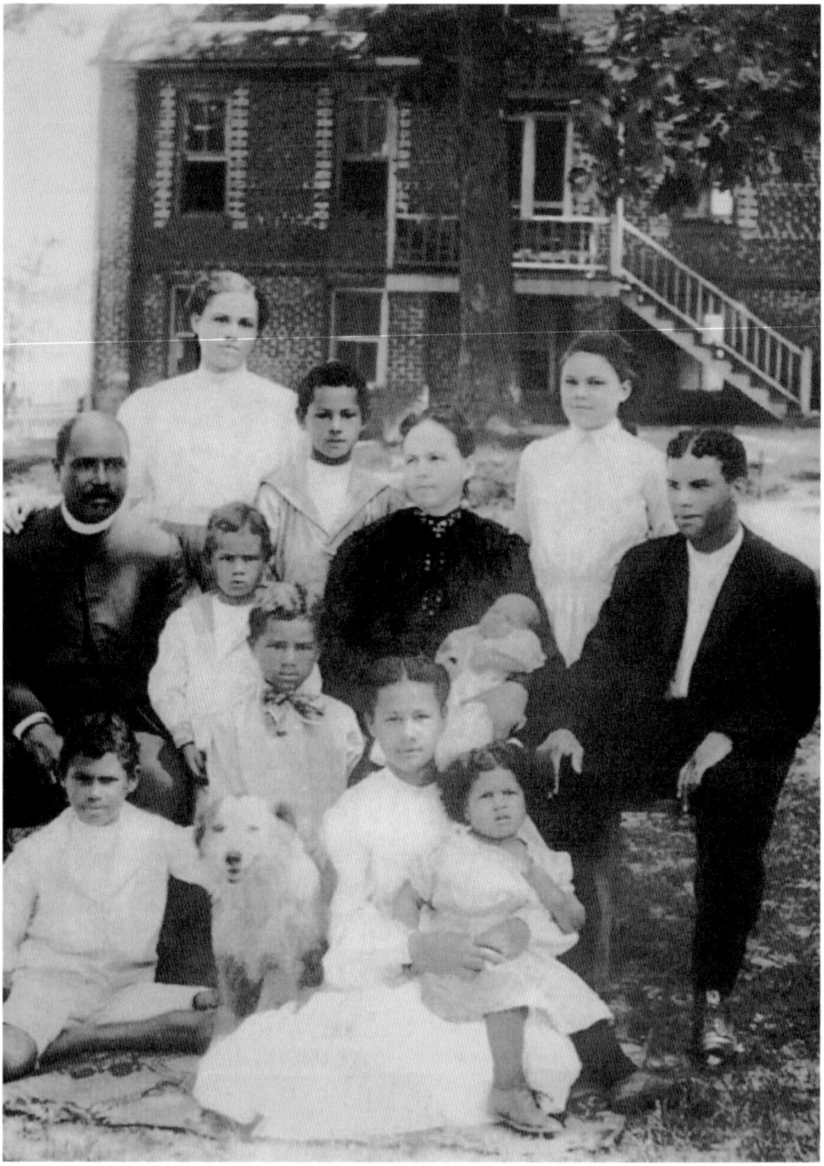

**Sarah Louise "Sadie" Delany and Annie Elizabeth "Bessie" Delany**

The Delany sisters grew up on the campus of St. Augustine's, where their father was vice principal and their mother a teacher, during the height of Jim Crow. The family is pictured here with Sadie standing at left rear and Bessie sitting at center front. Sadie (1889–1999) worked with the Negro Rural School Fund, educating black children in rural Raleigh with the help of Dr. Booker T. Washington, before leaving to teach in New York.

Bessie (1891–1995) followed Sadie to New York City in 1918, attending Columbia's School of Dentistry. In 1923, she became only the second licensed black female dentist in New York, sharing a practice with her brother. All three mingled with and took part in the Harlem Renaissance as important figures, although Bessie was the more radical sister. When they were both over 100, the sisters coauthored, with Amy Hill Hearth, the *New York Times* bestseller *Having Our Say: The Delany Sisters' First 100 Years* about their experiences. (Courtesy of St. Augustine's University.)

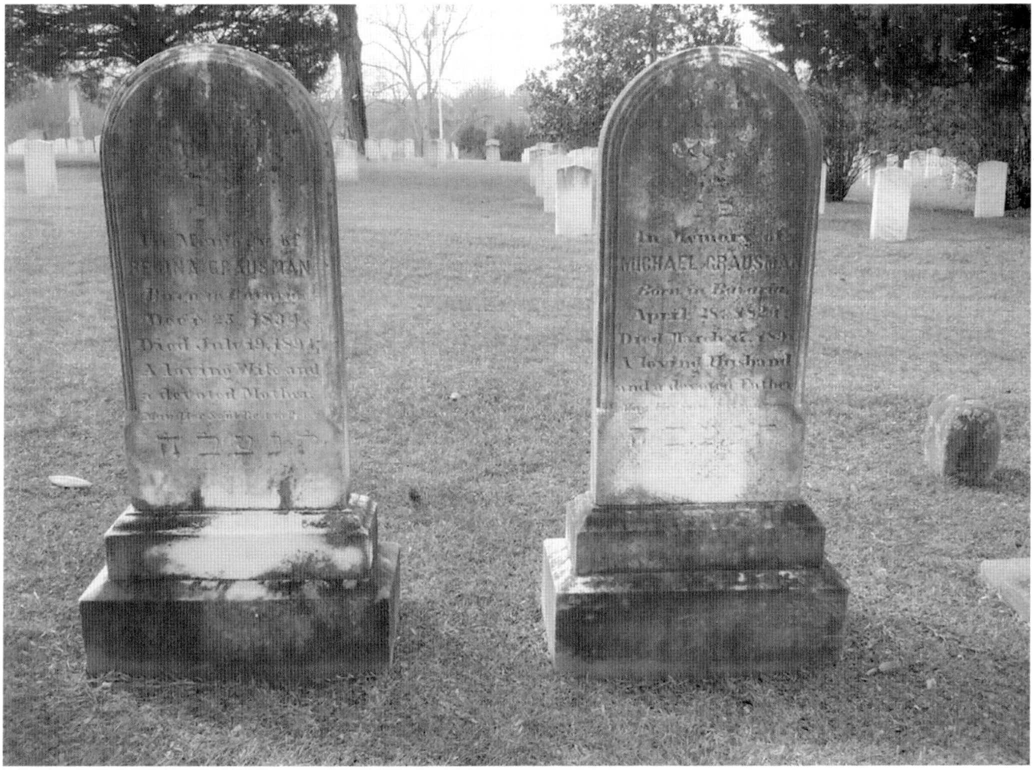

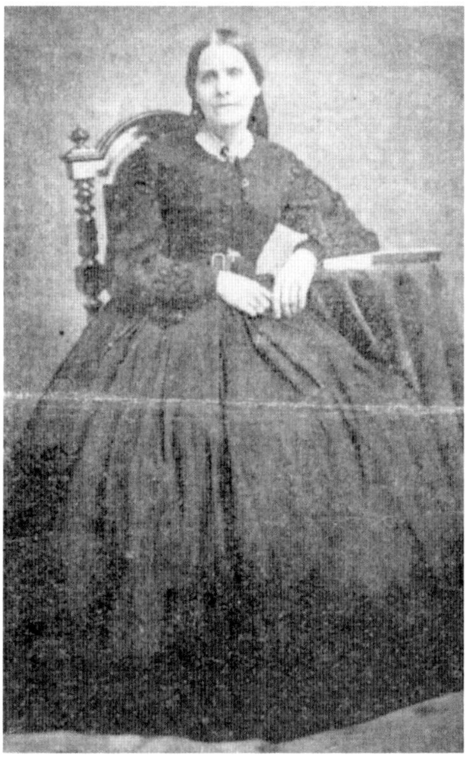

**Michael and Regina Grausman**

Michael (1824–1891) and Regina (1834–1894) Grausman are considered the first practicing Jewish residents of Raleigh. They emigrated from Bavaria in the 1850s, moving to Raleigh in 1862. They were commissioned to serve as tailors for the Confederate army, and they opened a grocery store. In 1874, the first Jewish services were held in Raleigh, in the former nursery of their home. Michael, who had studied to be a rabbi, led the service. (Authors' collection.)

**Sophia Arms Partridge**

Partridge (1817–1881) fell in love with Raleigh when visiting from New York. She ran the Select School for Young Ladies from 1846 to 1851 and from 1858 to 1865. During the Civil War, she ardently supported the Confederacy, painting flags, sewing, and serving in the local aid society. Partridge worked with the Wake County Memorial Association to get the Confederate Cemetery opened in 1867, on the grounds of what is now Oakwood Cemetery. (Courtesy of SANC.)

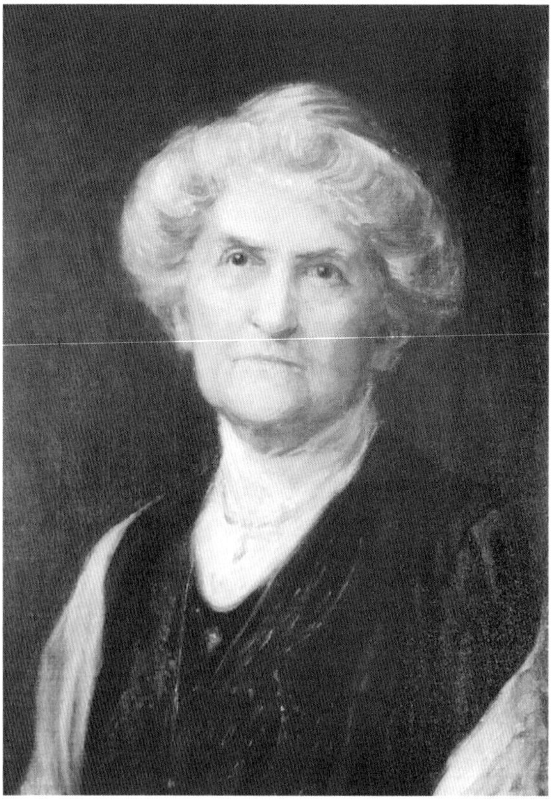

### Elvira Worth Moffit

Moffit (1836–1930) was always concerned with the well-being of other local women. In 1899, she set up the Woman's Exchange in downtown Raleigh, an organization that promoted industry and craft. In 1904, she helped to establish the Woman's Club of Raleigh, whose statement reads, "The object shall be the intellectual philanthropic, social and civic betterment of the community." (Courtesy of the Woman's Club of Raleigh.)

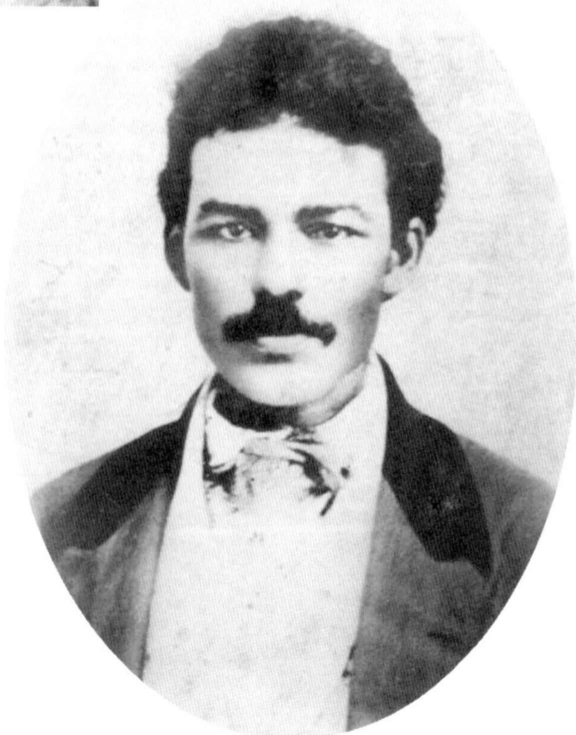

### John A. Copeland Jr.

A Raleigh native, freeman Copeland (1834–1859) moved with his parents to Oberlin, Ohio. He soon became involved in the abolitionist movement and found himself part of John Brown's Raid on Harper's Ferry in 1859. Copeland was caught and sentenced to death. Prior to his execution, he declared, "If I am dying for freedom, I could not die in a better cause. I had rather die than be a slave." (Courtesy of Library of Congress.)

# CHAPTER SIX

# Movers and Shapers

Historians and other social commentators often discuss how a city changes over time, how it adapts to its environment, evolves with fluctuating social mores, and grows or shrinks as geography or culture dictate. However, a city is just a collection of infrastructure and buildings without one key factor. What these observers are really seeing are the actions of the individual people who erect those buildings and whose beliefs and interests spur them to expression.

Raleigh has an impressive collection of modernist buildings, thanks in large part to the students of North Carolina State's School of Design and its dean, Henry L. Kamphoefner. He brought in architects like Matthew Nowicki, who designed the innovative and parabolic J.S. Dorton Arena at the State Fairgrounds in 1950. Prof. Harwell Hamilton Harris brought the colors and shapes of North Carolina's nature into his designs, and landscape architect Richard Bell combined his laboratory, classroom, and home all into one inspirational location outdoors.

Even before Raleigh had many buildings at all, in the 1820s, architect William Nichols transformed the statehouse, at the behest of the general assembly, so that it would look grand enough to match the giant, Neoclassical sculpture of Pres. George Washington they had just commissioned from Italy.

Raleigh's cultural landscape has been influenced to varying degrees by every person who has been lucky enough to spend time here, but sometimes, personal achievements have resonated long past the original events. NC State student Katharine Stinson made history by entering the engineering school as its first female student, but she just wanted to pursue her dreams, not make history. William H. Deitrick loved Raleigh's buildings, so he installed his office in an old water tower to save it from destruction. He did not imagine that, over 60 years later, people like Greg Hatem and J. Myrick Howard would be making their living preserving other historic buildings, including some of his own, and integrating them into Raleigh's modern landscape.

Each day, the people of Raleigh impact their city in sometimes subtle but real ways. What citizens do creates the future of this place as well as a piece of its history.

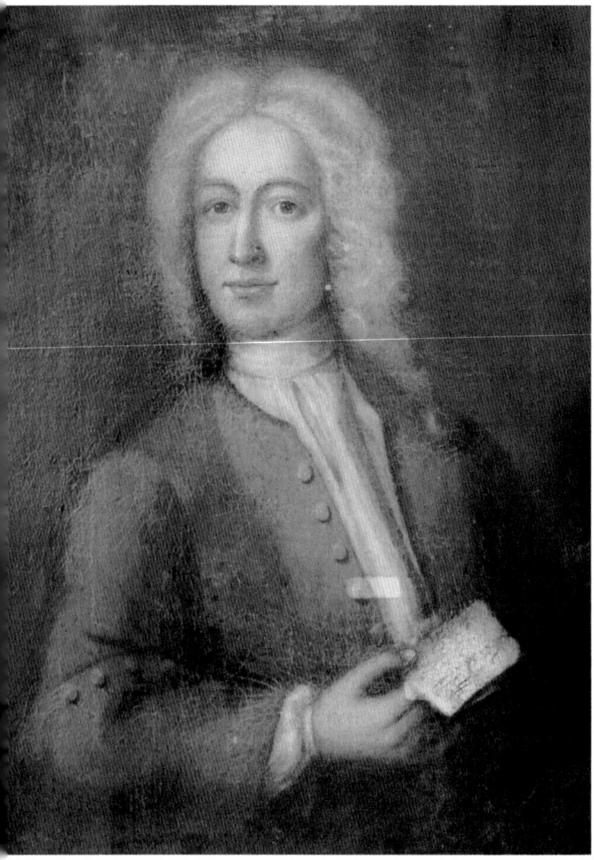

## John Lawson

Lawson (1674?–1711) was the official surveyor general of the Carolinas. In 1700, Lawson led an expedition to the Carolina back country. He was the first European settler to explore the area that would later become Raleigh and Wake County. In 1709, he published *Voyage to Carolina*, which led many to come to the North Carolina colony. In 1711, he was captured by the Tuscarora, who tortured and murdered him. (Courtesy of Eastern Carolina University.)

## The Tuscarora

When European settlers first approached what would become Raleigh, it was being used as a hunting ground for the Tuscarora, a Native American tribe. Many Tuscarora were enslaved, tortured, or raped by early settlers. In 1711, after murdering John Lawson, they attacked the city of New Bern, beginning the Tuscarora War. The war lasted until 1714, at which point the remaining Tuscarora left the area. This drawing depicts Lawson awaiting his death. (Courtesy of SANC.)

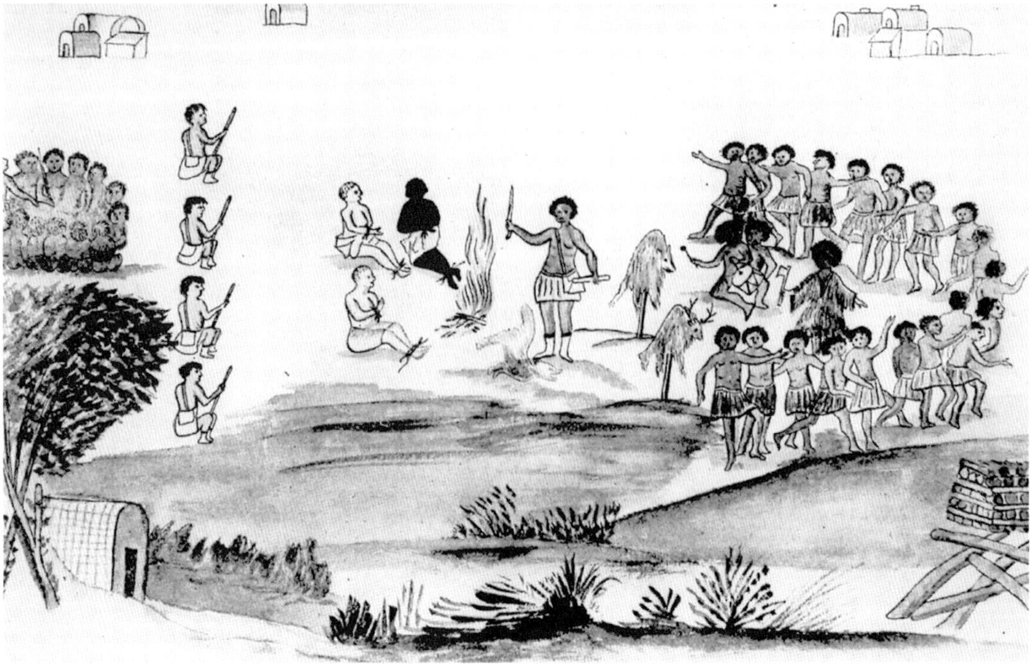

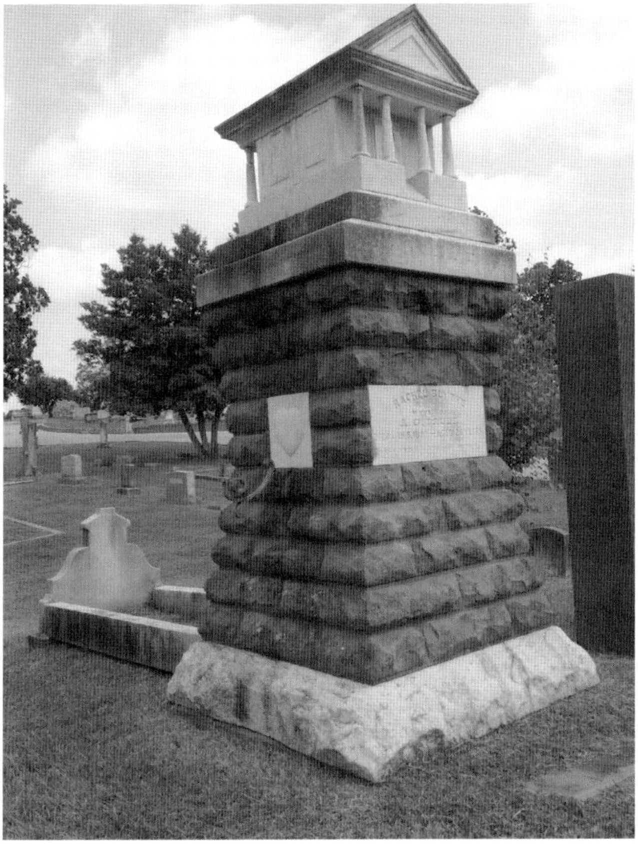

A.G. and Rachel Bauer

The life of A.G. Bauer (1858–1898) started full of promise but ended tragically. He was born in Virginia, and his work took him from Ohio to West Virginia to Pennsylvania. He came to Raleigh in 1883 as an assistant to a Philadelphia architect, but soon set up his own practice. His work was marked by dramatic towers and flamboyant designs in the Queen Anne style, and ranged from private residences to government buildings. North Carolina was in the process of rebuilding after the destruction of the Civil War, so Bauer had no trouble finding projects and clients, and his designs popped up all over the area. His best-known buildings included the new governor's mansion, North Carolina School for the Deaf, Park Hotel, Raleigh Fire Headquarters, and Baptist Female University, and he was rapidly gaining acclaim with each structure he built.

In 1891, Bauer met Rachel Blythe. Her mother was Cherokee, and at that time, North Carolina law forbade interracial marriage. They married in secret anyway, but after Rachel became pregnant, they held another ceremony out of state and lived openly in Raleigh with their daughter. Months later, Bauer's carriage was hit by a train, severely injuring him. His struggles with dizziness and concentration caused his work to suffer and many of his clients to leave. Rachel got pregnant again in 1896, but she was sick for much of the pregnancy, and died several days after giving birth to their second child.

Despondent, Bauer sent his children to live with Rachel's family. He settled his lawsuit against the railroad and used the money to pay for this elaborate memorial at his wife's grave, which he designed himself. He finished his three remaining projects, a residence and some remodeling, and then shot himself in his room. He and Rachel are buried next to each other in Historic Oakwood Cemetery. Unfortunately, most of his work was destroyed in the name of progress before his style became popular again, although the governor's mansion and one or two of his houses remain, recognizable by their distinctive towers and turrets. (Authors' collection.)

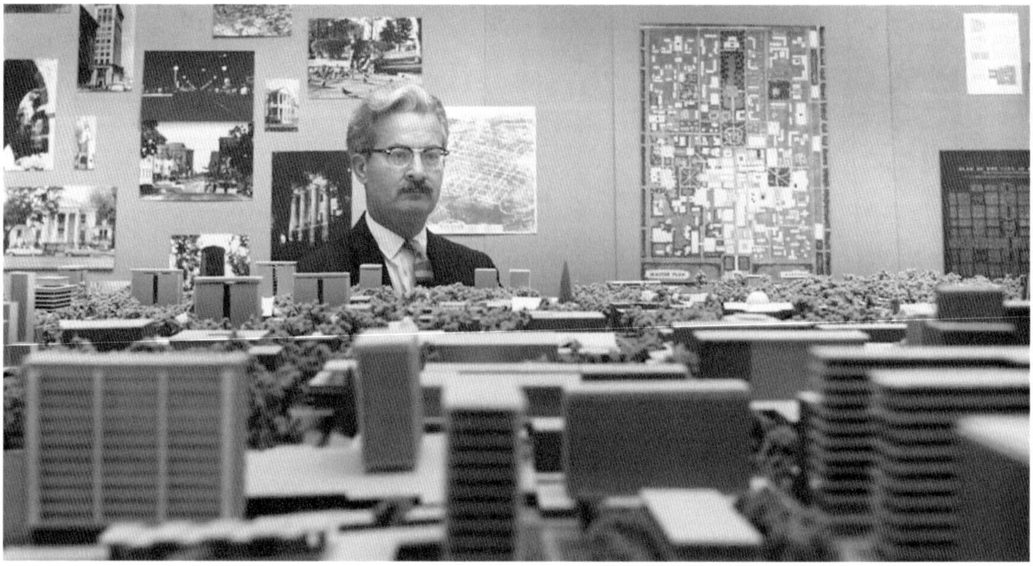

**Henry L. Kamphoefner**

North Carolina State hired Kamphoefner (1907–1990) to head its brand-new School of Design in 1948, which was to be "devoted to the development of an organic and indigenous architecture; its accompanying landscape architecture and the related arts; to meet the needs and conditions of the southern region." Kamphoefner hired modernist leaders to teach and brought in visiting lecturers such as Mies van der Rohe, Walter Gropius, Frank Lloyd Wright, and Buckminster Fuller. Kamphoefner is pictured here in a School of Design classroom in 1960. (Courtesy of Oversize Photographs: People (UA023.030.070), 0229235, Special Collections Research Center, North Carolina State University Libraries.)

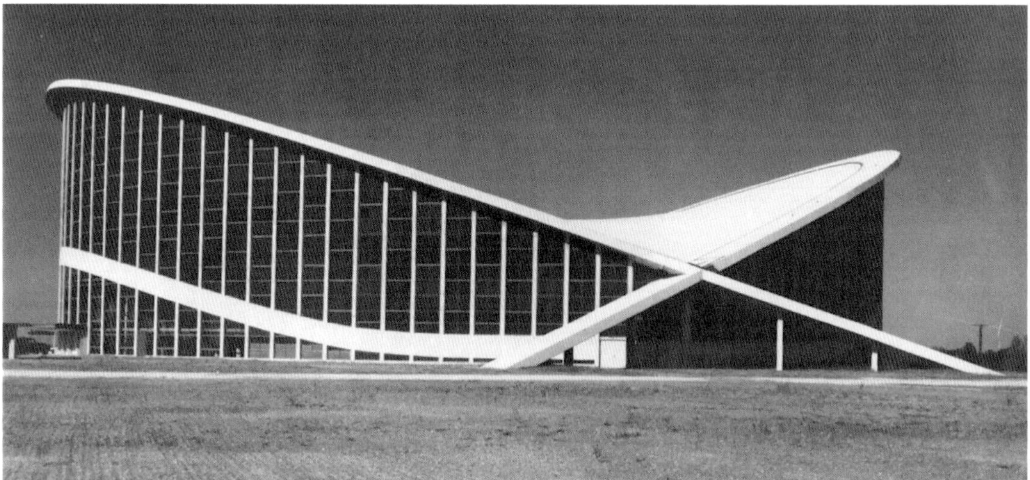

**Matthew Nowicki**

The design for the J.S. Dorton Arena at the North Carolina Fairgrounds is simple, dominated by two intersecting parabolas, yet challenging to produce and unlike anything else in the world at the time of its construction. After creating the initial design, School of Design Department of Architecture head Nowicki (1910–1950) died when the plane he was taking to visit another job site crashed. William Henry Deitrick, a friend and colleague, completed Dorton Arena based on the surviving plans. (Courtesy of RCM.)

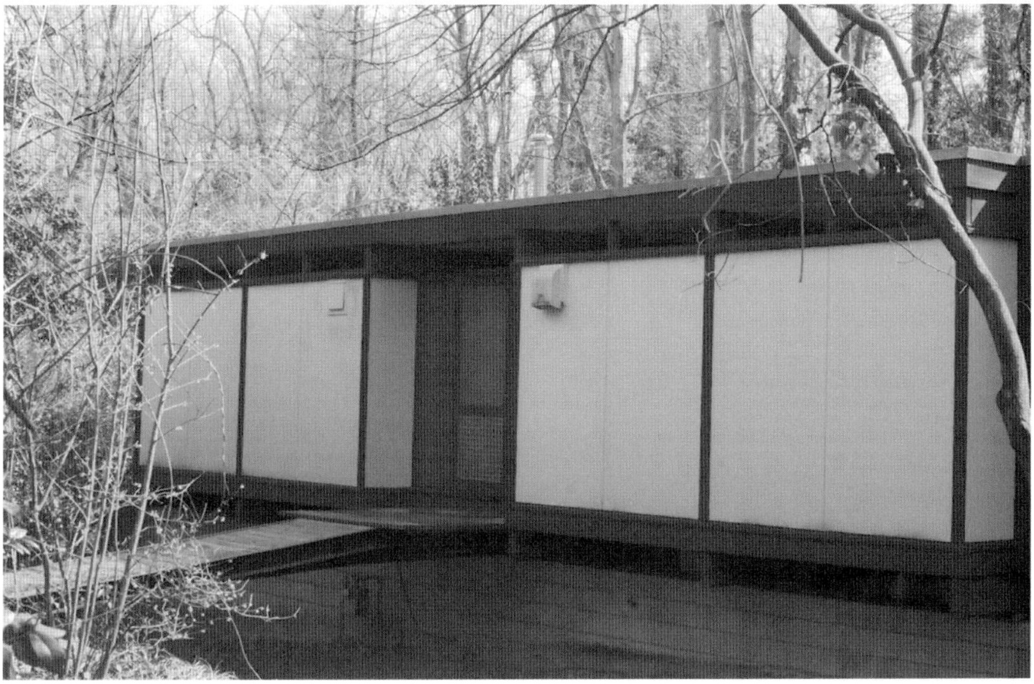

**George Matsumoto**
The US government sent Japanese American George Matsumoto (1922–present) to an internment camp during World War II, yet he went on to become an award-winning architect. He taught at NC State's School of Design, and his Modernist work was known for its flat roofs, natural wood walls, and small but functional kitchens. Matsumoto returned to California in 1961, but his houses, such as this one, remain in neighborhoods around Raleigh. (Courtesy of Dmitri Medvedev.)

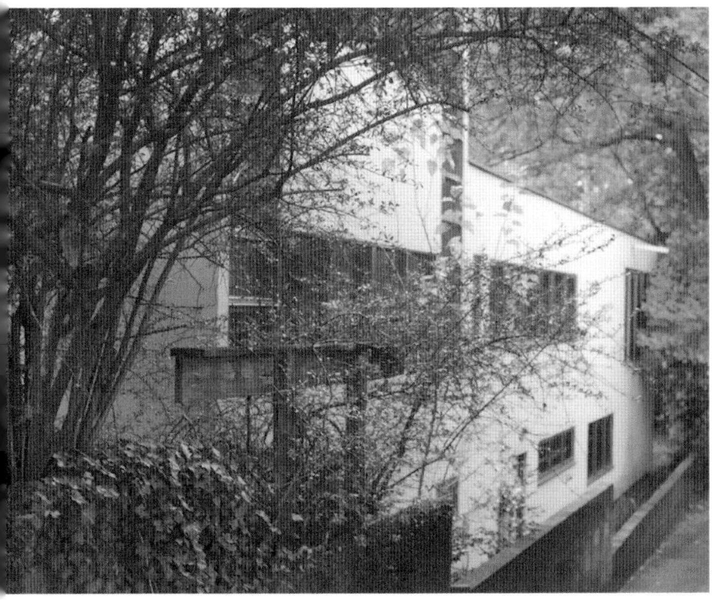

**Harwell Hamilton and Jean Bangs Harris**
Known for work that "embodied a gentle modernity and a strong sense of place," Harwell Hamilton Harris (1903–1990) honed his style by drawing inspiration from the landscape around him on his career path from California to Texas to NC State's School of Design. He incorporated the shape of pine needles, the shadows of trees, and flashes of color like a trout in a stream, as observed in North Carolina, into his modernist style. His house and office, which he shared with his wife, Jean, is pictured here. (Courtesy of Dmitri Medvedev.)

**William H. Deitrick**

Deitrick (1895–1974) started experimenting with Modernist elements in the late 1930s and encouraged the creation of the School of Design to help modernize the entire state of North Carolina after World War II. He executed the plans for Dorton Arena after designer Matthew Nowicki's passing, and is also credited with instigating historic preservation in Raleigh, starting with his 1938 reclamation of the old Raleigh Water Tower for use as his office. Jones Hall at Meredity College is an example of his Modernist buildings. (Courtesy of OR.)

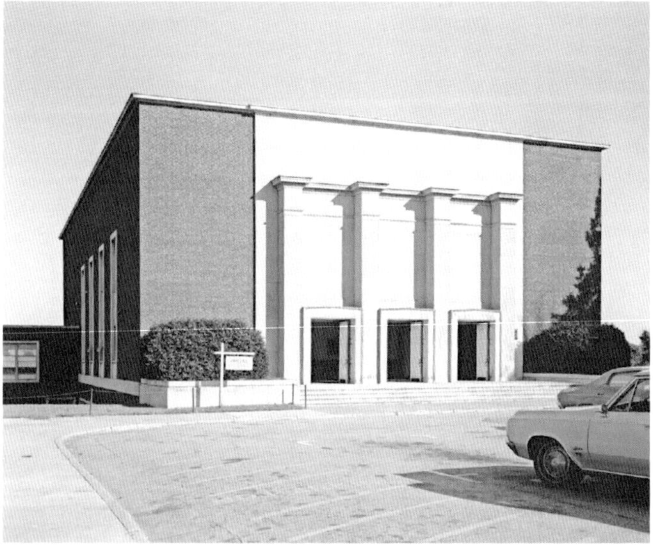

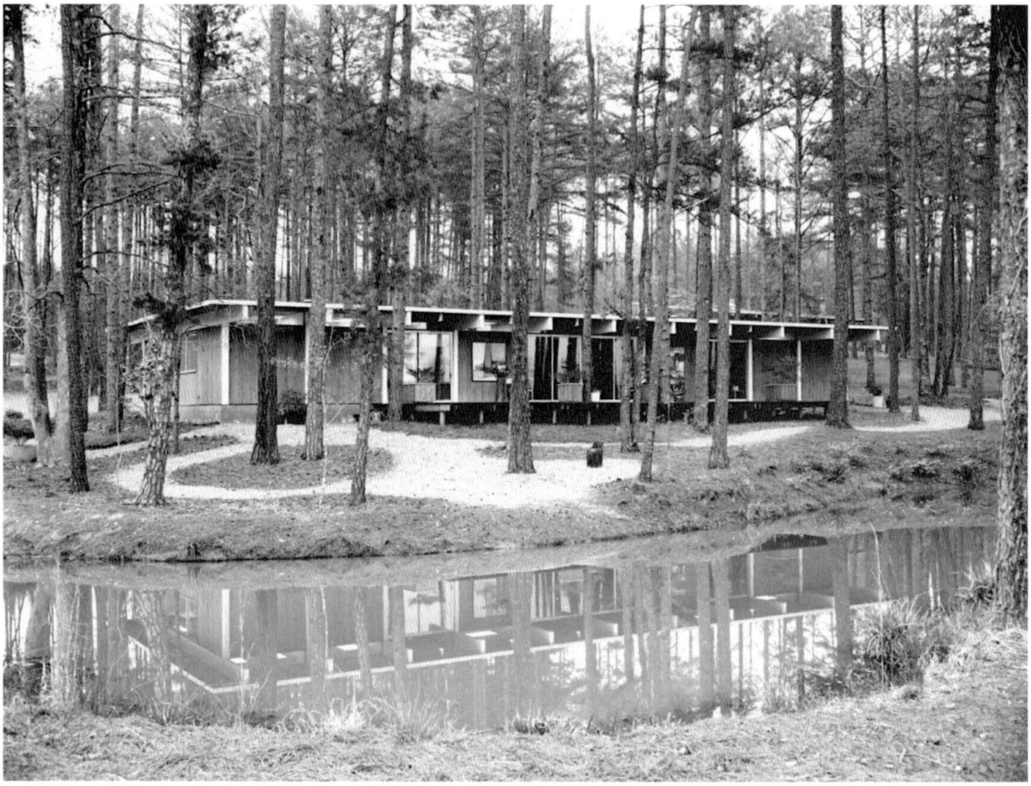

**Richard Bell**

Bell (1931–present) graduated in the first class of NC State's School of Design and introduced North Carolina to the field of landscape architecture as a registered profession. Bell literally shaped Raleigh's appearance with over 2,000 projects, notably the Brickyard at NC State and Pullen Park. One of his most innovative endeavors was the Water Garden (pictured here), a combination of his own home and an artist gallery. His "laboratory" for testing plants was the landscape itself. (Courtesy of OR.)

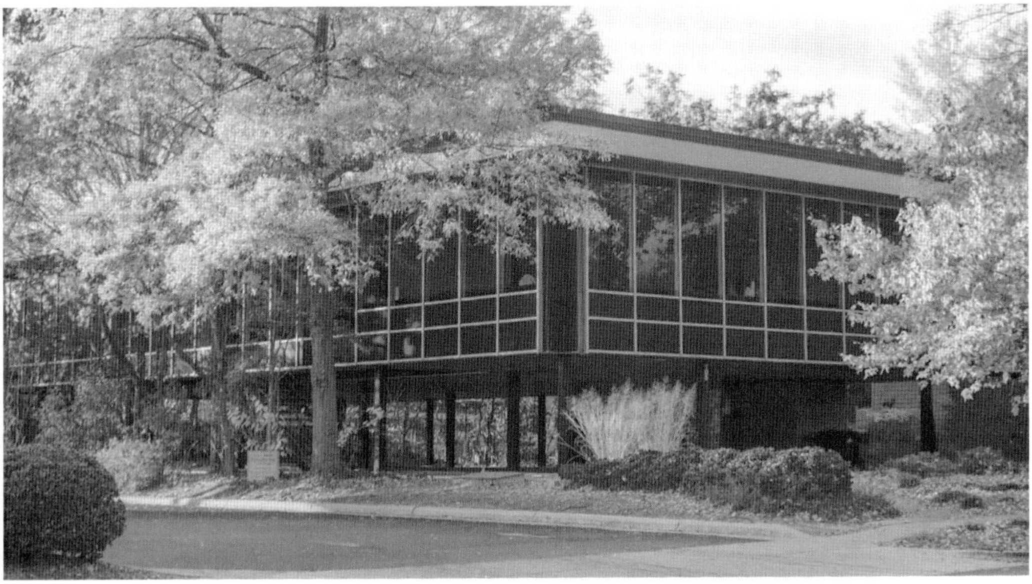

**G. Milton Small**
Another recruit of Henry Kamphoefner, Small (1916–1992) came to Raleigh in 1948 as the chief designer for William Henley Deitrick. Having studied under famed architect Mies van der Rohe in Chicago, Small brought this style of Modernism to Raleigh, and soon branched off to form his own firm in the 1950s, shown here. NC State's Carter-Finley Stadium and Talley Student Center, WRAL-TV studios, and numerous Modernist houses across Raleigh are of his design. His son, G. Milton Small III, continues the family name at the firm, now known as Small Kane Architects. (Courtesy of Dmitri Medvedev.)

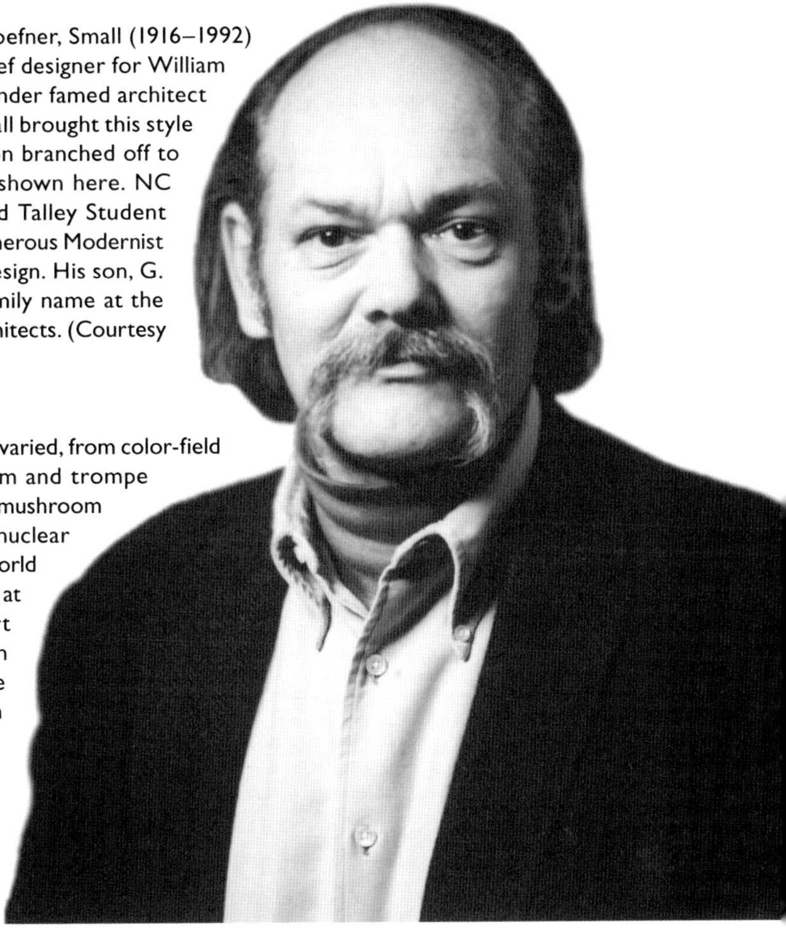

**George Bireline**
Bireline's (1923–2002) artistic style varied, from color-field painting to abstract impressionism and trompe l'oeil, and even included allusions to mushroom clouds in reference to the impact nuclear war had on him after his service in World War II. His work has been exhibited at the Guggenheim Museum and in art museums across the southeastern United States. A professor at the School of Design at NC State from 1955 to 1986, he chose Raleigh as his home base. (Courtesy of People: administrators, faculty, and staff, B(UA023.024.012), 0006678, Special Collections Research Center, North Carolina State University Libraries.)

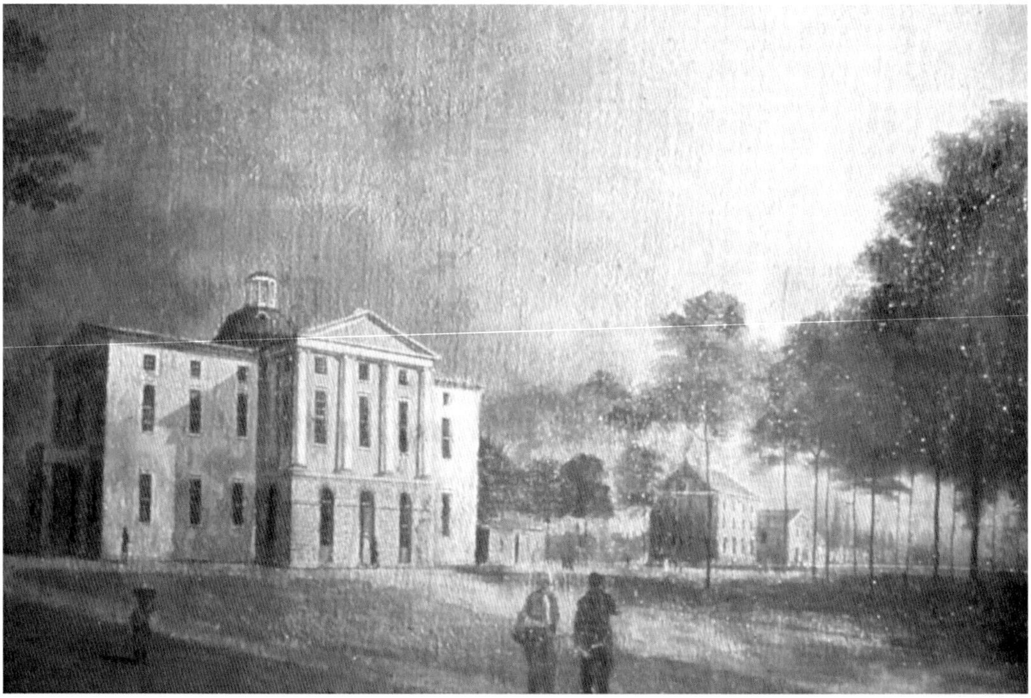

### William Nichols

Nichols (1780–1853), state architect, began upgrades to the statehouse (pictured here) in 1820, after North Carolina commissioned a Neoclassical statue of George Washington. The changes included adding another story, enlarging the general assembly space, and constructing a rotunda with a skylight to shine on Washington's statue. Unfortunately, both the statehouse and statue burned down in an 1831 fire. Nichols's extensive Neoclassical expansion of the Mordecai House still stands in Raleigh. (Courtesy of OR.)

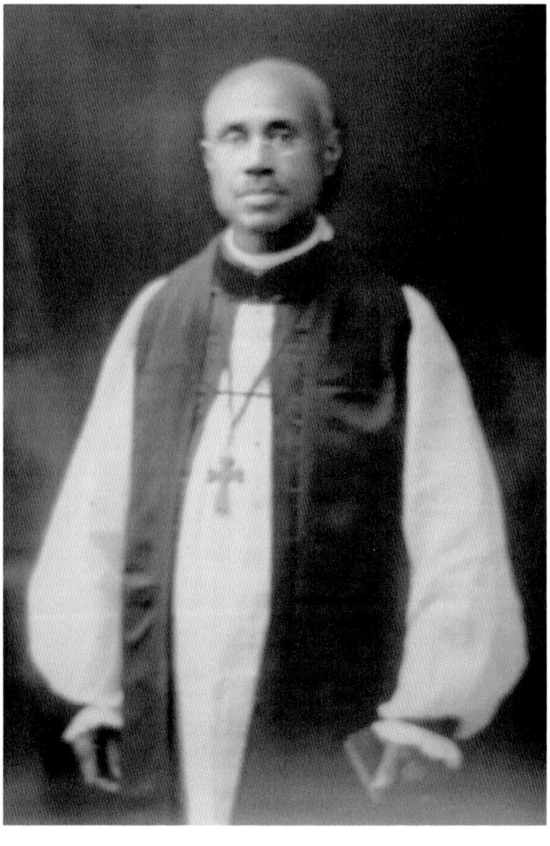

### Henry Beard Delany

After graduating as salutatorian of St. Augustine's in 1885, Delany (1858–1928) married valedictorian Nanny Logan, and both began teaching at the college. He led the students in reconstructing the campus after a fire and designed St. Augustine's Chapel in 1895, his only surviving structure. Delany began attending church while in school and in 1918, became North Carolina's first black Episcopal bishop and only the second in the country. (Courtesy of OR.)

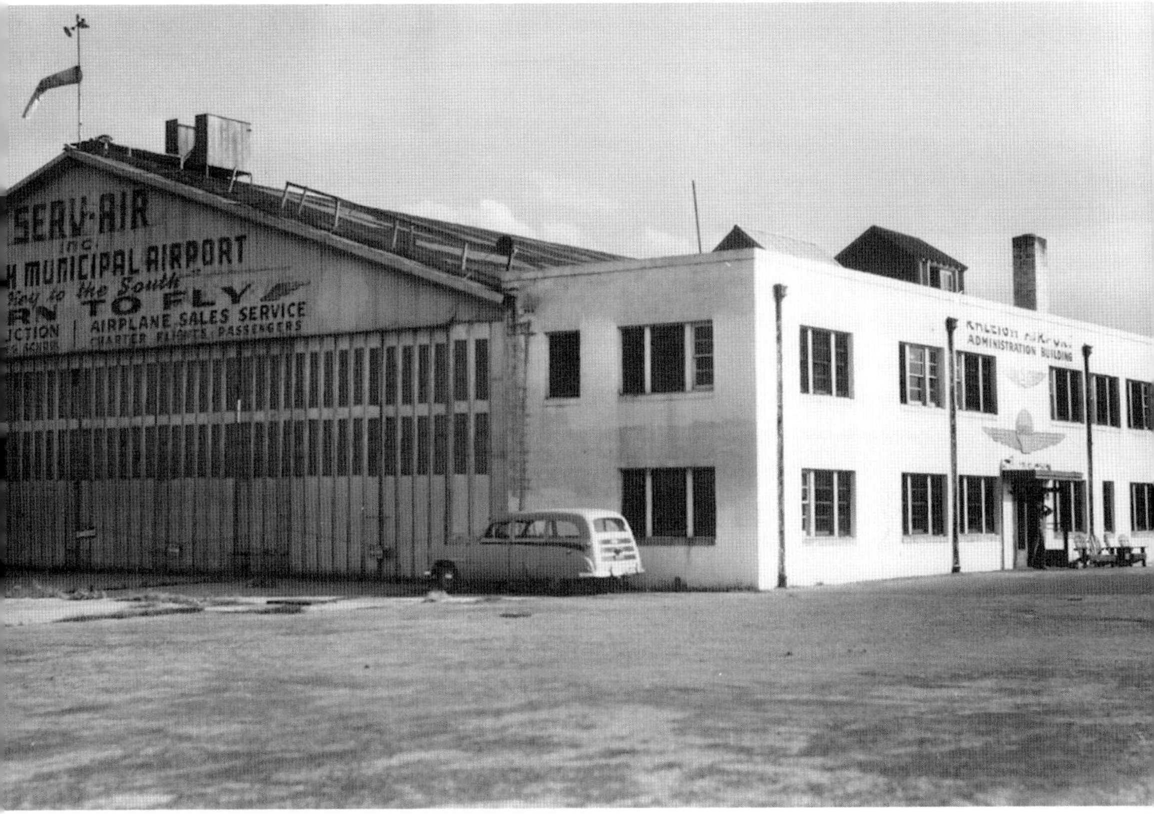


**Katharine Stinson**

Stinson (1917–2001) can claim a distinction shared by few: Amelia Earhart gave her career advice. Stinson was born in a small town outside of Raleigh. Growing up at the advent of flight, she was captivated by airplanes and idolized Earhart, pioneer of air travel and trailblazer for women. When the Raleigh Municipal Airport (pictured) opened in 1929, the teenaged Stinson started work as a mechanic's assistant and traded her wages for flying lessons, envisioning herself as the next Earhart. In 1932, Stinson's dream came true, as Earhart flew into Raleigh on a barnstorming publicity trip across the country. Stinson had dreamed of this moment for years and was lucky enough to meet and speak with the inspirational aviatrix. Stinson excitedly told Earhart about her plans to become a female pilot as well, but Earhart surprised her by advising against it. Instead, she counseled, go to school and become an aviation engineer so that she could design airplanes, for that was where the future was most promising.

Stinson took her hero's advice, and applied to be the first female student in the Engineering School at NC State. After initial resistance from the dean, Wallace C. Riddick, forced her to enter all-female Meredith College for a year, he relented and admitted her. Stinson graduated with a BS in mechanical engineering, with an aeronautical option, in 1941, just in time for World War II. The Civil Aviation Administration (later the Federal Aviation Administration) made her its first female employee the next year as a junior aeronautical engineer, and she retired in 1973 as the technical assistant chief of the aircraft engineering division.

Among her many honors, Stinson helped organize and held the office of president of the Society of Women Engineers, was named Aviation Pioneer of the Year by the Institute of Aeronautics and Astronautics in 1987, and in 1999, was awarded an honorary doctorate by NC State. In 1944, the local newspaper, the *News & Observer*, wrote that she was the "answer to all the questions about women stacking up in a man's world without asking or needing concessions because she is a woman. She marks up another Raleigh 'first' of which we may be very proud." (Courtesy of RCM.)

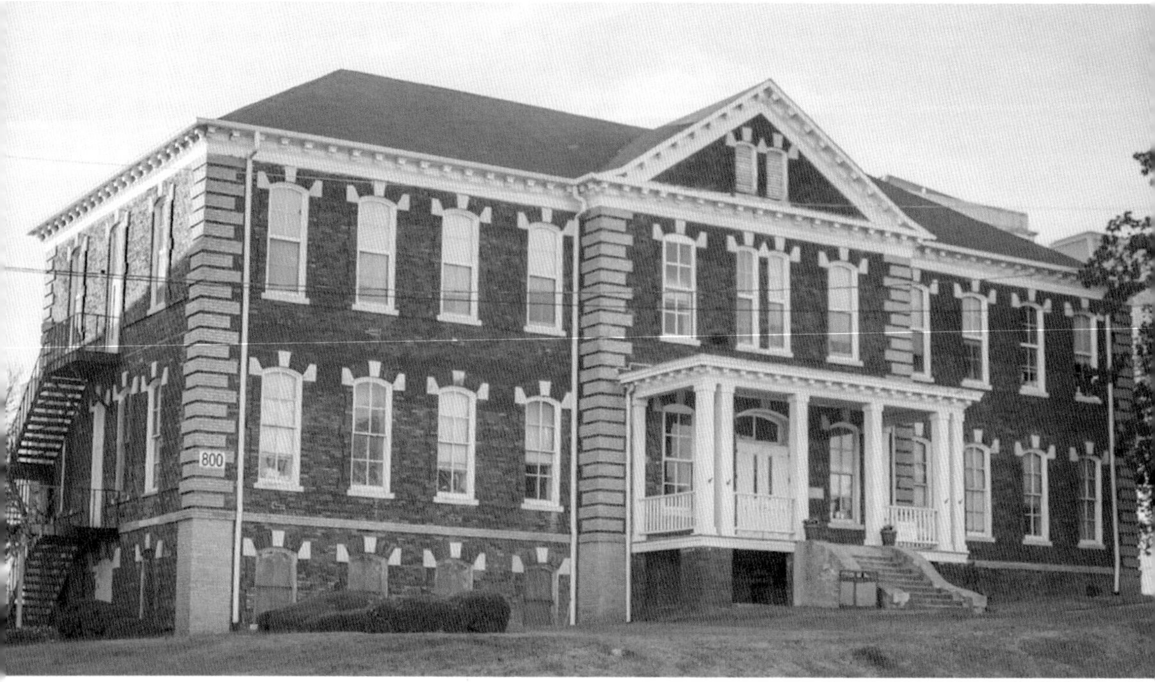


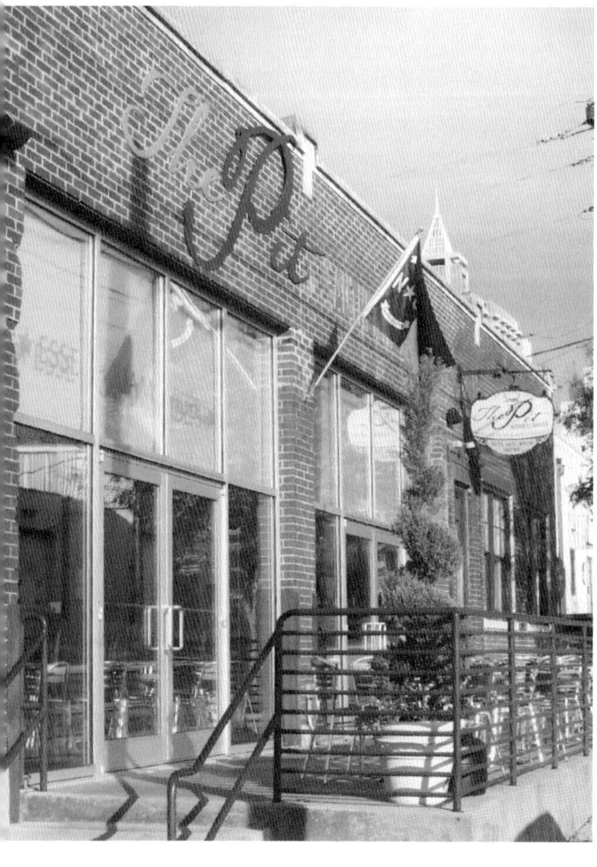


## Gaston Alonzo Edwards

Edwards (1875–1943) was North Carolina's first licensed black architect. He taught at both the North Carolina Institution of the Deaf and Dumb and the Blind for African American students, and at Shaw University. In his own practice, he designed the new hospital for Leonard Medical School (shown here) and the Masonic Building in Raleigh. Edwards is credited with many other buildings and residences in Raleigh and Durham, although surviving records are scarce. (Courtesy of Dmitri Medvedev.)

## Greg Hatem

Hatem is the developer and investor behind downtown Raleigh's current revitalization. He created Empire Properties in 1995 for the preservation, adaptation, and celebration of some of downtown's most historic spaces. Hatem has received national attention and numerous awards, and the restaurants of Empire Eats, like The Pit (pictured here), Sitti, and Raleigh Times, have been featured on *The Today Show* and the Food Network. He remains invested in Raleigh's future, serving on several preservation and arts boards and being active on planning committees. (Courtesy of Dmitri Medvedev.)

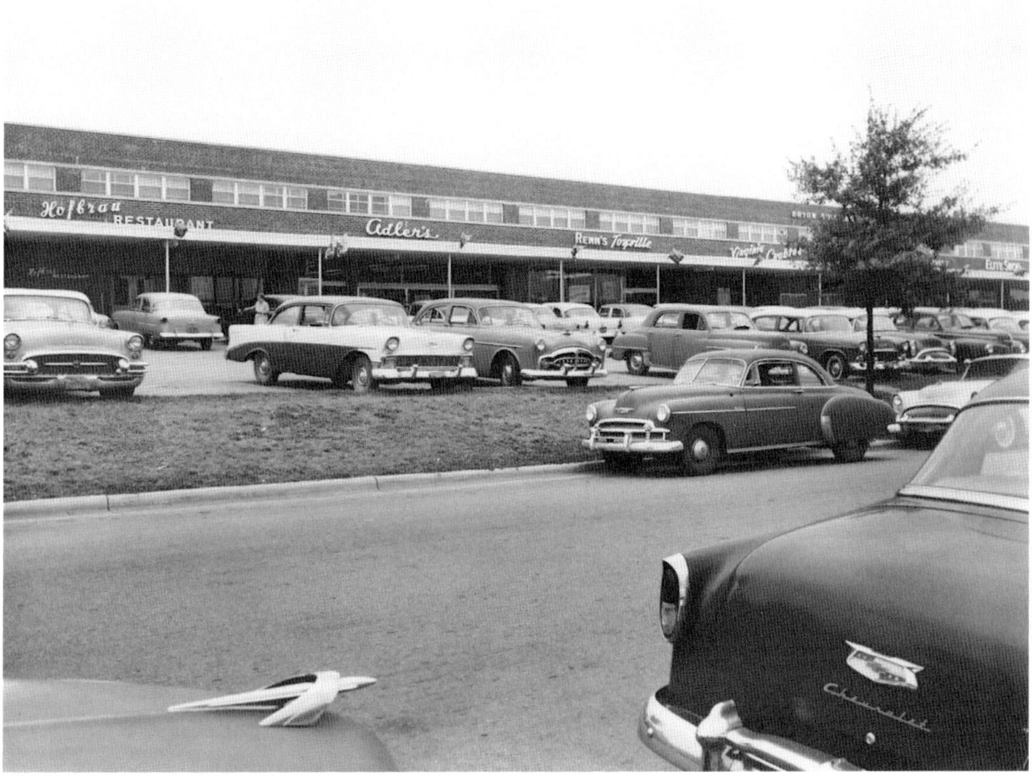


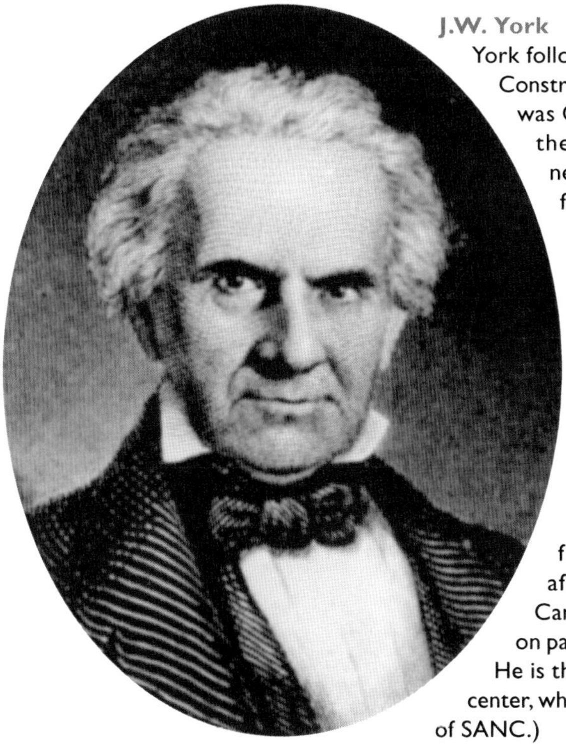

**J.W. York**

York followed in his father's footsteps, taking over York Construction Company in 1941. His centerpiece project was Cameron Village, shown here, which combined the first shopping center in the region with neighborhood housing. York also built Raleigh's first industrial park in 1951 and was instrumental in the creation of Raleigh-Durham International Airport. From the NC State Bell Tower to the State Farmers Market, Raleigh has been "York-built" since 1910. (Courtesy of RCM.)

**Duncan Cameron**

Cameron (1777–1853) was a judge and investor in the state's early commerce. He facilitated the survival of St. Mary's School after it experienced financial trouble, and helped rebuild the capitol after the 1831 fire. Following the Civil War, Cameron's former slaves founded Oberlin Village on part of his plantation, possibly with his assistance. He is the namesake for the Cameron Village shopping center, which was built on his former plantation. (Courtesy of SANC.)

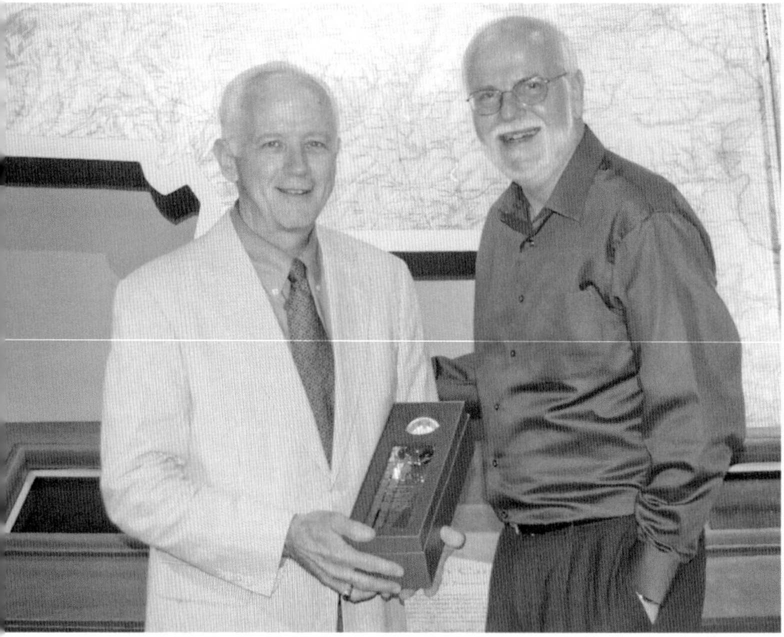

## Myrick Howard

As the executive director of Preservation North Carolina since 1978, the state's only private, nonprofit preservation organization, Myrick Howard (1953–present), pictured here on the left with Steve Schuster, has helped protect over 600 historic properties in more than 70 of North Carolina's 100 counties. Growing up in a Durham home built by his grandfather, and witnessing the razing of other historic homes, inspired Howard's career choice. His headquarters is located in the historic Briggs Hardware Building in downtown Raleigh. (Courtesy of Myrick Howard.)

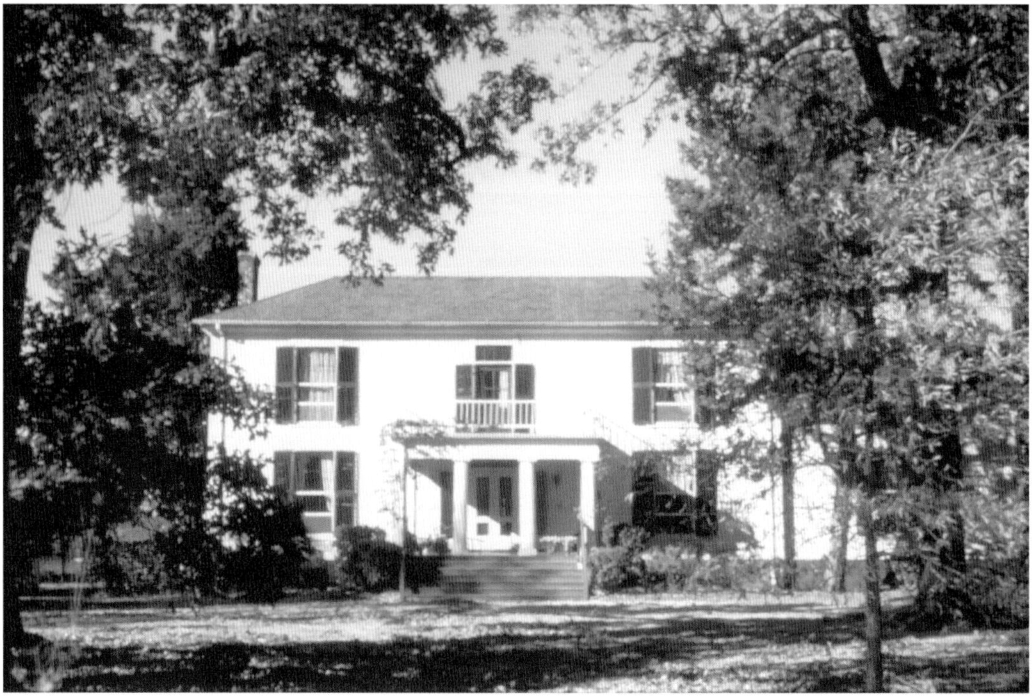

## Hinton Family

The Hinton family has been in Raleigh since the city's earliest days, and several of the family's 19th-century homes still stand in and around Raleigh. One of these homes, Midway Plantation, built in 1848, was threatened in 2005 when plans were drawn up to install Interstate 540 through its property. The family decided to move the house to save it. A documentary, *Moving Midway*, has been produced about the process. (Courtesy of OR.)

# CHAPTER SEVEN

# Talk of the Town

Beginning when Raleigh *Register* editor Joseph Gales traded punches with rival editor William Boylan in the middle of Fayetteville Street during the capital's first decades, Raleigh's media sources have not shied away from "hard-hitting" news. Newspapers, then radio and television stations, kept their subscribers informed about the latest goings on in the capital city, the state, and the country.

Located in North Carolina's capital city, Raleigh journalists formed close relationships with the politicians they covered. Local establishments like Mecca Restaurant and the Sir Walter Hotel doubled as legislative lounges for off-duty lawmakers and reporters who wanted to build relationships. In these locations, legislators made deals not possible to broker on the statehouse floor, and newsmen blurred the lines between profession and friendship.

Journalists in Raleigh used their influence and access to pursue a variety of issues. One of Raleigh's award-winning citizens was V.C. Royster, who started out in Raleigh before his 35-year career at the *Wall Street Journal* resulted in two Pulitzer Prizes and the Presidential Medal of Freedom. Nell Battle Lewis used her position at the *News & Observer* to comment directly on the progressive shortcomings and failures of politicians in the 1920s statehouse.

Walter Hines Page also spent his early career in Raleigh, writing about how North Carolina needed to improve itself. He ended up in New York City, serving as the British ambassador during World War I. The most influential journalist-turned-politician in Raleigh, though, was Josephus Daniels, whose commitment to the Democratic Party led him on the paradoxical paths of both inciting a military government overthrow in the United States and then leading one of its military branches during World War I. Daniels, the politician, contributed a great deal to the news that Daniels, the newspaper editor, reported.

Thanks to some of Raleigh's "firsts," like the Irving-Swain Press, Raleigh's first African American owned and operated printing press, and the city's first television station, WRAL-TV, no matter how powerful any one outlet gets, they are not the only voice. Now, in the era of constantly updated social media, everyone's voice can be heard, and it is even clearer that Raleigh continues to make news every day.

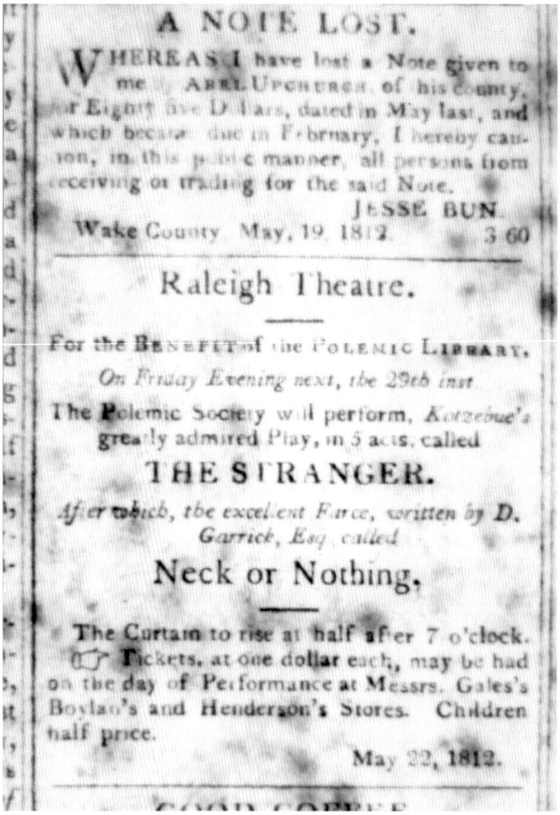

A NOTE LOST.

WHEREAS I have lost a Note given to me by Abel Upchurch, of this county, for Eighty five Dollars, dated in May last, and which became due in February, I hereby caution, in this public manner, all persons from receiving or trading for the said Note.

JESSE BUN.

Wake County May, 19, 1812. 3 60

Raleigh Theatre.

For the Benefit of the Polemic Library.

*On Friday Evening next, the 29th inst.*

The Polemic Society will perform, *Kotzebue's* greatly admired Play, in 5 acts, called

THE STRANGER.

*After which, the excellent Farce, written by D. Garrick, Esq. called*

Neck or Nothing.

The Curtain to rise at half after 7 o'clock.

☞ Tickets, at one dollar each, may be had on the day of Performance at Messrs. Gales's Boylan's and Henderson's Stores. Children half price.

May 22, 1812.

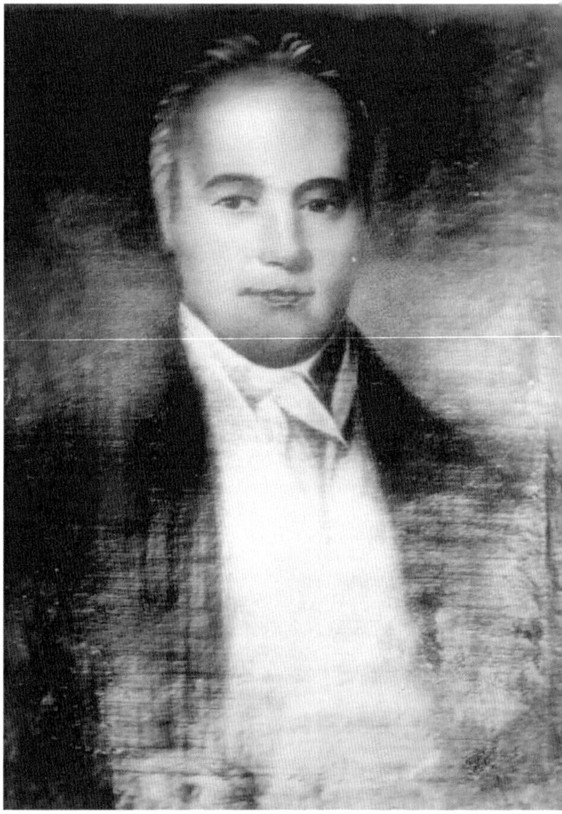

## Joseph Gales

Gales (1761–1841) was born in England, where he had published the Sheffield *Register* until he got into a conflict with the government for being too liberal. He arrived in Raleigh from Philadelphia in September 1799, and put the first issue of Raleigh's second newspaper, the Raleigh *Register*, on sale on October 22, 1799. The *Register* remained in print for over six decades. Among its highlights was issuing the first daily newspaper edition in the state in 1859, which Gales's grandson edited. The advertisement for the Raleigh Theatre (above) appeared in the May 1812 *Register*.

In order to participate in state and national politics as a capital city should, one of the first industries in Raleigh was necessarily journalism. Gales's position as newspaper editor gave him a position of both power and practical influence among his fellow citizens, and he wasted no time diversifying his involvements. He used his printer not just for newsprint, but for books and booklets, including the first work of fiction printed locally, authored by his wife, Winifred Marshall Gales, in 1804, and George Moses Horton's volume of poetry. He used his editorial position to advance his own causes, and he advocated for Raleigh to "relish [more] of the refined arts," including promoting a commercial railroad, the insurance and silk industries, and the creation of Raleigh's first successful school, which became Raleigh Academy in 1804.

Gales gained the respect of most of Raleigh's residents, winning election to several terms as mayor, then known as intendant of police, over 20 years. He advocated strongly for greater fire prevention and protection in Raleigh, having suffered firsthand when his printing office burned down in 1804, and was responsible for acquiring a fire engine from Philadelphia. He had a notable feud with the other newspaperman of Raleigh, editor William Boylan of the *Minerva*. In addition to a professional contest to gain the official state printer's office, Gales and Boylan shared a personal dislike for each other, erupting in a fistfight on Fayetteville Street, after which Boylan was required to pay Gales £100 in restitution. Neither the *Register* or the *Minerva* is still in publication, but the journalistic legacy begun by Gales and Boylan remains strong in Raleigh. (Courtesy of OR.)

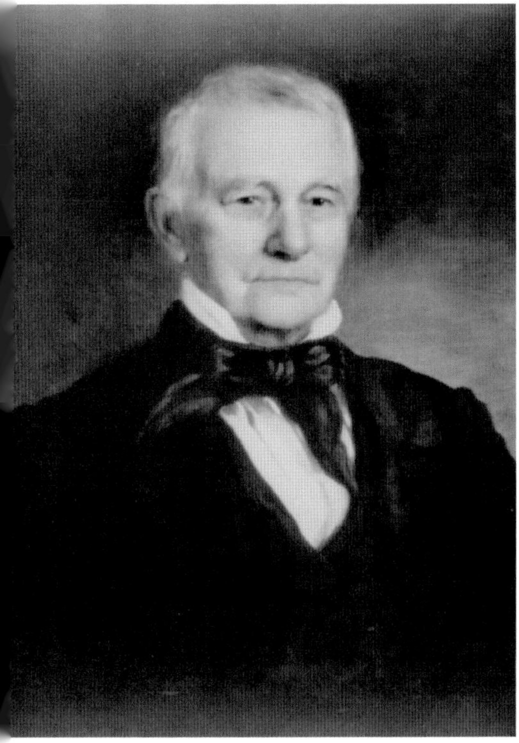

**William Boylan**
New Jersey native Boylan started the Fayetteville *Minerva* in the 18th century. In 1799, he moved to Raleigh and started the Raleigh *Minerva*, which he published until 1810. Boylan was active in local politics, serving as justice of the county court, on the board of commissioners, and as the treasurer of the State Agricultural Society. In 1810, he opened a bookstore, and continued to promote local civic activity. (Courtesy of OR.)

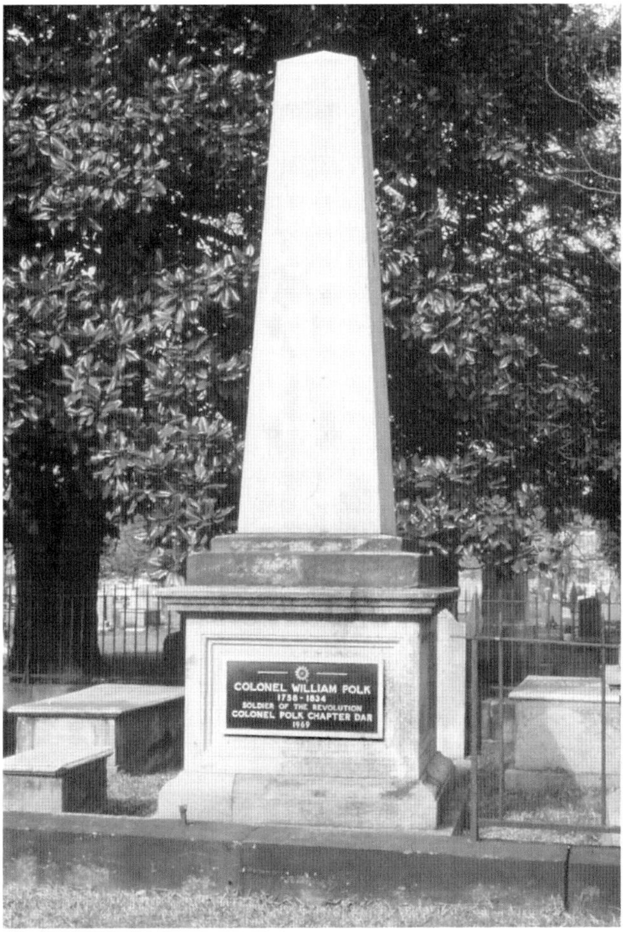


**Leonidas Lafayette Polk**
Polk (1837–1892) was North Carolina's first commissioner of agriculture, and started the *Progressive Farmer*, a magazine still published today, to educate and organize farmers. Locally, he founded the Watauga Club, which successfully lobbied for the creation of a "People's College" for agricultural and mechanical studies, now North Carolina State. Polk helped create the national Populist Party and likely would have been their nominee for president in 1892 had he not died months earlier. (Courtesy of OR.)

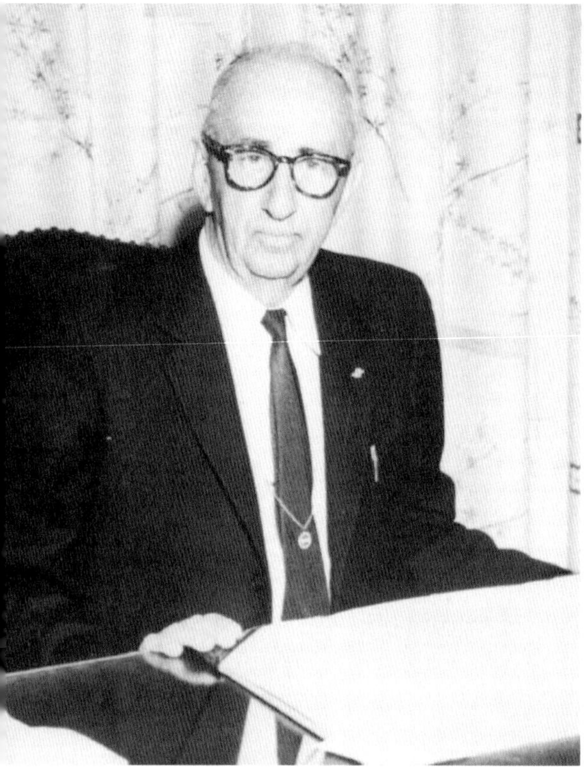

## A.J. Fletcher

Capitol Broadcasting Company founder Fletcher (1887–1979) aired the first broadcast of WRAL-AM in 1939. Aided by son Fred and irreplaceable employee Scottie Stephenson, Fletcher won the fight for the first television channel granted to Raleigh, and WRAL-TV aired *Miracle on 34th Street* on December 15, 1956. After Fletcher's death, the A.J. Fletcher Foundation has supported nonprofits working to improve North Carolina's community. (Courtesy of RCM.)

## Fred Fletcher

After graduating from high school, Fletcher (1910–2000) moved to Chicago and became a lawyer with the newly founded FCC before moving back to Raleigh to help his father, A.J. Fletcher, found WRAL-FM. Despite his father's big shadow, Fletcher found his own voice in Raleigh, broadcasting his *Tempus Fugit* show to thousands. Audiences were entertained by his storytelling Fairy Tale Man and kept informed with tips, such as where police had set up speed traps. Fletcher is pictured below, at right, on the set of one of his popular programs. (Courtesy of RCM.)

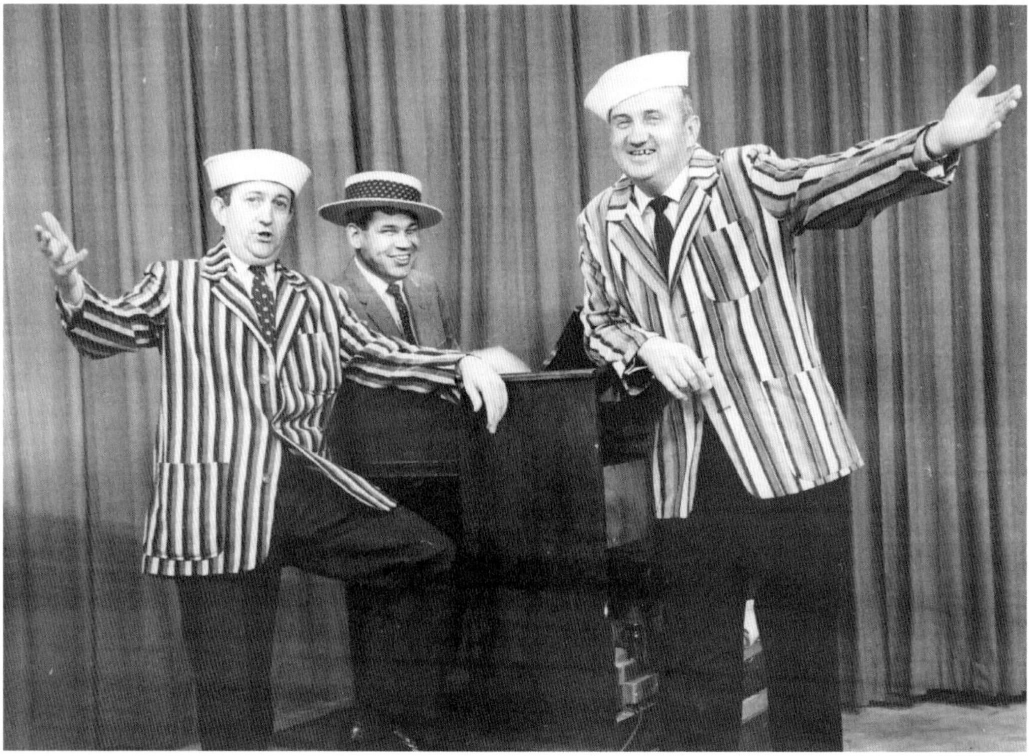

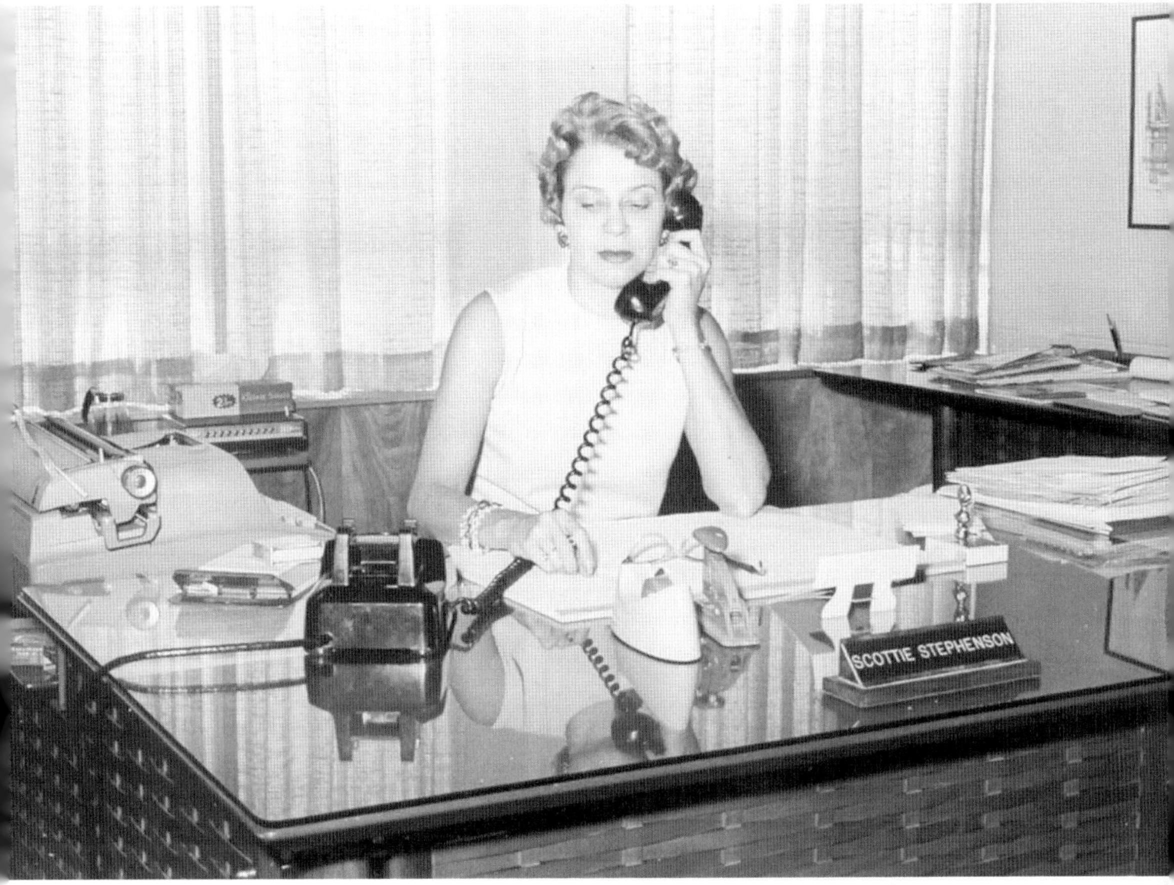


**Louise Scott Stephenson**
"Scottie" (1921–2001) described her role with the Capitol Broadcasting Company as "housemother," but that sells her work short. She started with WRAL-AM in 1944, writing advertising copy for the radio, answering phones, and announcing daily casualty lists during World War II. When the FCC requested over 3,000 official documents and reports during the fight for Raleigh's first television license, she helped research and prepare them. By the time WRAL-TV went on the air in 1956, she had created almost every position in the department.

In addition to her work with the company, Stephenson helped her city, serving on the boards of multiple charities and organizations for the underprivileged, children, and the arts. The Raleigh Little Theatre named its outdoor amphitheater for her, and when she retired from Capitol Broadcasting after 58 years, she had served longer than any other employee, including founder A.J. Fletcher. (Courtesy of RCM.)

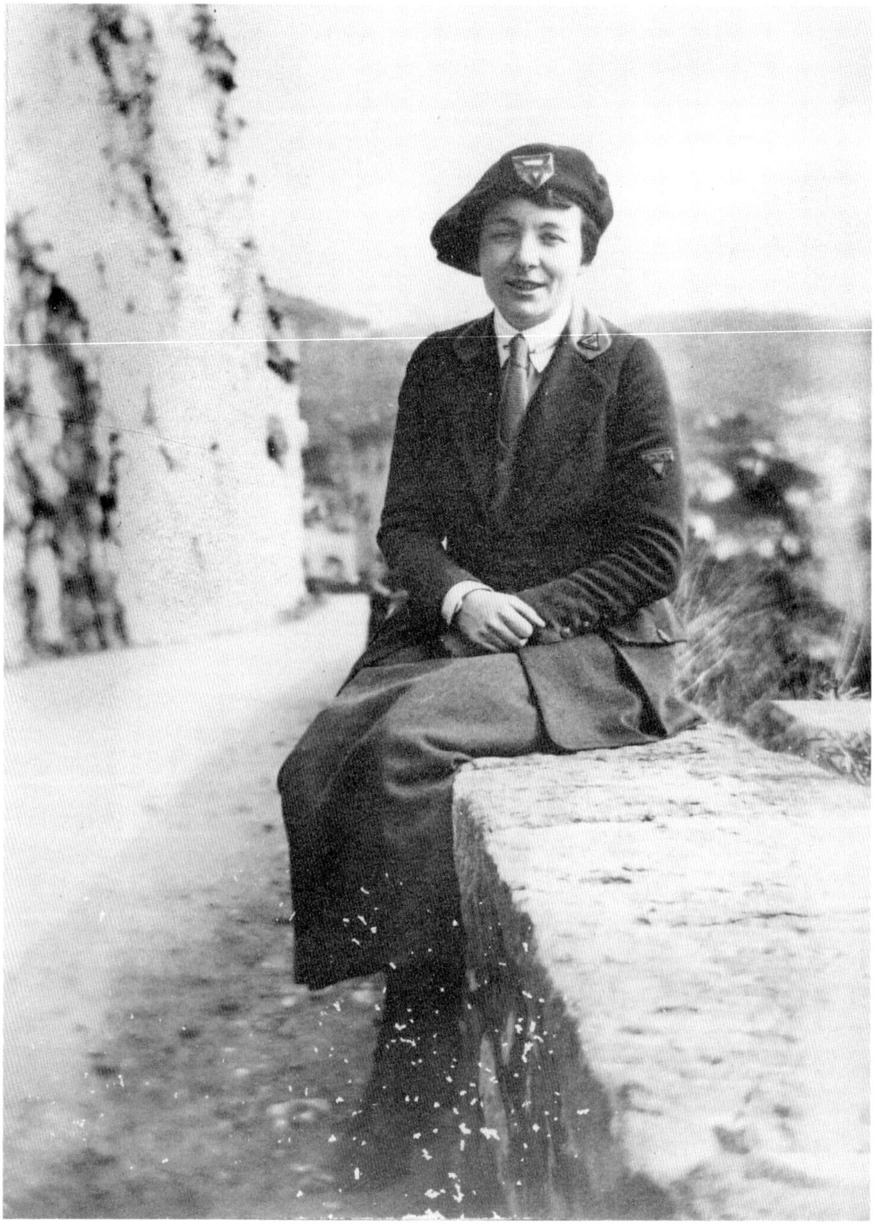

**Nell Battle Lewis**
Lewis (1893–1956) embodied the opportunities of the "New South" early in life, first leaving home for college, then spending 1918–1919 in war-torn France assisting soldiers. During the 1920s, she became one of the most prominent voices of liberalism in the South, writing for the *News & Observer*. She used a regular column, "Incidentally," as her soapbox, supporting women's rights, African American rights, evolution, and labor unions, while denouncing the KKK and the death penalty, among other issues.

However, her life took a drastic turn in the 1930s after she was hospitalized for what were described as nervous breakdowns. She attacked her old positions and friends in her column and earned the nickname "Battling Nell." The *News & Observer* kept her on their staff, but she never regained her standing as an incisive, progressive voice of the South. (Courtesy of University of North Carolina Library at Chapel Hill.)

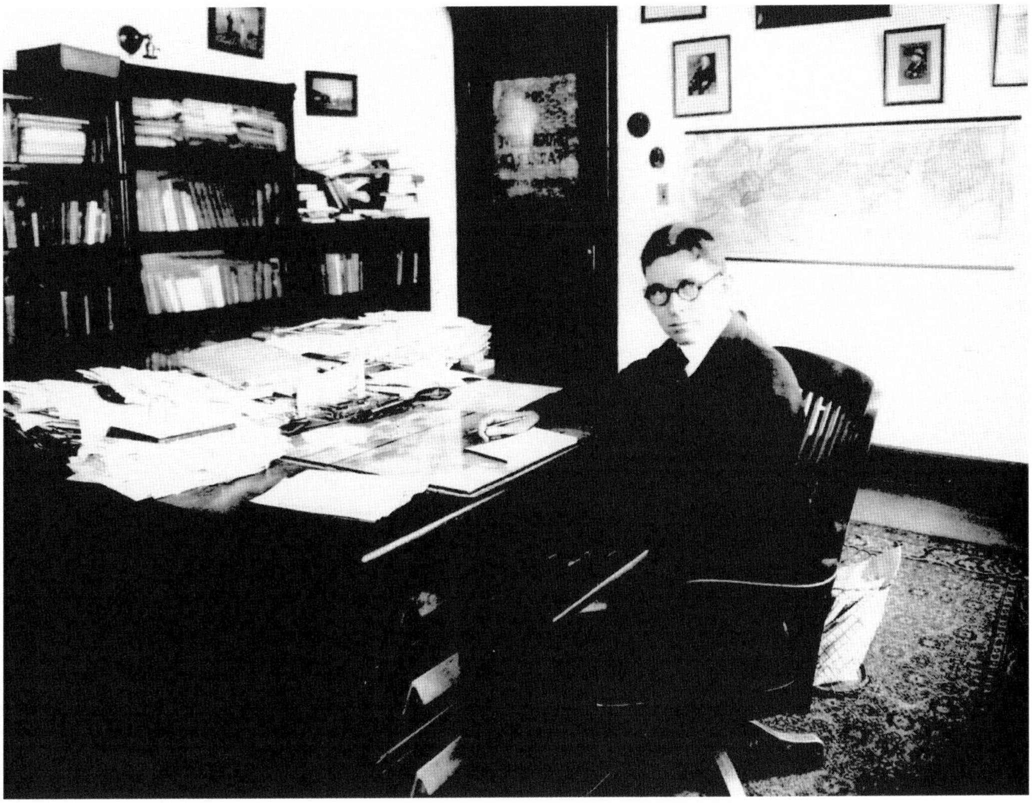

**Clarence H. Poe**

Raleigh native Poe (1881–1964) took over Leonidas Polk's *Progressive Farmer* in 1899 as an 18-year-old, and by 1908, it had gone from a weekly newspaper with 5,000 readers to the largest farm publication in the South. Poe believed farmers could benefit from a greater awareness of social conditions, so he combined his agricultural knowledge with tales about his travels and discoveries. (Courtesy of SANC.)

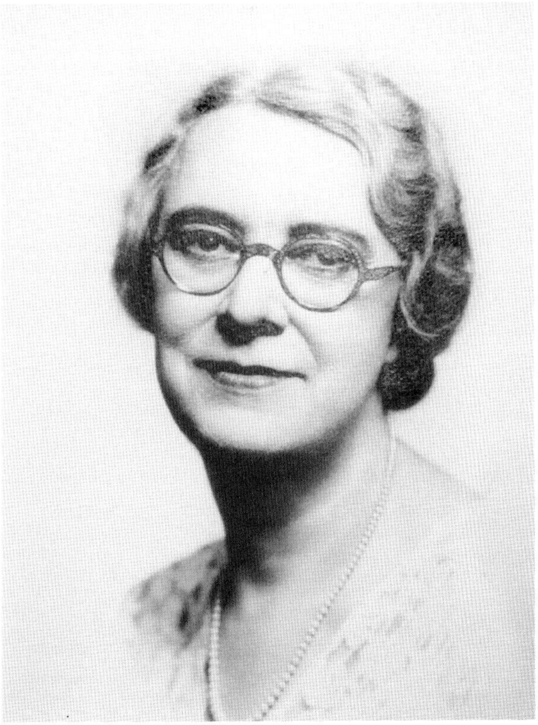

**Susan Iden**

The *Raleigh Times* newspaper hired Iden (1885–1944) in 1908 to write its society column. She was promoted to city editor during World War I, but after the soldiers came back, she resumed her reporting position. Iden was also responsible for the creation of the Raleigh Garden Club, after the overwhelming popularity of her series of articles on the subject necessitated a meeting. The club celebrated its 85th year in 2010. (Courtesy of the Raleigh Garden Club.)

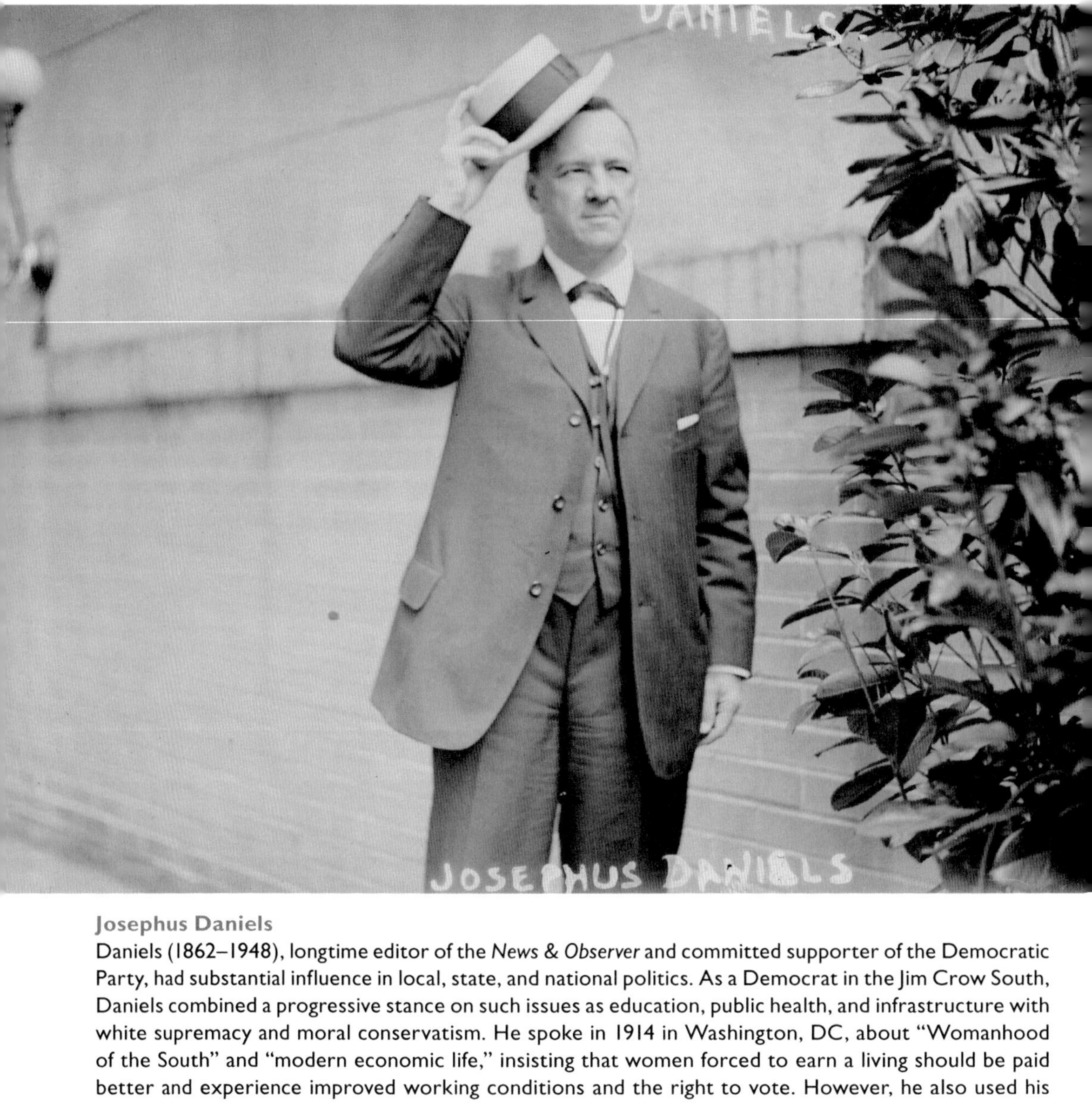

**Josephus Daniels**
Daniels (1862–1948), longtime editor of the *News & Observer* and committed supporter of the Democratic Party, had substantial influence in local, state, and national politics. As a Democrat in the Jim Crow South, Daniels combined a progressive stance on such issues as education, public health, and infrastructure with white supremacy and moral conservatism. He spoke in 1914 in Washington, DC, about "Womanhood of the South" and "modern economic life," insisting that women forced to earn a living should be paid better and experience improved working conditions and the right to vote. However, he also used his newspaper to incite racial conflict, leading to the 1898 Wilmington Race Riot, a white-led coup d'état of the legitimately elected government. Daniels's work for the national Democratic Party earned him a seat in Pres. Woodrow Wilson's cabinet as secretary of the Navy, a position he held through World War I. (Courtesy of RCM.)

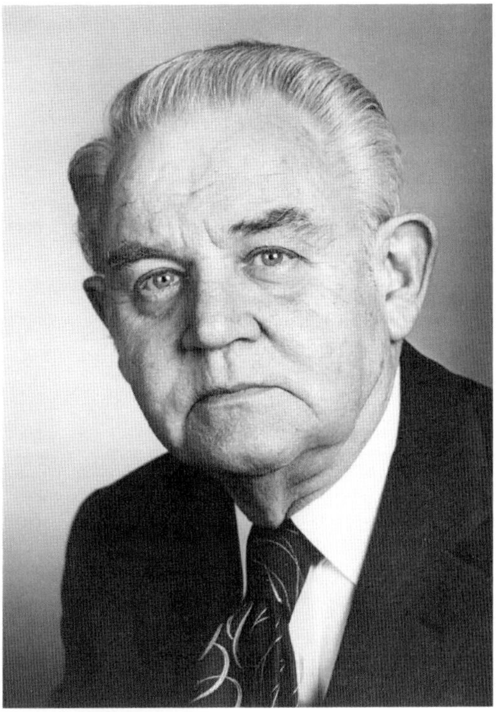

**V.C. Royster**
Royster (1914–1996), grandson and namesake of one of the founders of Royster's Candy Store in downtown Raleigh, turned his career to words rather than wrappers. He started with the *Wall Street Journal* as a reporter in 1936, and retired as editor in 1971, with two Pulitzer Prizes and a Presidential Medal of Freedom for his writing. (Courtesy of SANC.)

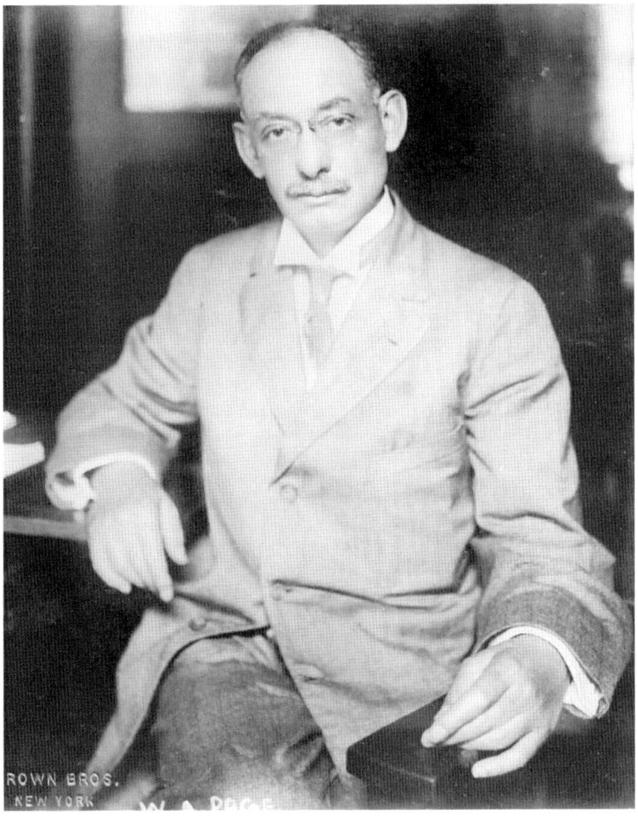


**Walter Hines Page**
Son of the founder of neighboring Cary, Page (1855–1918) founded the *State Chronicle* in 1883 to attack North Carolina's politicians for driving away the state's best talent. He called these officials "mummies," attached to a dead way of life. After he left for New York, Page went on to become a nationally respected writer and editor, as well as the US ambassador to Great Britain during World War I. (Courtesy of RCM.)

### Lawrence Macauga Cheek

Cheek (1886–1920) founded Raleigh's first regularly published African American–owned weekly publication, the *Independent*, to provide a "voice for the voiceless" in the community during the Jim Crow era. Cheek, along with several other African Americans, ran for a seat on the all-white Raleigh City Council in 1919. He was unsuccessful, but his newspaper lives on today as the *Carolinian*. (Courtesy of RCM.)

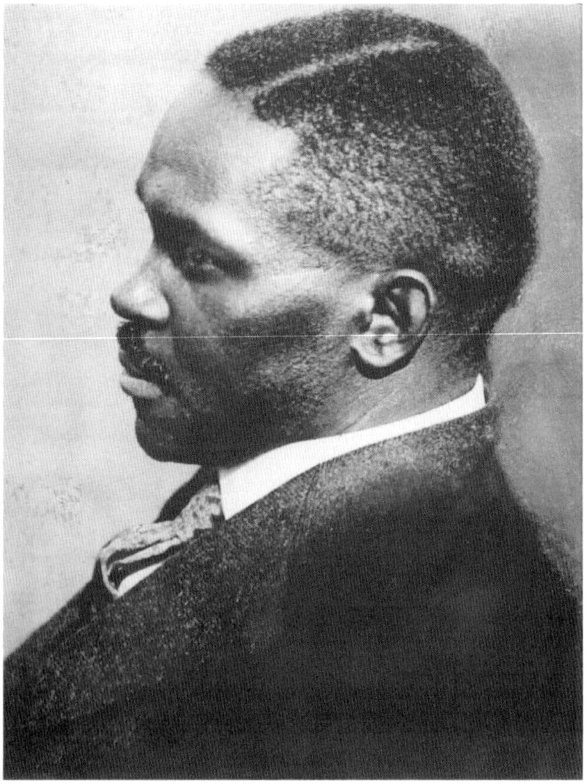

### P.R. Jervay

Jervay got his start aiding his father in publishing the *Cape Fear Journal* in Wilmington. He moved to Raleigh in 1940 and assumed the position of editor-publisher-owner of the *Carolinian*, a prominent newspaper in Raleigh's black community. Jervay promoted education in the pages of the *Carolinian*, realizing that education is the cornerstone of success. Pictured is Jervay's colleague, C.R. Swain, working the press. (Courtesy of RCM.)

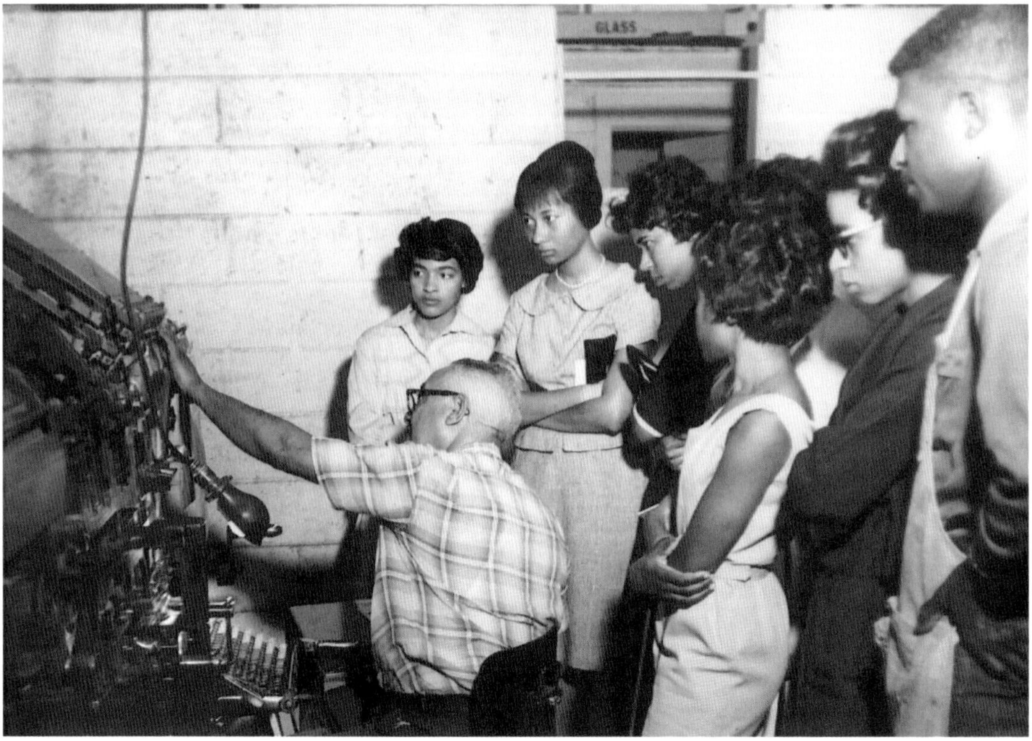

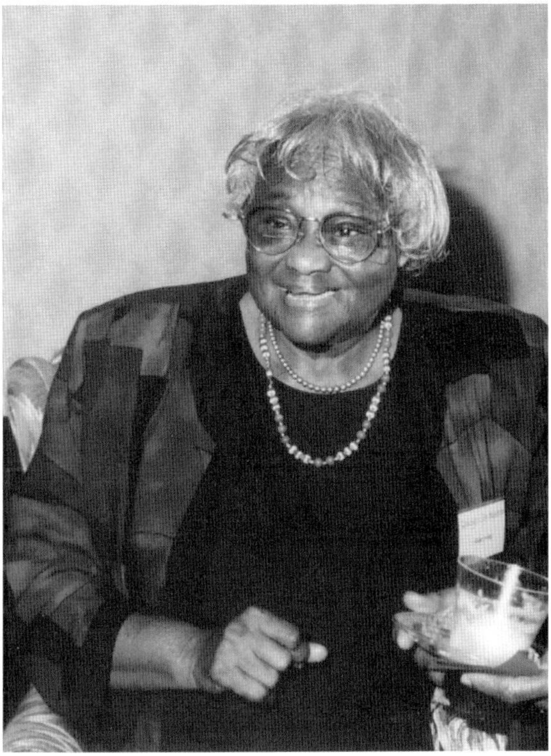

**Vivian Irving**
Charles and Vivian Irving were a father-and-daughter business team, as well as civil rights activists. The family moved to Raleigh in 1920, when Charles worked at the Raleigh *Independent*, founded by Lawrence M. Cheek, and later, the *Carolinian*. Vivian grew up to become a schoolteacher, but during World War II, she gained skills in printing and went to work at the *Carolinian*. In 1947, the Irvings founded Irving-Swain Press. (Courtesy of RCM.)

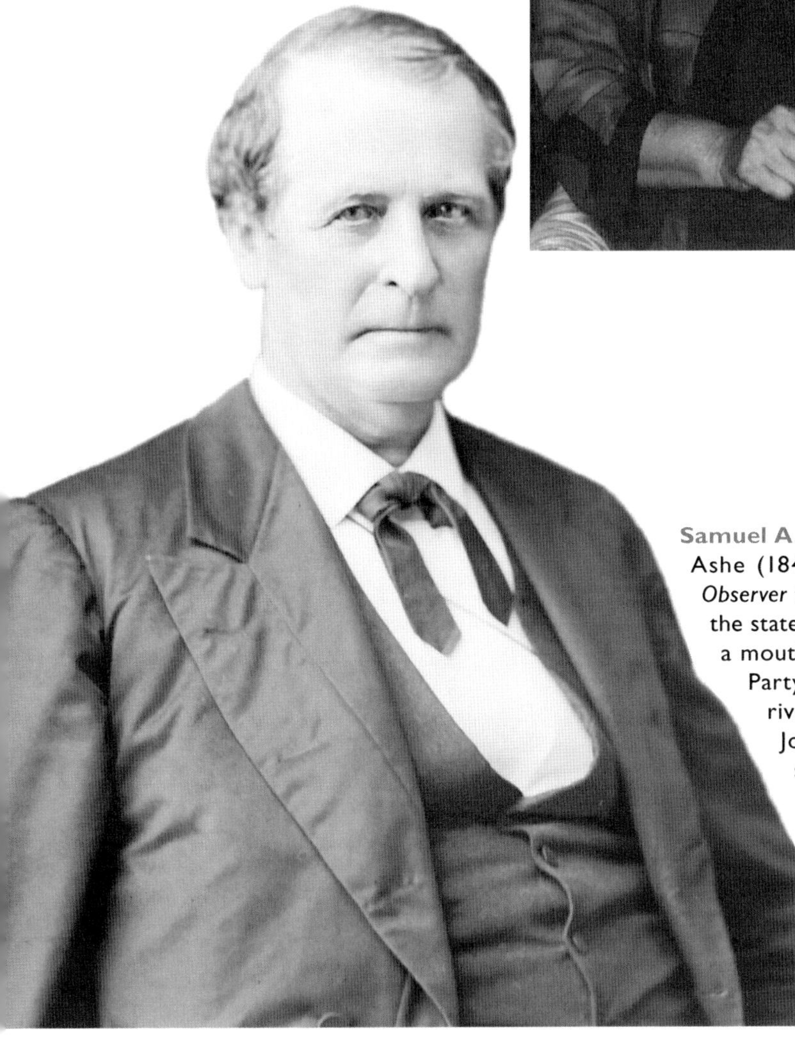

**Samuel A. Ashe**
Ashe (1840–1938) led the *News & Observer* to the highest circulation in the state and used the newspaper as a mouthpiece for the Democratic Party. However, he developed a rivalry with fellow Democrat Josephus Daniels, The two sparred back and forth in their rival newspapers, and the feud escalated to the point of a physical fight on the capitol grounds. Ironically, after getting into financial trouble, Ashe sold his newspaper to Daniels. (Courtesy of RCM.)

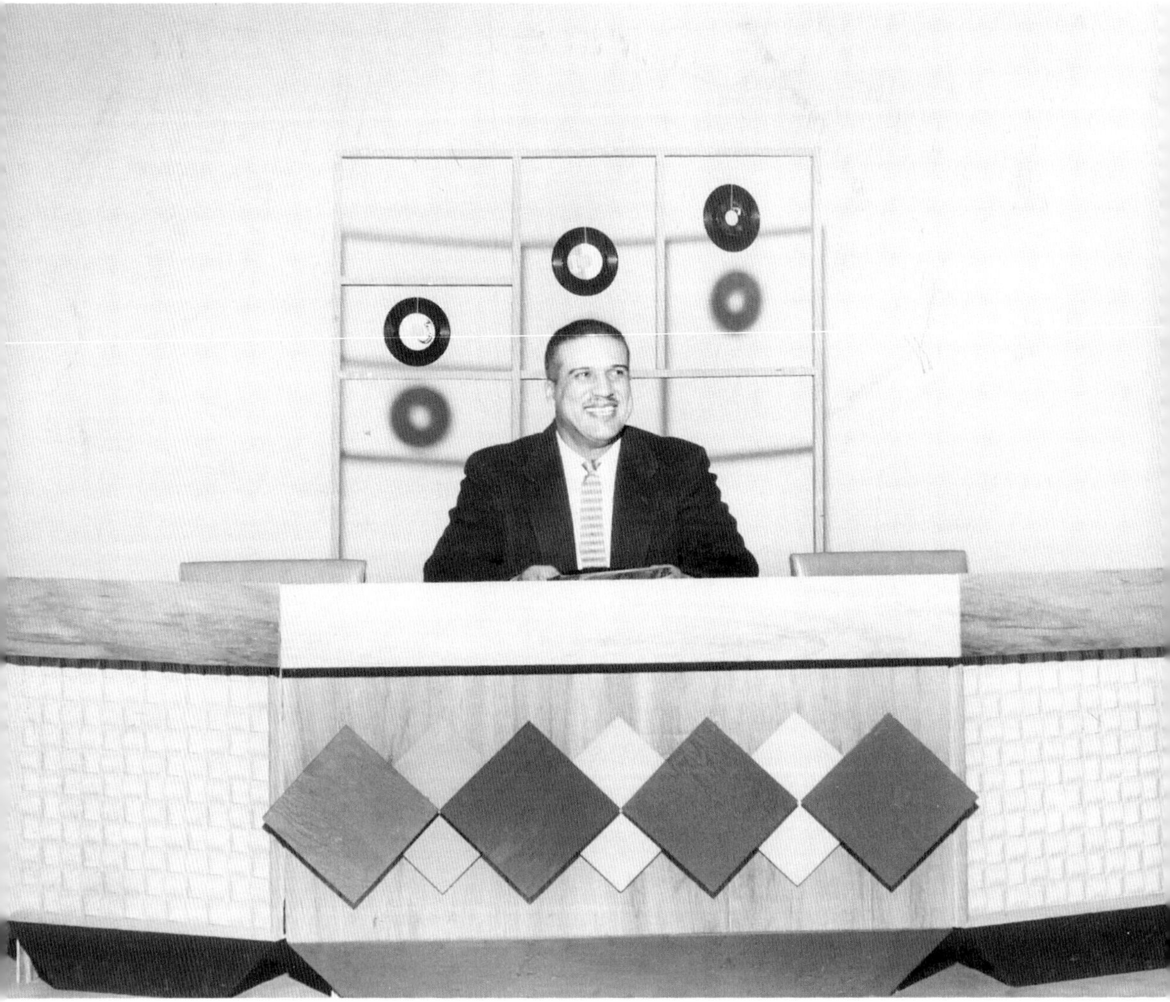

**J.D. Lewis**
Lewis (1919–2007) was born in Raleigh and went to Morehouse College in Atlanta. After college, he became one of the first black members of the US Marine Corps, where he trained to be a radio technician. Following the war, he applied his skills stateside, and in 1947, returning to Raleigh, opened a radio repair business. He built a mobile sound truck that he used to announce games for the Negro Baseball League. One day while announcing, Fred Fletcher of Capitol Broadcasting overheard him and recognized Lewis's radio talent. Lewis joined Capitol Broadcasting, WRAL's parent company, in 1948. When the company transitioned to television in the 1950s, Lewis became the host of "Teenage Frolics," making him the first African American to host his own local television dance program. Later, in 1974, Lewis was named the company's first human resources director. He went on to record editorials for WRAL and served as its first minority affairs director. Lewis retired from WRAL in 1977 and passed away in 2007. (Courtesy of Yvonne Holley.)

# CHAPTER EIGHT

# Capital of Industries

Because Raleigh did not exist as a city before 1792, the Christmas street plan preordained the location of the city center and its most trafficked areas. In this sense, Raleigh's path to development was purely hypothetical. However, the entrepreneurial spirits of residents like Peter Casso, eponymous owner of Casso's Inn during the early 1800s and brothers Benjamin R. and Frank M. Jolly, whose Jolly's Jewelers opened in 1881, ensured that Raleigh had a successful business center downtown on Fayetteville Street.

The statehouse, with its comings and goings of politicians and visitors, supplied a steady stream of people while the legislature was in session, and the numerous local colleges and schools provided plenty of students and teachers looking for something to do downtown. Steadily, residents began filling those needs and giving people in Raleigh a place to spend their money.

The Dombalises opened Mecca Restaurant in 1930, and it quickly drew the political crowd as a place for lunch and conversation. Kids begged their parents to stop by the Roysters' candy store, and at Christmas, the Briggs family devoted an entire floor of their hardware store to a display of toys. For more practical needs, the Hamlin Drug Store served Raleigh's "Black Main Street" on Hargett Street, as did many other stores required by the segregation laws of the Jim Crow era.

Thanks to businessman Rufus Tucker, a chamber of commerce has helped unite Raleigh businesses since 1888, although owners had worked together on an informal basis in support of Raleigh's economy for years. In addition to helping each other, many of Raleigh's businesspeople have made it their priority to aid their neighbors in the community. Restaurateur Ashley Christensen's commitment to ending hunger, SAS founder Jim Goodnight's contributions to education, and Quail Ridge Books & Music owner Nancy Olson's focus on childhood literacy all demonstrate the belief that true success is measured in how much a community is enriched, not just how large one's bank account is.

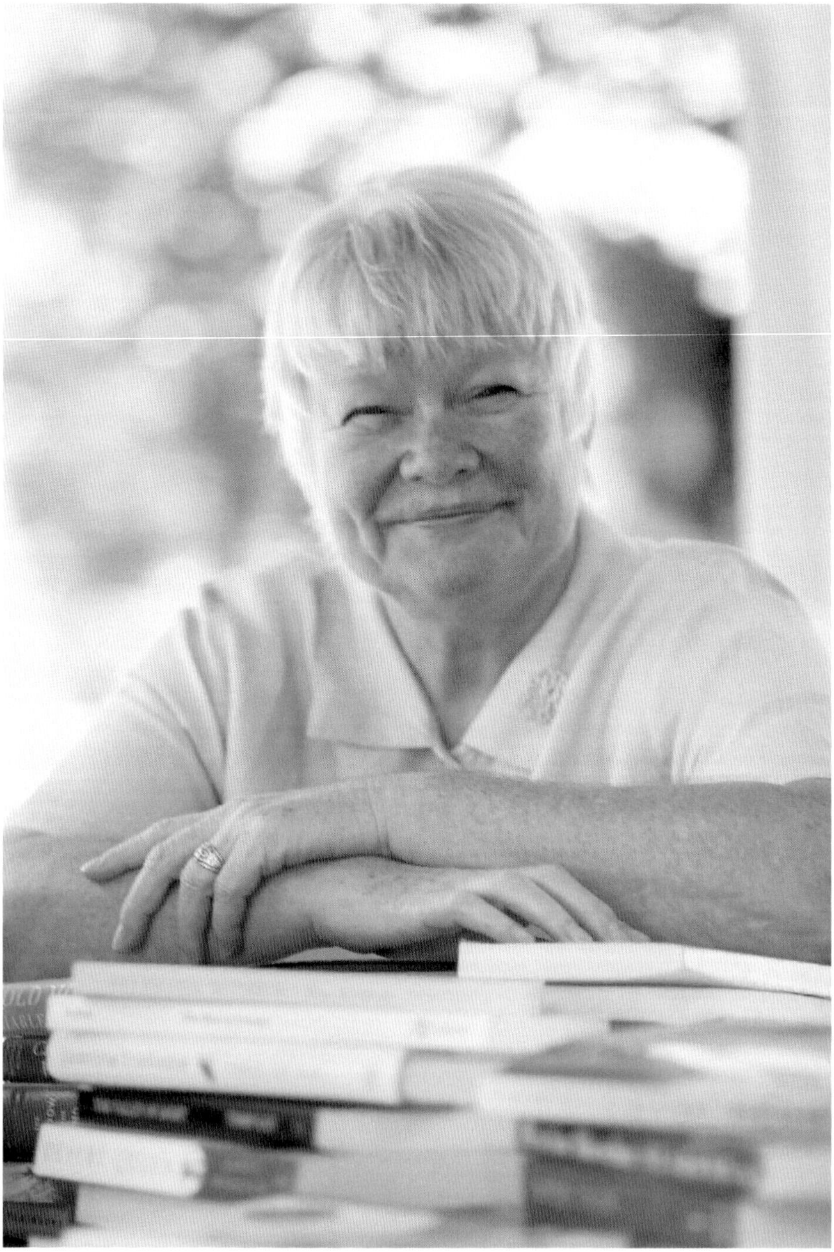

**Nancy Olson**

Quail Ridge Books & Music has been a staple for local readers since 1984. Owner and founder Olson tells her employees, "We have to be better than the chains." Olson strives to make sure her customers are more informed about authors, signings, and reading in general than in any other store. Quail Ridge draws thousands of readers for events, from local town meetings to readings with national authors and politicians, such as Jimmy Carter and Al Gore. Olson has supported the careers of Raleigh and North Carolina authors. She also nurtures readers and future writers through book donation programs Books for Kids and the Angel Tree. She also contributes to charities and organizations across Raleigh. (Courtesy of Nancy Olson and York Wilson Photography.)

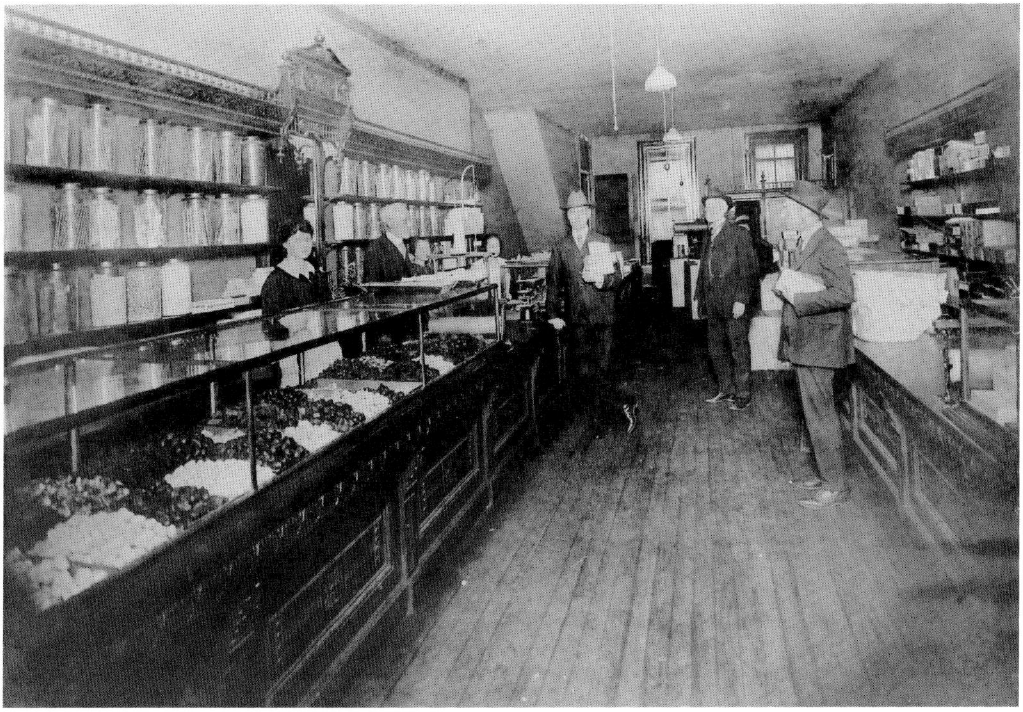

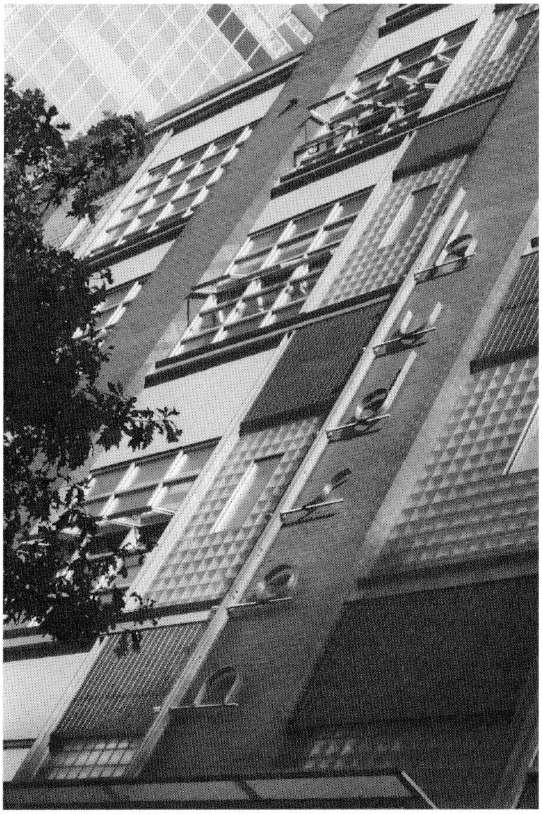

**Vermont Connecticut and Arkansas Delaware Royster**

Brothers Vermont Connecticut and Arkansas Delaware Royster began working at Wierner's grocery and confectionery in 1865. The store was opened by a Union sutler following the Civil War. The brothers soon opened Royster's Candy Store at the Fayetteville Street location, shown here in the 1920s. The popular sweet shop survived for 95 years following the brothers' transfer of the business to employees during the Great Depression. (Courtesy RCM.)

**Karl Grier Hudson Jr.**

Hudson (1919–2006) took over operations of the Hudson Belk department store on Fayetteville Street from his father in the 1960s. In response to protests by local black students and despite threats of boycotts by white citizens, Hudson deliberately included African Americans in his store. After the lessee of the store's restaurant refused to serve black patrons, Hudson ran the restaurant himself and served everyone, initiating the end of segregated businesses in Raleigh. (Courtesy of Dmitri Medvedev.)

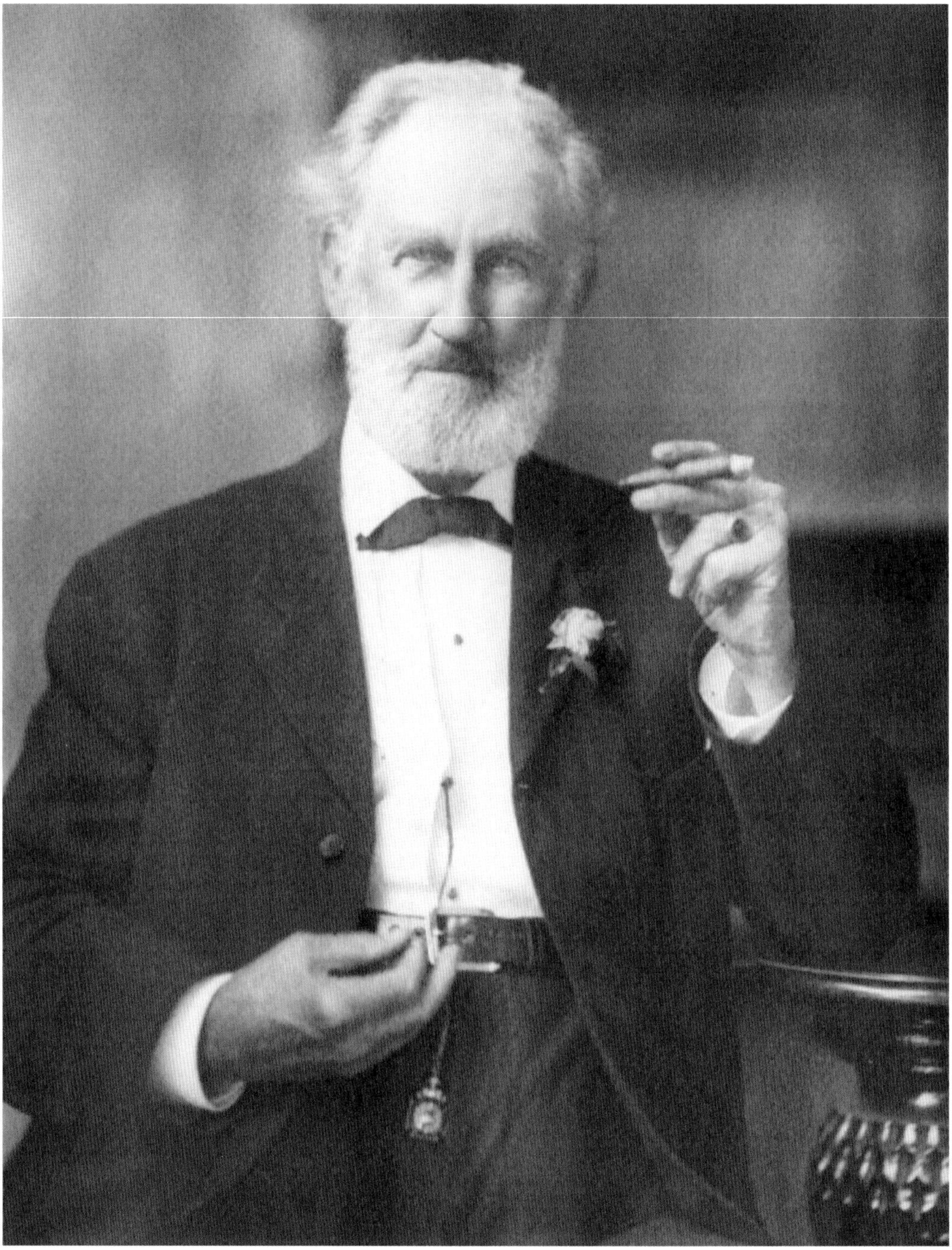

**Col. William J. Hicks**

Central Prison was North Carolina's first state prison and one of the first contracting jobs for Raleigh resident Hicks (1827–1911). The project was so successful that Hicks became the de facto state architect of North Carolina. His designs—and the "penitentiary bricks" the future residents made to build their own walls—were soon in use all over town, including the governor's mansion, the supreme court building, and on the campus of North Carolina State. (Courtesy of Marshall Wyatt.)

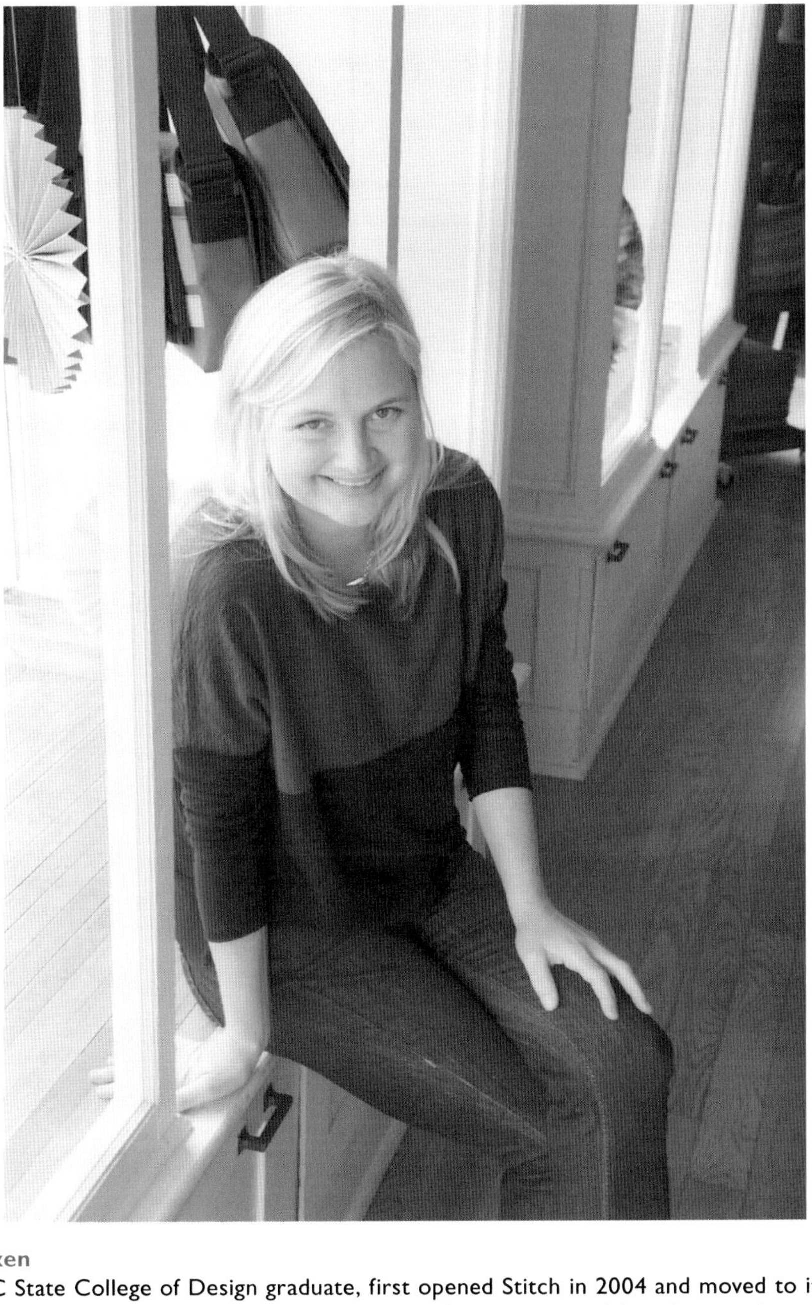

**Holly Aiken**
Aiken, NC State College of Design graduate, first opened Stitch in 2004 and moved to its current location on Hargett Street in 2008. In addition to retail space, owner Aiken devotes the second floor to manufacturing her distinctive purses, bags, and accessories, using brightly colored vinyl in a variety of customizable designs. This local business bridges decades of Raleigh history, from the "Ladies Shop" sign still painted on the front window as a remnant of Goodman's Ladies Shop, opened in 1933 by Celia Goodman, to its arrival downtown as one of the first retail stores following the reopening of the Fayetteville Street Mall to vehicular traffic in 2006. As evidenced by the ubiquitous sight of Aiken's bags on arms all over Raleigh, Stitch is playing an important role in the revitalization of downtown. (Courtesy of Holly Aiken; photography by Elizabeth Galecke.)

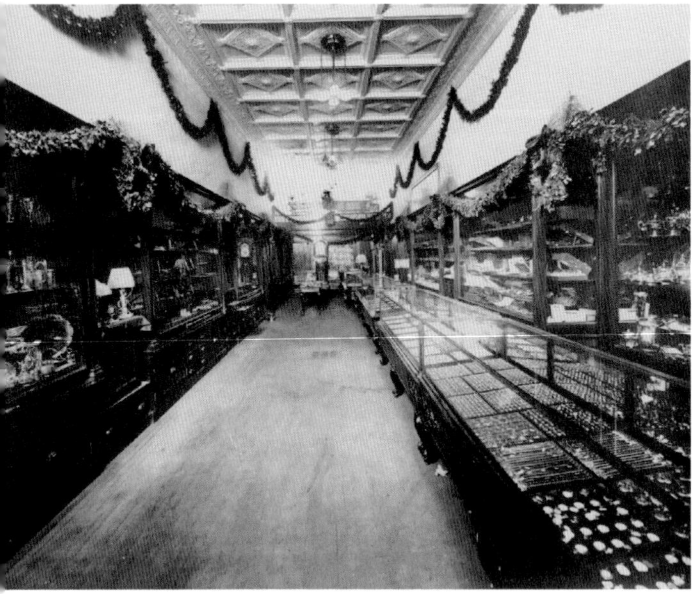

### The Jolly Family

When Jolly's Jewelers closed its store in North Hills after 130 years in business, it marked the end of a Raleigh family business that had been sustained by five generations of Jollys, since Benjamin and Frank Jolly opened it in 1881. Jolly's invented the "Jolly Bracelet Watch" for children, which sold nationwide in Woolworth's and kept official time for local Seaboard Air Line Railroad workers. The business secured several patents for various other industry-related improvements. The store interior is pictured here in 1913. (Courtesy of RCM.)

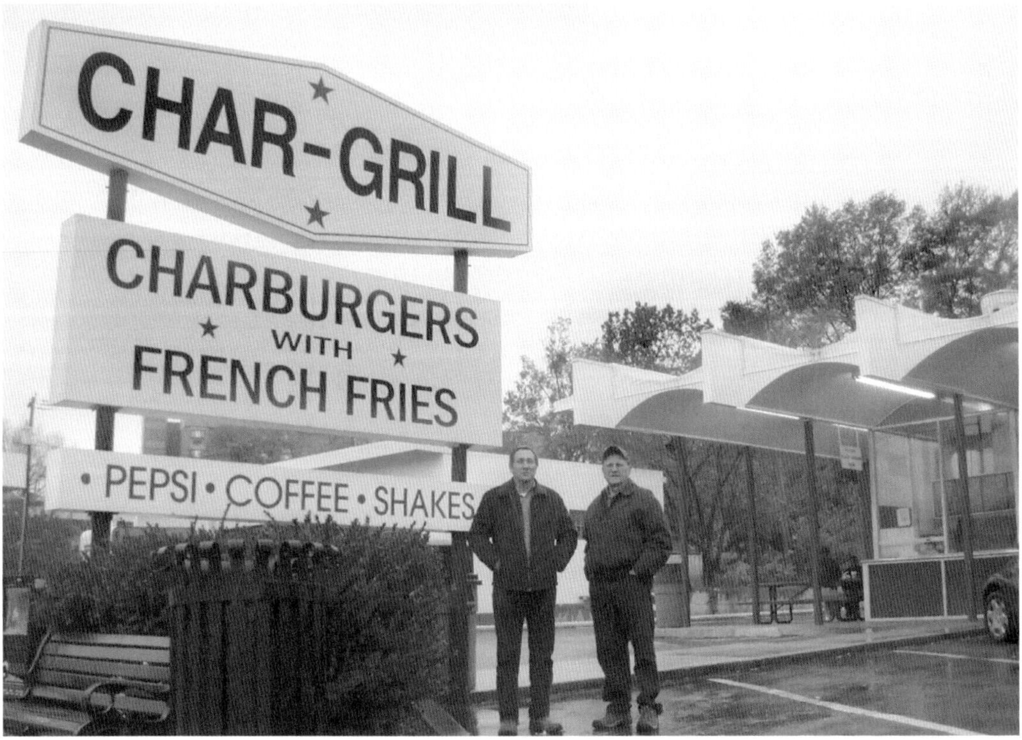


### Ryon Wilder and Mahlon Aycock

Char-Grill was opened in 1960 on Hillsborough Street by Bruce and Dorothy Garner. Bruce died in 1961, and Dorothy ran the popular establishment for several years. In 1974, she was approached by friends Ryon Wilder (right) and Mahlon Aycock. Char-Grill was slated for demolition at that point. They reopened Char-Grill the next year, and purchased the building in 1977. Char-Grill is still a great downtown place to get a delicious burger and shake. (Authors' collection.)

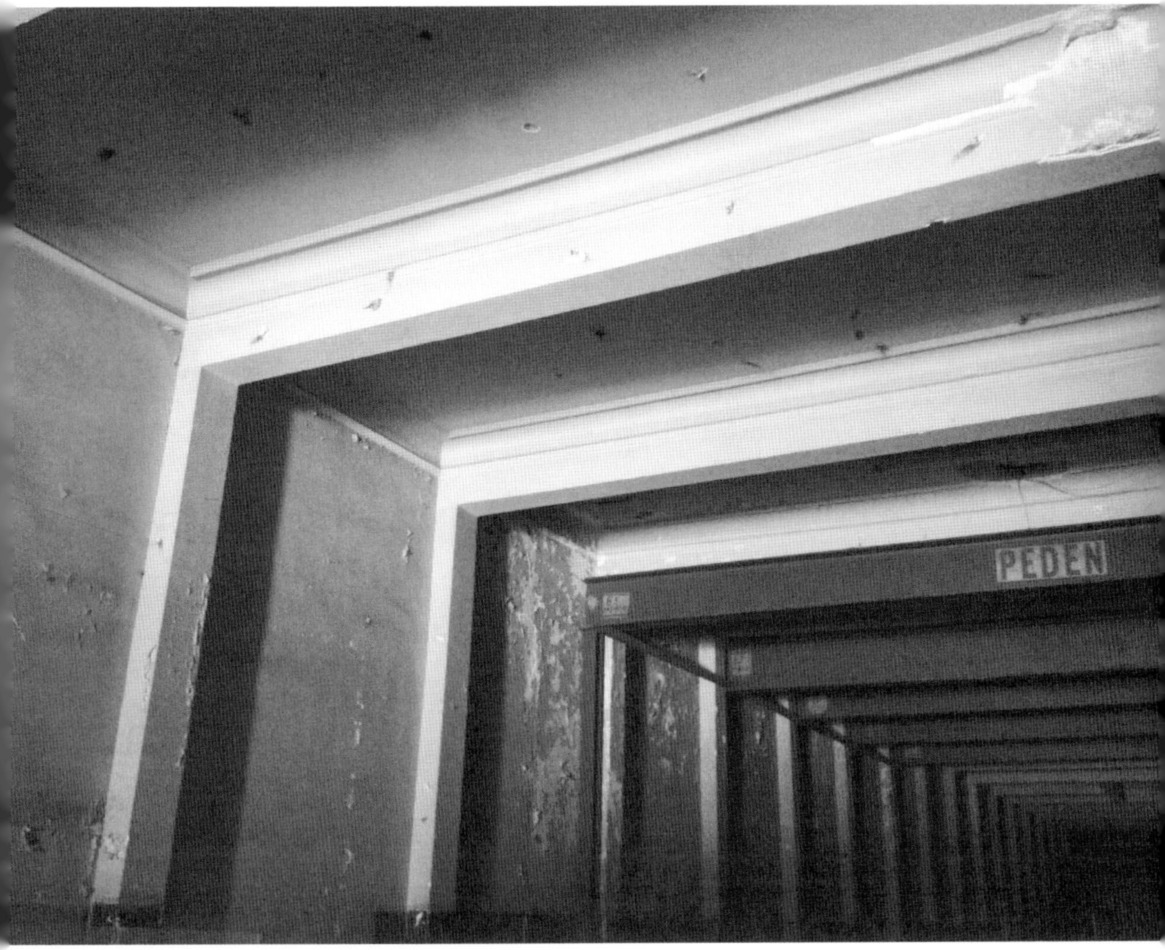


**James Peden Sr.**

Along with Brown-Wynne Funeral Home, which cabinet- and coffin-maker Henry J. Brown founded in 1836, Peden Steel Company traces its origins to the 1830s, making these the two longest-surviving businesses in Raleigh. Blacksmith Silas Burns came to Raleigh in 1831 to help rebuild the burned statehouse and construct railroad cars for the North Carolina Railroad. As a member of an early skilled workers' "union" in Raleigh, Burns partnered with William Stronach to open the Novelty Iron Works factory, which was powered by a steam engine at West and Hargett Streets. Peden (1898–1988) bought it in 1931, 100 years after it was opened. During the post–World War II boom, developers all over Raleigh used Peden Steel to support their new buildings. The Wake County courthouse, Cameron Village, and Edenton Street Church are just a few sites that relied on Peden. Shown here are Peden Steel beams in the Boylan-Pearce Department Store building. (Authors' collection.)

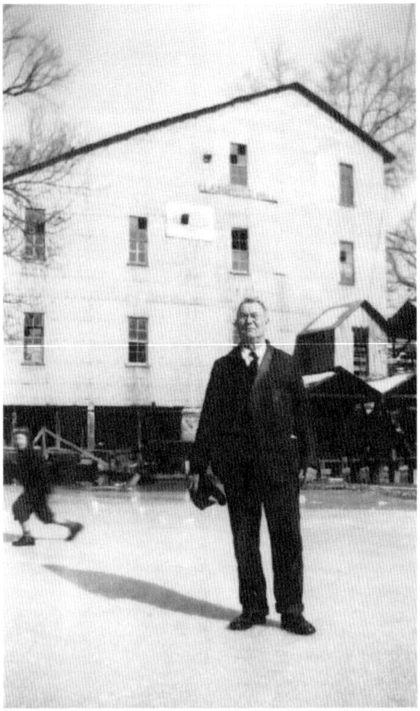

### Cornelius Jesse "C.J." Lassiter

In 1908, Lassiter, pictured at right at Lassiter Pond and below with his wife, built a gristmill at one of the oldest mill sites in the county, at the "Great Falls of Crabtree." Mills had been on that spot since at least 1764. Lassiter was so successful that he built a lumber mill and cotton gin on the same location. The mill was a popular spot for picnicking and swimming, and remained open until 1958, when it burned down. (Courtesy of RCM.)

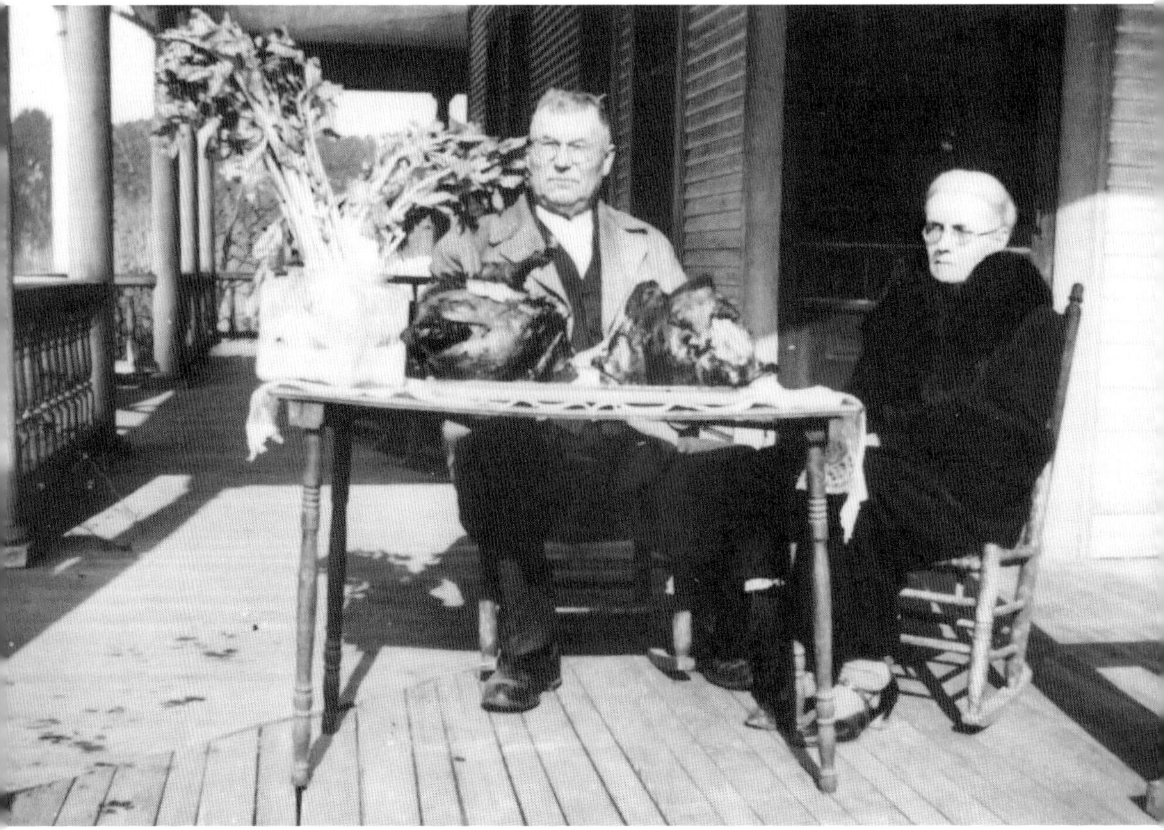

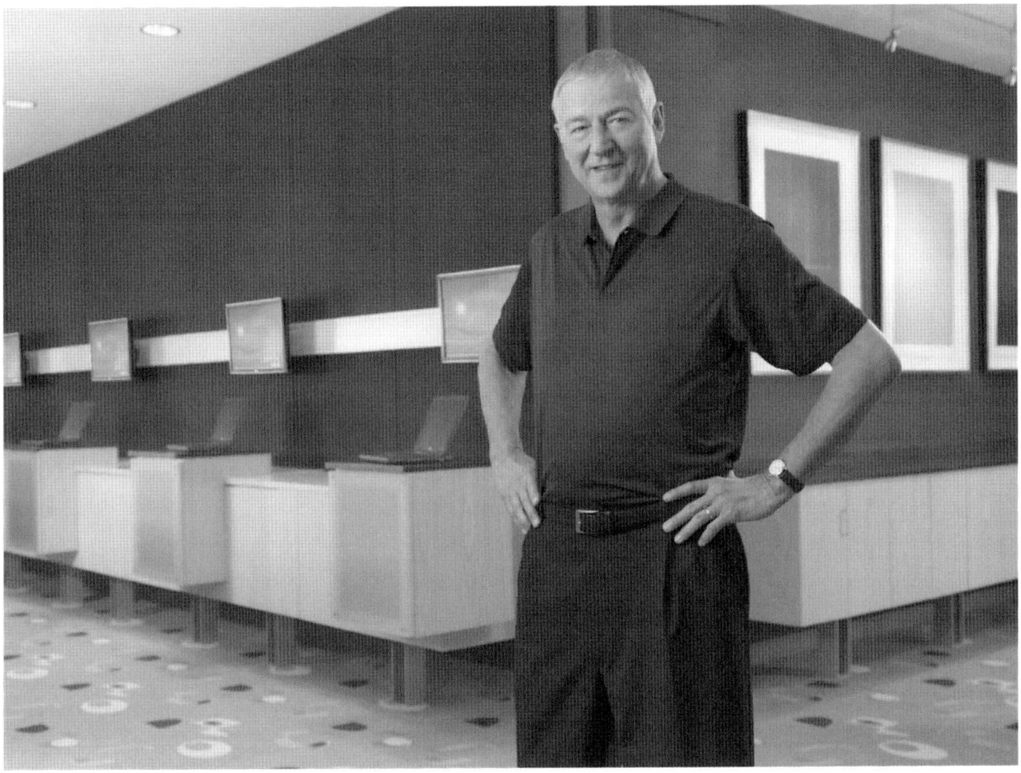

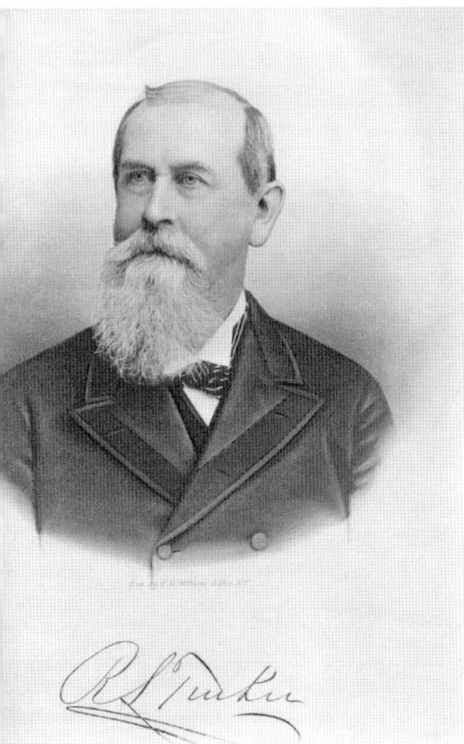

**Dr. James H. Goodnight**
President and CEO Goodnight (1943–present) founded SAS Institute in 1976, originating from a summer job at North Carolina State analyzing agricultural research data for the economics department. SAS is the largest privately held software company in the world and regularly tops lists of the best places to work, a result of the company valuing its workers' creativity and innovation. SAS's philanthropy is focused on education, with an aim of integrating technology into the teaching and learning skills of a new generation. (Courtesy of www.sas.com.)

**Rufus S. Tucker**
Businessman Tucker (1829–1894) observed in 1888 that "Raleigh . . . appeared to be at a stand still. The trades, manufactures, and business generally seemed dull and without energy. . . . Business men and traders were somewhat disheartened." In response, a group of 185 people met, paid dues of $1, and elected Tucker the first president of the new chamber of commerce. It focused on growing downtown manufacturing. The Raleigh Cotton Mill, in operation between 1890 and the 1930s, was its first major achievement. (Courtesy of RCM.)

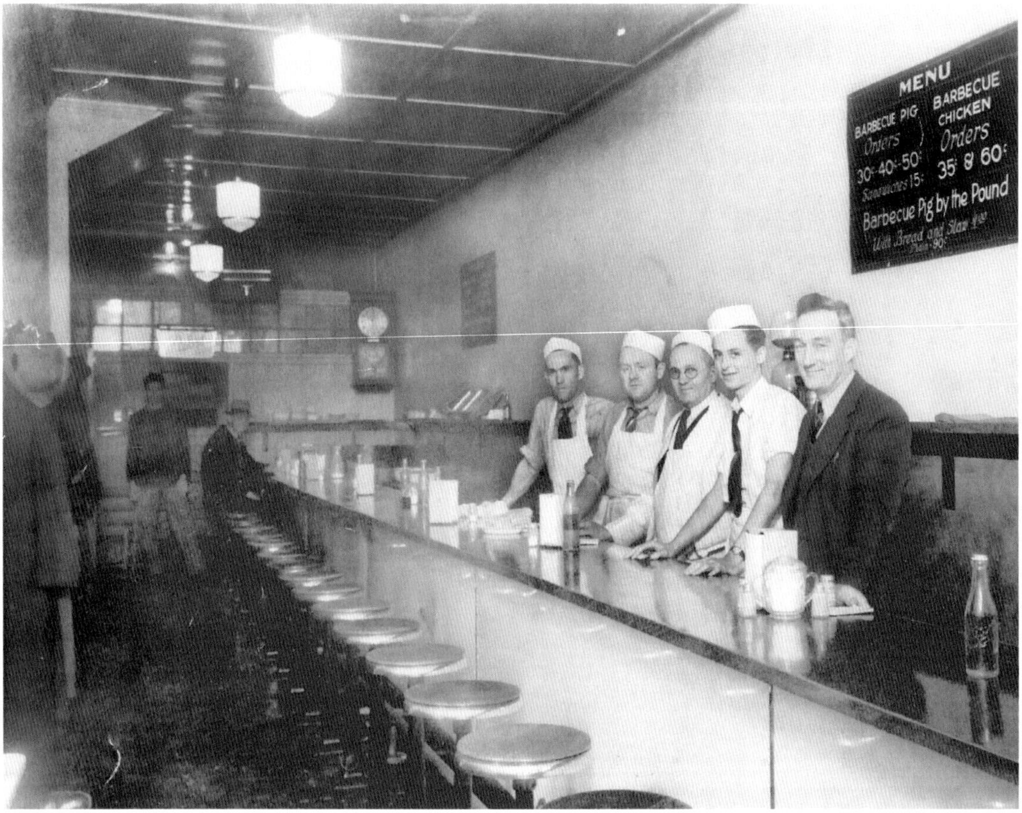


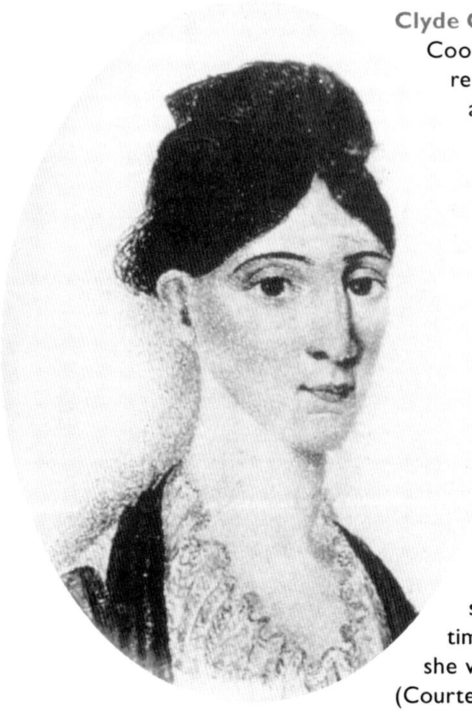

### Clyde Cooper

Cooper (pictured above at right, with staff) opened his restaurant on Davie Street on New Year's Day in 1938, and continued to work there for 50 years. Today, Clyde Cooper's BBQ is owned by Debbie and Randy Holt, who have fought to keep the historic building from being torn down, while still offering tasty barbecue to Raleigh residents. One of their customers has been coming there since 1938, except for the three years he served in World War II! (Courtesy of Clyde Cooper's BBQ.)

### Elizabeth Haywood

Elizabeth "Betsey" Eagles Asaph Williams Haywood (1796–1840) was the wife of state treasurer John Haywood. She presided over hundreds of dinners attended by many prominent politicians. John passed away in 1827 and left Betsey $70,000 in debts to the state. Betsey again opened her home to politicians, this time as a high-class boardinghouse. When she died in 1832, she was one of the most popular entertainers in the city. (Courtesy of OR.)

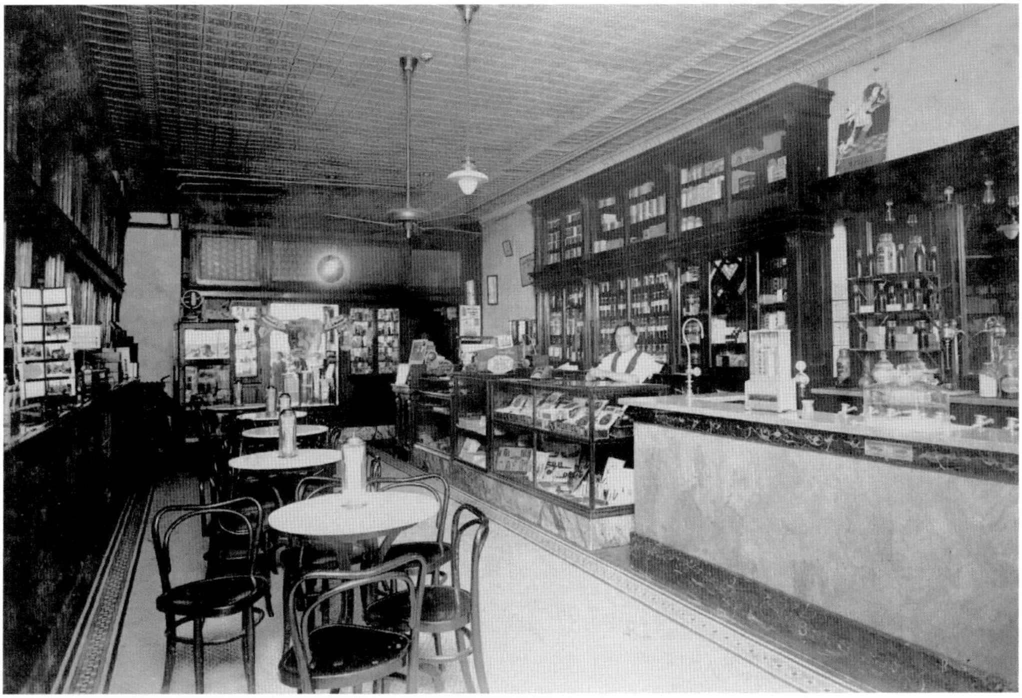

**James E. Hamlin**

Opened by Hamlin in 1904, Hamlin Drug Store is the oldest African American–owned pharmacy in the country. As the druggist for the black community, Hamlin saw almost everyone, and was well connected and well respected as a result. Dr. John Mitchell Johnson has owned and operated the store since 1956, maintaining its local focus and community atmosphere through the civil rights movement, integration, and into the 21st century. (Courtesy of SANC.)

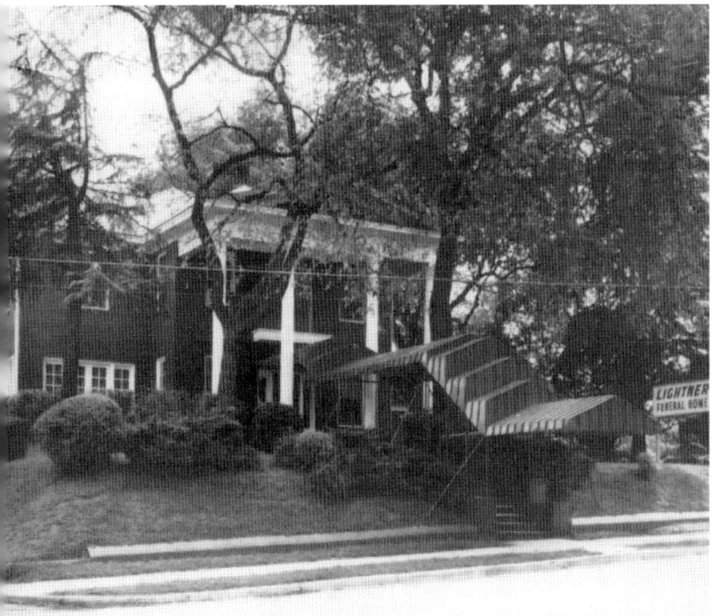


**Calvin Lightner**

Lightner (1877–1960) was one of the most influential African American builders of his time. He constructed the Davie Presbyterian Church and the original Mechanics and Farmers Bank building. In 1921, he built Lightner Arcade, which housed Hamlin drugstore, a restaurant, the *Carolina Tribune,* a hotel, and more, and hosted such famous musicians as Duke Ellington and Count Basie. The Lightner Arcade succumbed to the Great Depression, and Calvin started Lightner's Funeral Home, pictured here. (Courtesy of RCM.)

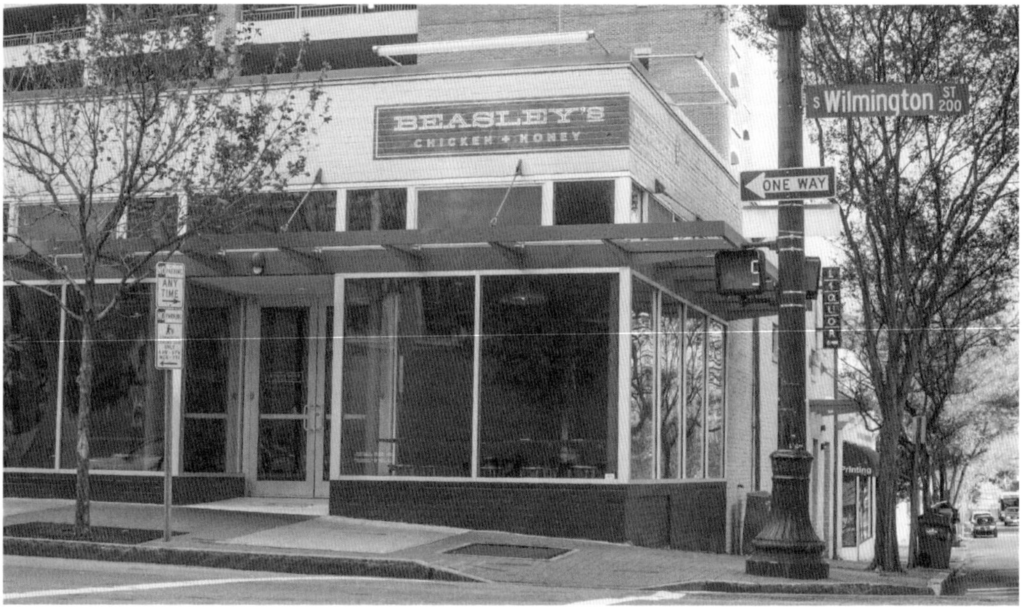


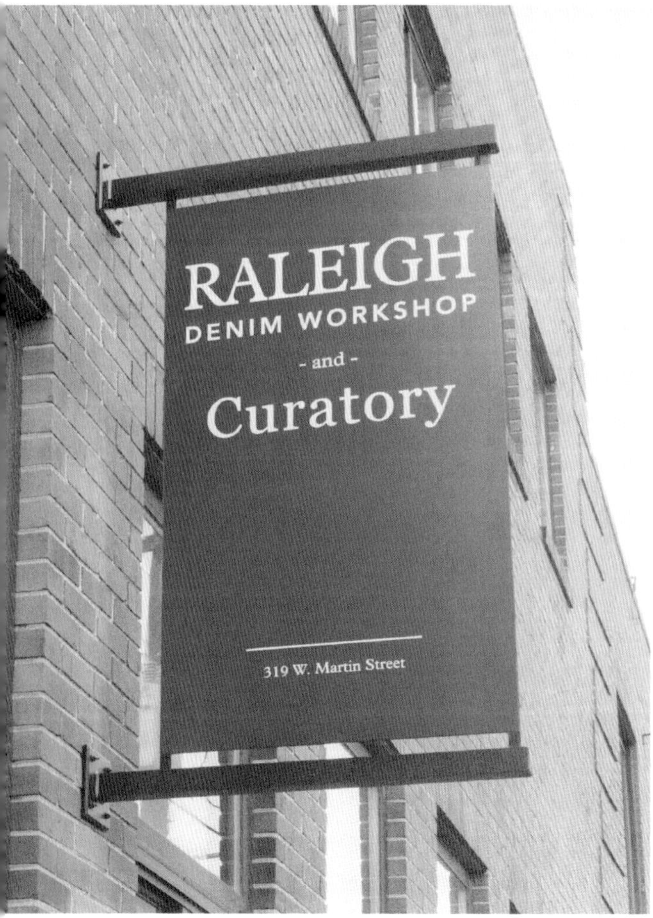


**Ashley Christensen**
Christensen opened Poole's Diner in a largely forgotten part of downtown Raleigh in 2007, but her simple yet creative take on local ingredients soon created a loyal following. The growth of Raleigh, aided by her efforts, has allowed her to open three new restaurants, all sharing a converted Piggly Wiggly with one giant kitchen. Christensen has plans for further development in the future and also devotes a great deal of her time to charities focused on children and hunger. (Courtesy of Dmitri Medvedev.)

**Victor and Sarah Lytvinenko**
The Lytvinenkos, cofounders of Raleigh Denim, sell their handmade and locally sourced jeans out of their downtown storefront on Martin Street. After meeting and collaborating in college, this husband-and-wife duo celebrates North Carolina's rich textile history by combining traditional production methods with modern styles to create their unique brand. Their jeans are produced entirely in their store, which is also their workshop, using fabric from Cone Denim Mills in Raleigh. (Courtesy of Dmitri Medvedev.)

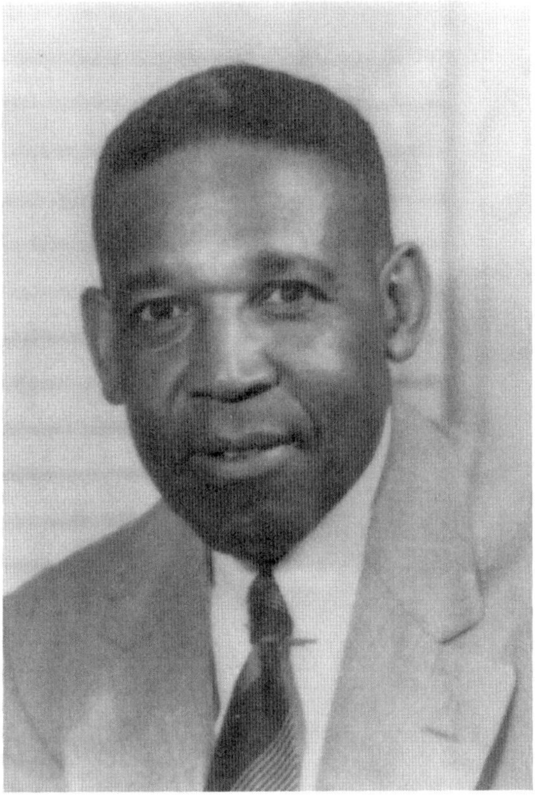

**Samuel Harris**

Harris (left) started Harris Barber College (below) in 1930 in the back of a barbershop, next to what is now the Hamlin Drug Store. He believed that African American males should possess a skill that would help them improve their economic status. In 1942, a new college was built on South Blount Street, where the school still stands today. The new facility offered opportunities for students to room and board. (Left, courtesy of Geraldine Burroughs; below, RCM.)

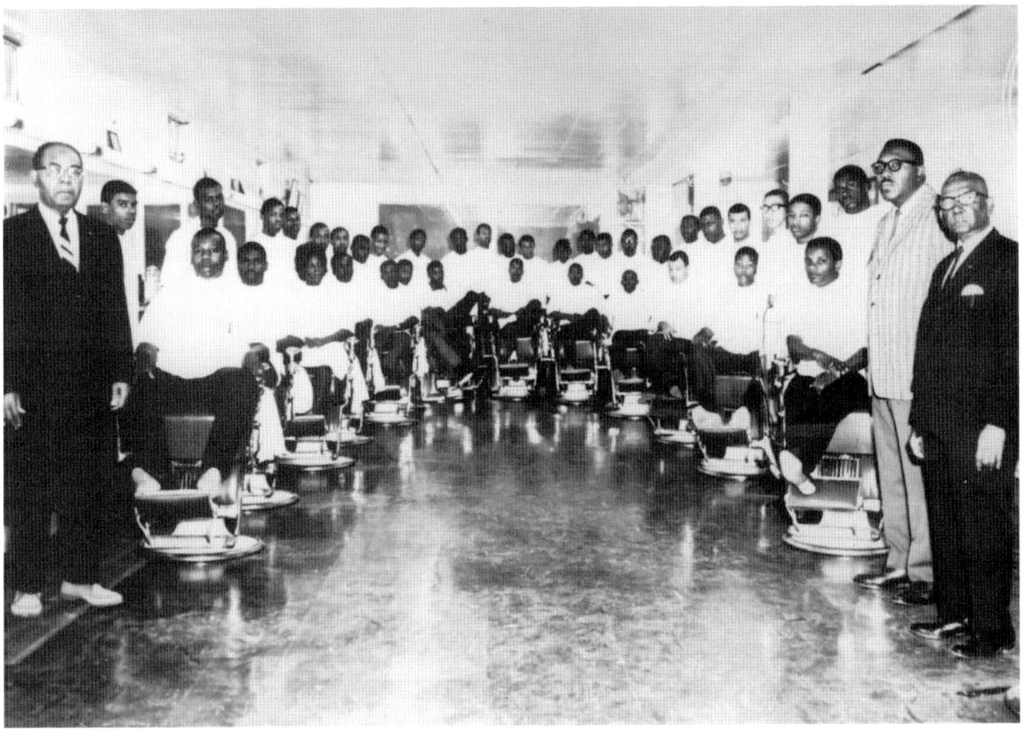

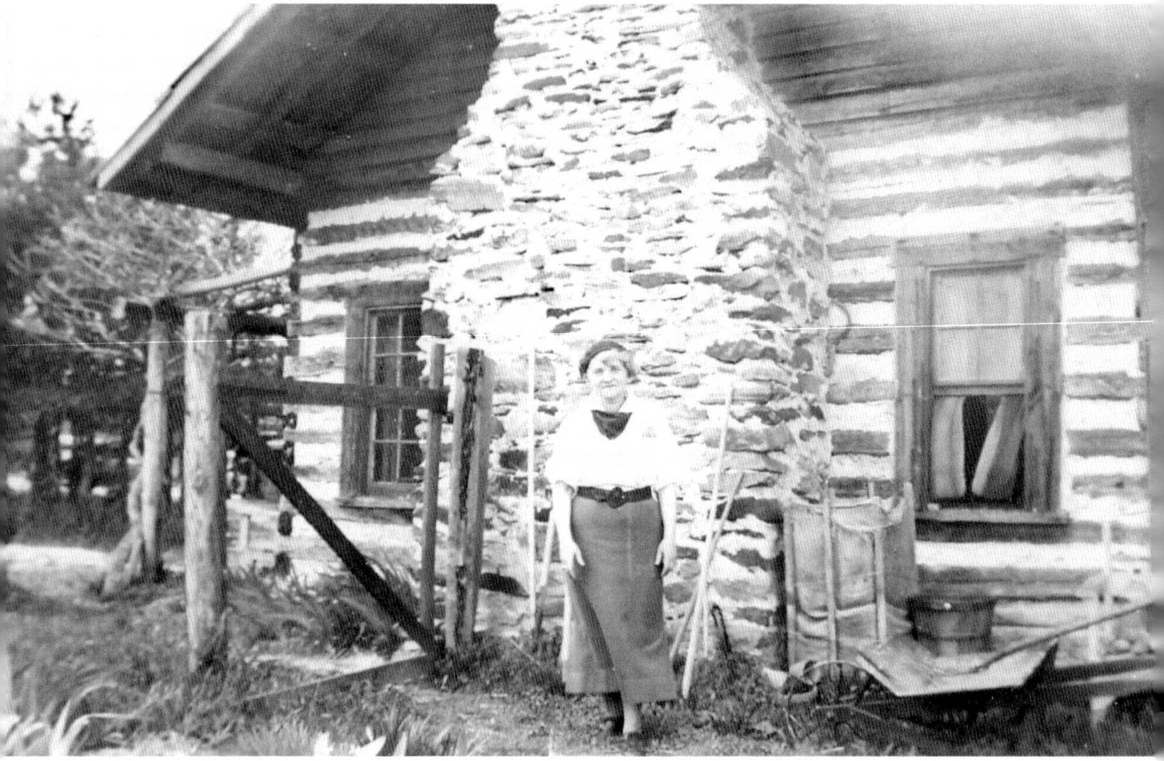

**Juliana Royster Busbee**

In 1917, Juliana (1876–1962) and her husband, Jacques (1870–1947), started their own company to bring the traditional pottery of Moore County to a wider audience. Juliana had purchased an orange-colored glazed pie dish and traced its origins back to Moore County, North Carolina. Under their initiative, the pottery trade and old traditions of the potters were revitalized. In 1918, the couple moved to Greenwich Village, New York, and opened the Village Store. They later moved to Seagrove, North Carolina, and renamed the business Jugtown Pottery, where they taught potters old traditions to create new pieces. To this day, Jugtown Pottery focuses on earthenware and salt glazes and carries on the traditions of North Carolina pottery. Jugtown has sold pieces made by many of its potters, who have been greatly admired over the past 100 years. (Courtesy of Jugtown Pottery.)

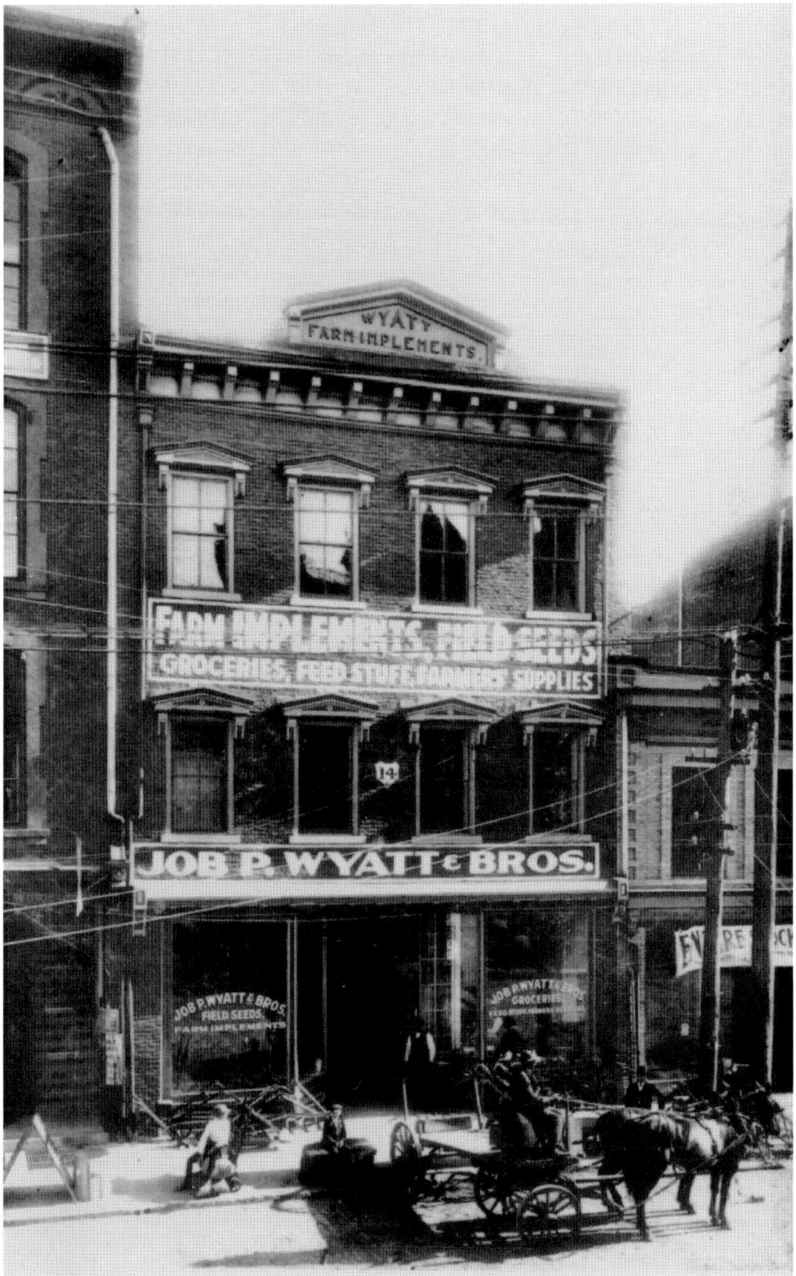


**Job P. Wyatt**

From a single shared general merchandise store on East Martin Street in 1881, Wyatt created what would become two different nationally successful companies. After his original partner relocated, Wyatt hired two of his brothers, Edgar and Patrick, to sell hardware and farm goods as part of Job P. Wyatt and Bros. A third man, W.G. Quarles, headed the seed department. In 1955, they formed the separate company of Wyatt-Quarles Seed Company as a result of large demand in the seed industry, with Quarles as president and Edgar Wyatt vice president. The remaining business became Job P. Wyatt and Sons, and both operate in Raleigh today. (Courtesy of RCM.)

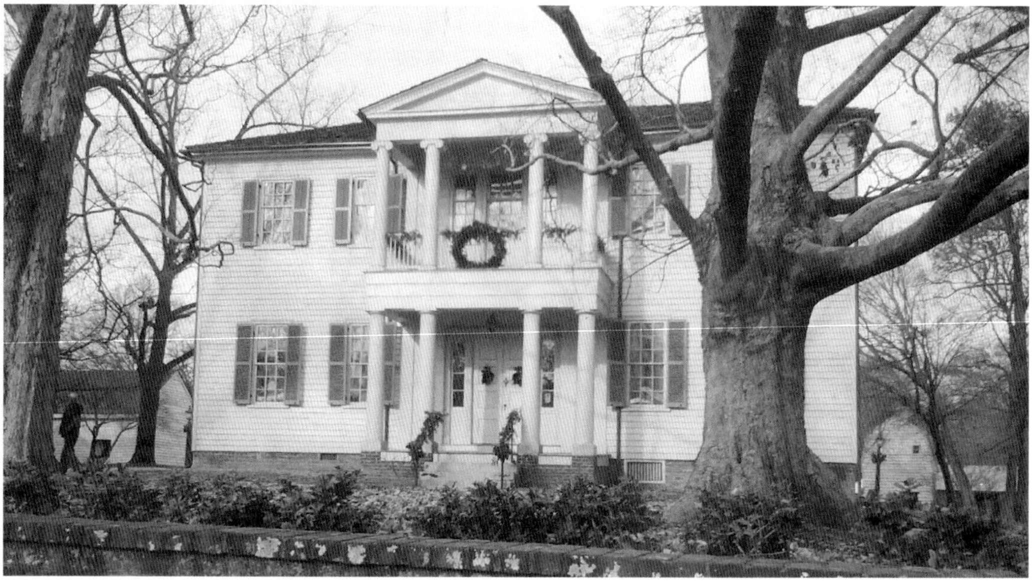

**Moses Mordecai**

Mordecai was the first Jewish person to move to Raleigh, although he was not a practicing Jew and changed the pronunciation of his name from "kye" to "key." Moses came from a prominent Wilmington family and set up a successful law business in Raleigh. The family lived in the Mordecai House (pictured here), one of the oldest residences in Raleigh. Moses's son, Henry, donated a portion of land on which the first Jewish cemetery in Raleigh was established. (Authors' collection.)

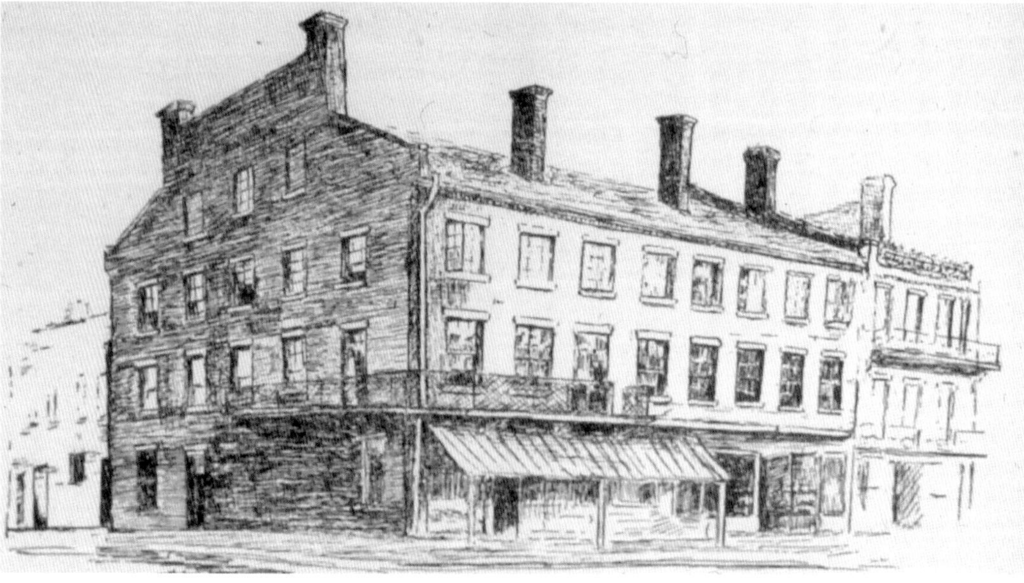

**Peter Casso**

Casso, a native of France, was a prominent Raleigh businessman. In 1795, he purchased a lot across from the statehouse. His main business was Casso's Tavern (pictured here), well known for its 25 beds, bar, and kitchens. In addition, Casso hosted a variety of entertainments, including cock fights and catered public dinners. Casso also had several side businesses, including a profitable general store located next to the tavern. (Courtesy of OR.)

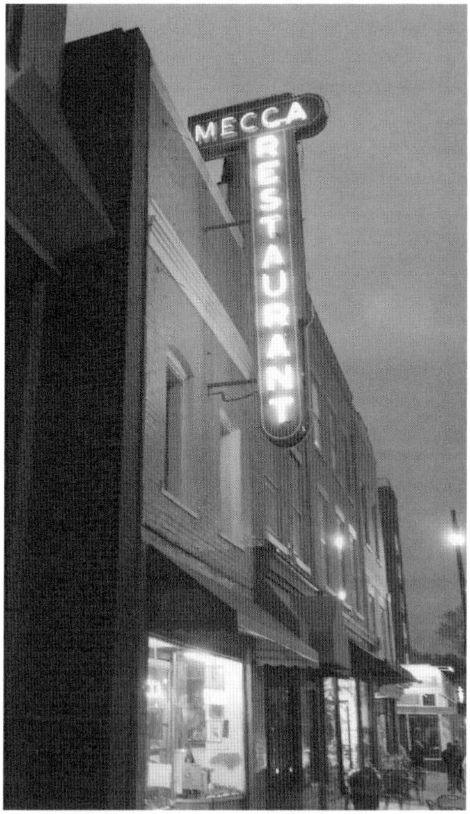


### Mecca Restaurant

Mecca Restaurant, the oldest family-run restaurant in Raleigh (and possibly North Carolina), opened its doors in downtown Raleigh in 1930. Greek immigrants Nicholas and Helen Dombalis greeted everyone from children to politicians with a warm smile and a warm plate. Their son John and his wife, Floye, took over operations in the 1950s, although Nick still worked the cash register almost every day during lunch.

Today, the original neon sign still welcomes hungry Raleighites inside, where delicious aromas waft over the same cherry wood booths and mirror-backed counter from over 80 years ago. Guests are still welcomed by Floye, although her son Paul now makes sure everyone gets a tasty, soul-filled experience at Mecca, and the memories of Raleigh's past mingle with the voices of its present. (Left, authors' collection; below, courtesy of RCM.)

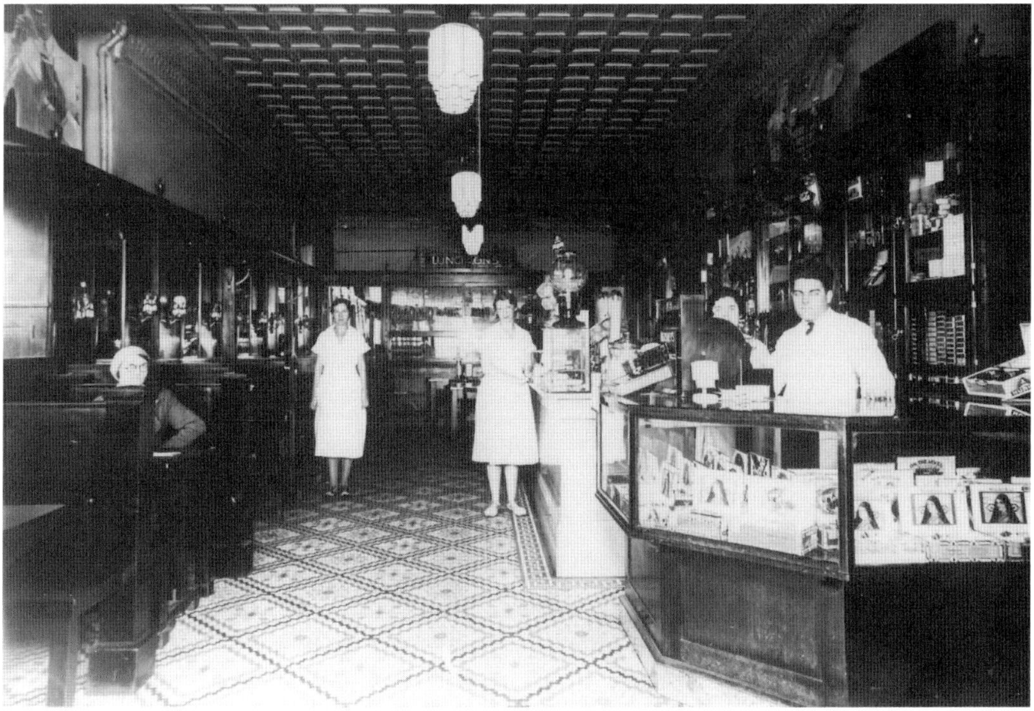

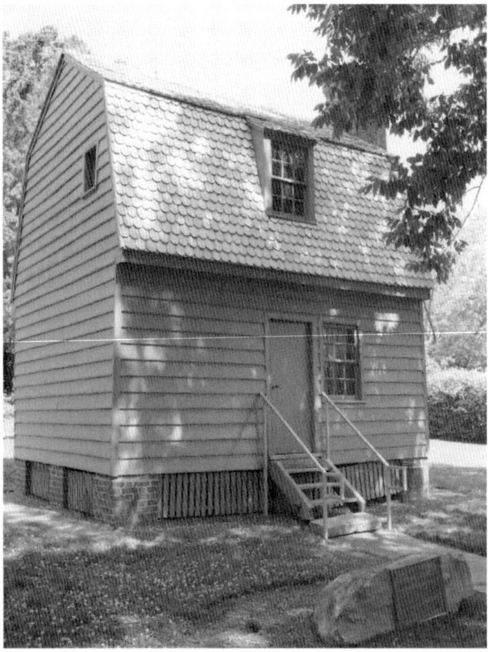

### Mary Johnson's House

Johnson's husband died after rescuing two drowning men, leaving her with two sons, eight-year-old William and three-year-old future president, Andrew (see page 11). She purchased a loom and became known as "Polly the Weaver." Mary, concerned for the future of her sons, apprenticed them both to a tailor. Her determination to support the family helped Andrew achieve success, even though she would not live to see him assume the presidency after Abraham Lincoln's assassination. (Courtesy of RCM.)

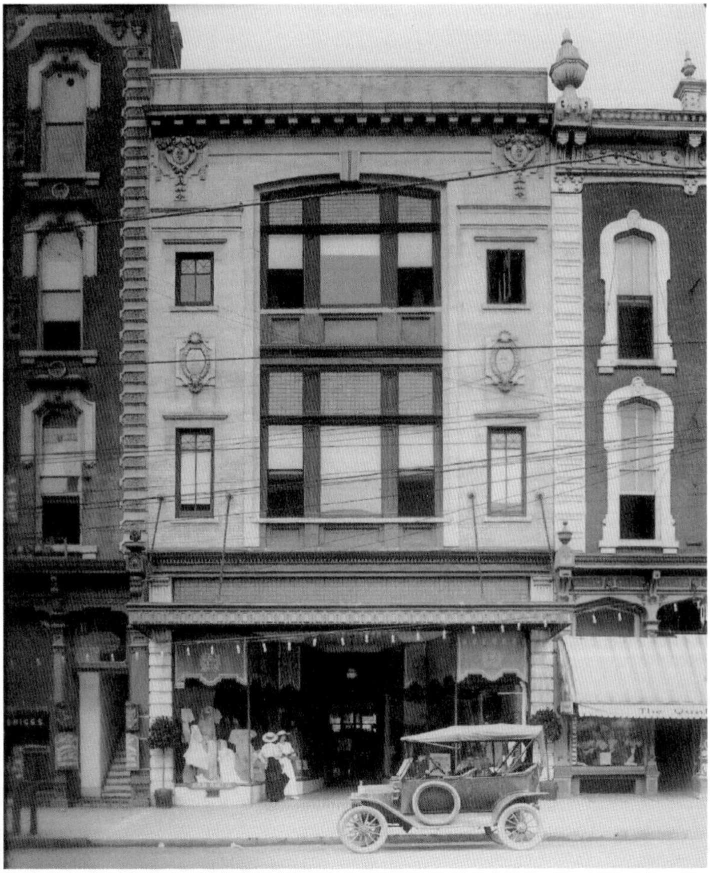

### James Boylan and J. Burrell Pearce

The origins of the Boylan-Pearce Department Store reach back to 1899. The store officially opened in 1905, and by 1919, had a popular ready-to-wear department and millinery department, and offered dry goods, carpets, furnishings, and more. It opened a mail-order department and was one of the city's largest corporations in the 1920s. The store moved to Cameron Village in the 1950s, and eventually closed its doors, though the building remains standing. (Courtesy of RCM.)

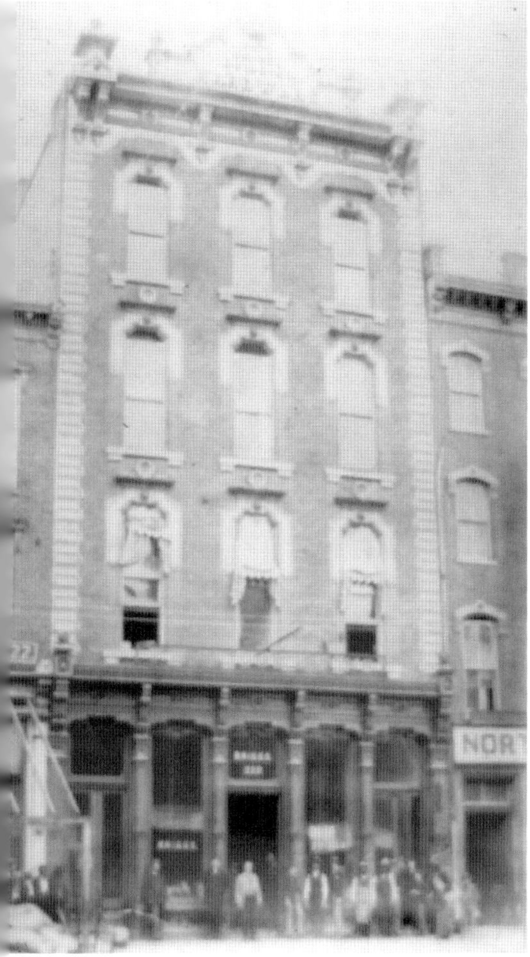

### Thomas Briggs

Briggs (1821–1886) became one of the most prominent local businessmen in Raleigh, but started out as an architect in the 1850s. During the Civil War, he was contracted to erect the main building of Peace Institute, which was used as a hospital. Briggs brought the building close enough to completion that the first patients were received in less than a month.

In August 1865, Briggs and his partner, James Dodd, opened a combination hardware and general merchandise business. Dodd left the partnership three years later, and in 1874, Briggs built a four-story structure at 220 Fayetteville Street. It was the tallest building in Eastern North Carolina, and is the oldest remaining building on the street. The business, pictured left, remained open at that location until 1995. It is still operated by the family to this day at a new location. (Left, courtesy of OR; below, courtesy of RCM.)

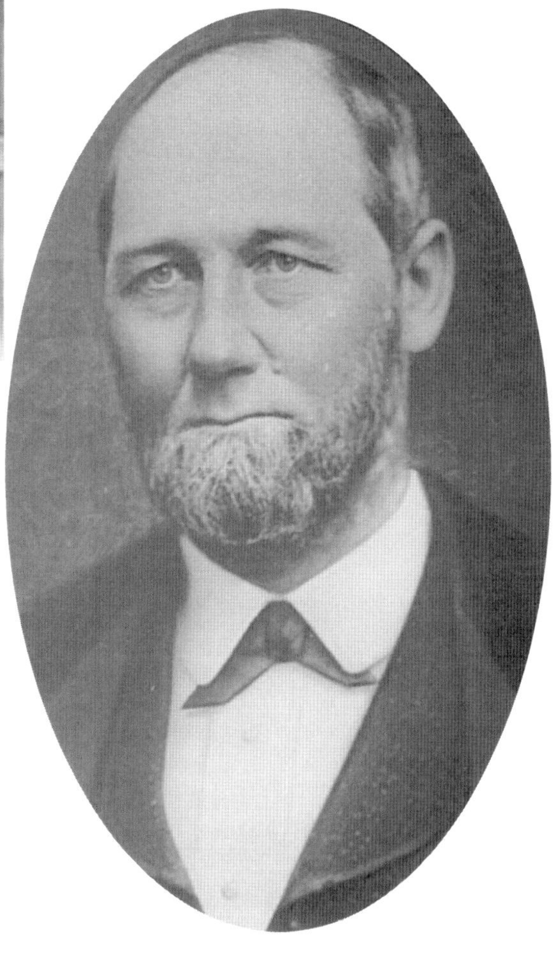

# INDEX